Dream Books and Gamblers

Dream Books and Gamblers

Black Women's Work
in Chicago's Policy Game

ELIZABETH SCHROEDER SCHLABACH

**UNIVERSITY OF
ILLINOIS PRESS**
Urbana, Chicago, and Springfield

Furthermore:
a program of the J. M. Kaplan Fund

This publication is made possible with support from
Furthermore: a program of the J. M. Kaplan Fund.

Library of Congress Cataloging-in-Publication Data
Names: Schlabach, Elizabeth Schroeder, author.
Title: Dream books and gamblers : Black women's work in
    Chicago's policy game / Elizabeth Schroeder Schlabach.
Description: Urbana : University of Illinois Press, [2022] |
    Includes bibliographical references and index.
Identifiers: LCCN 2022013234 (print) | LCCN 2022013235
    (ebook) | ISBN 9780252044786 (cloth) | ISBN
    9780252086878 (paperback) | ISBN 9780252053832 (ebook)
Subjects: LCSH: Lotteries—Illinois—Chicago—History—20th
    century. | Women, Black—Illinois—Chicago—Economic
    conditions—20th century. | Women, Black—Illinois—
    Chicago—Social conditions—20th century. | Informal
    sector (Economics)—Chicago—History—20th century.
Classification: LCC HG6126 .S37 2022 (print) | LCC HG6126
    (ebook) | DDC 795.3/80977311—dc23/eng/20220321
LC record available at https://lccn.loc.gov/2022013234
LC ebook record available at https://lccn.loc.gov/2022013235

Dedicated to the memory of my mentor,
Jonathan C. Smith, who taught us by example.

Contents

Acknowledgments

The initial concept for this book stemmed from a footnote in my first book, *Along the Streets of Bronzeville: Chicago's Literary Landscape*. In the second chapter of that book, I mention how the South Side Community Art Center and the *Chicago Defender*'s charities were funded by Bronzeville's policy kings. Through a series of editorial decisions and encouragement, the footnote turned into the third chapter of that book, "Policy, Creativity, and Bronzeville's Dreams," which analyzed policy as a form of performance art. I argued that the style and substance of Bronzeville's renaissance art and literature was synonymous with the ability of patrons to see themselves beyond the scope of poverty—a fictive imagination of oneself outside one's current context. I was stuck on the fact that newspapers mentioned only the men who ran policy gambling, always referring to them as "kings." I guessed that if there were kings, there had to be queens, right? And if so, how did Black women navigate the expectations of gender alongside the informal labor, sexism, and racism that defined life in Bronzeville?

The question kept bothering me, as most historical questions do. I needed to know more about the women. I reached out to LaShawn Harris to ask her about her article on Harlem's numbers running and Black mediums. She generously offered to send me her research and read my work. I also revisited Victoria Wolcott's work on policy gambling and Detroit that I had read years ago in my graduate Urban History Seminar. I sent her an email and she, too, volunteered to read my work and collaborate with me on a conference presentation. It's through these types of acts of generosity that this project was born, that I found encouragement and the wherewithal to make it through years of revision. Harris continually told me, "We need your book. Is it ready?" Thank you, LaShawn. Thank you, Victoria. Thank you so very much for your scholarship and friendship.

The world of historians of informal economies reflects this generous spirit, too. I am indebted to LaShawn and to Victoria Wolcott, and also to Davarian Baldwin, Matthew Vaz, Will Cooley, and Cynthia Blair. Historians of Black Chicago were omnipresent in their mentorship, guidance, and encouragement on this project. In particular I want to thank Lionel Kimble, Donald Hayner, Matthew Cressler, Erik Gellman, Melanie Newport, Christopher Robert Reed, and Bradford Hunt.

I really sank into archival research on this project and found a love for old papers and file boxes. I truly felt like this was my "historian's book." This comfort level with historical research would never have been possible without the help of many archivists and librarians. Thank you to the archivists at the Vivian Harsh Research Center of the Chicago Public Library, the Newberry Library, University of Illinois Chicago Special Collections, University of Chicago Special Collections, Chicago State University Special Collections, the Chicago History Museum, Cook County Circuit Court Archives, *Chicago Tribune*, *Chicago Defender*, the Library of Congress, the National Museum of African American History and Culture, the National Archives, and the Schomburg Center for Research in Black Culture of the New York Public Library. Thank you to Amy Bryant, interim director of the Lilly Library at Earlham College; Jose Ignacio Pareja, Earlham College librarian, and his student workers for their collaboration on the geographic information system for the project; and Martha Higgins, the library director of the Carnegie Endowment for International Peace Library, for your friendship and willingness to help me tie up never-ending loose ends to this manuscript. Librarians and archivists truly are the most giving in this profession, especially during a global pandemic that made tidying up a manuscript nearly impossible.

Numerous colleagues and friends read iterations of the manuscript. My writing cohort at Earlham College—members of our covert writing group aptly titled "Midnight Manuscripts"—you encouraged me and kept me going. Ryan Murphy, Matthew Cressler, Eric Cunningham, Nora

Taplin-Kuguru, Emily Filler, Womai Song, Callie Maidhoff, Rebekah Trollinger, Danielle Steele, Ahmed Khanani, Wayne Soon, and Honghong Tinn—
thank you all for reading and offering criticism. My work and life at Earlham
College were all the better for our conversations when we didn't have to
focus on teaching or meetings but could recharge in the intellectual world
of our research. Thank you, Robert Hawkins, for reading the manuscript
when I nearly gave up. You spent hours on it—and the finished product
reflects it. I can't thank you enough. Thank you to Jamie Schmidt Wagman
and Corrine Mason for the many conference collaborations. Thank you to
my lawyer friends: my sister-in-law Caitlin Schroeder, JD; Associate Professor of Law Erin Sheley; and my former student Meagan Monohan, JD
(William & Mary Class of 2013), who lent their expertise as I navigated the
waters of legal history. Thank you to the members of the Newberry Library
Women's History Seminar who offered me direction and tips on how to
focus my study very early on. Thank you to the American Studies Brown
Bag Series and History Department Colloquium at the College of William
& Mary. This is where I was first asked what does "policy" mean? And "who
printed the policy slips?" Thank you, especially, to Jody Allen and Susan
Kern for being sounding boards for the project in its earliest stages.

This book was richly funded by internal grants from Earlham College.
My sincere thanks go to Dean James Logan for his constant support of my
scholarship. I was incredibly unsuccessful in obtaining external funding
(not that Sara Paule and I didn't try)—thank you, Sara, for helping me with
numerous external applications. Thank you to Rebekah Trollinger, LuAnn
Homza, and Charles McGovern for reading those applications. Thank you
to the scholars who sent me samples of successful applications. Despite
my lack of success in obtaining external grants, Earlham College never
wavered in supplying me with the resources to travel to archives and hire
undergraduate research assistants to help with my work. Thank you, Jackson Gage (Earlham Class of 2019) and Eli Tienen (Earlham Class of 2020),
for your work on my manuscript.

I am so happy to publish this monograph with the University of Illinois
Press, a press where I feel always welcome. Thank you to Dawn Durante
(now with University of Texas Press); Alison Syring, who stepped in after
Dawn's departure; and Dominique Moore, who carried me through the final
round of revision and production. This book would not have been possible
without the support and collaboration of Nicole Roccas, my developmental

editor, and copyeditors Kerry Fast and Jill R. Hughes. Finally, a sincere note of thanks to Keisha Blain for her words of encouragement when I thought Reviewer 2 would do me in. Thank you for your counsel and support.

None of this would be possible without the privilege I enjoy in academia. I've enjoyed stable employment since 2013 and tenure since 2016; these privileges can't be underestimated. Not everyone is so fortunate. I am very lucky; stable employment put me in a place where I could access resources for my research as well as support from my department, students, and scholars worldwide. Many thanks to my colleagues in History and African and African American Studies at Earlham College: Tom Hamm, Joanna Swanger, Elana Passman, Ryan Murphy, James Logan, Rebekah Trollinger, Ahmed Khanani, and Womai Song. And a new note of thanks to my colleagues in the History Department at Lawrence University. Thank you, students, for your enthusiasm and curiosity about my work; your questions and passion were motivating beyond a doubt.

It took me nine years to write this book. Wonderful life events got in the way: marriage, the birth of my two wonderful kids, two new jobs with cross-country moves, and a not so wonderful global pandemic. Support from friends, scholars, and family never stopped. I am indebted especially to my family, many of whom happen to live in Chicago. Thank you for giving me a place to stay while I visited archives. Thank you for checking in on my book with care. But, more importantly, thank you for always believing in me when I doubted myself. I wanted to give up and nearly did. Thank you, Joel, Anders, and Ingrid, most especially. I work to make you proud. Thank you for loving me and asking me, "Mommy, when will your book be done?" I'm happy to say, "It's done. Let's go play."

Introduction

On February 8, 1947, a slightly grainy photograph appeared on page 11 of the *Chicago Defender*. It pictured four distinguished-looking African American men who wore polished three-piece suits, with two of the men sporting black-rimmed glasses. The men stood at a wooden desk littered with scattered papers that sat in a neutral-painted office with a framed piece of art on the wall behind the desk. A skilled photographer arranged the men around the determining action of the photograph. Each man's eyes were fixed on the action that took place at center scene. Following any one of the men's line of sight, viewers were carried to the man handing a piece of paper to another. The photograph's caption explained the transaction further: "Aaron Payne, Chicago Attorney, presents Dr. Homer V. Wilburn, medical director of Provident Hospital, a check for $1000 as a contribution of Mrs. Harriet [sic] Jones. The Jones family makes a contribution to the hospital annually."[1] Payne was the shorter of the two men, with Dr. Wilburn towering over him. Payne appeared intent in his gesture, his thick eyebrows arching, and the beginnings of a smile crept across his face. Dr. Wilburn appeared stiff, casting a shadow across the desk and framed picture behind him, but receptive to the donation. Also pictured were Clyde L. Reynolds, hospital administrator, stationed to the left of Payne, and Theophilus M. Mann, chairman of the South Side Committee of the hospital's drive for funds, who anchored the photograph to Wilburn's right. Reynolds appeared relaxed, with a more discernable smile on his face. Mann squinted care-fully at the check, as if to decipher its script. The four men—an attorney, a doctor, a businessman, and a fund-raiser—represented the professional upper echelons of Black Chicago's elite, putting on display their investment in maintaining the financial wellness of Chicago's first Black-owned and -operated hospital. It was an important moment to capture for readers of the *Defender*. But the most important person of this moment, Harriett Jones, isn't personally visible in it, except in the form of the check delivered by her attorney.

As the caption points out, Jones donated to Provident annually, but she was far more recognizable as the mother of Chicago's trio of gambling kings known as the "Jones brothers," three brothers who were infamous for their philanthropic efforts and numerous illegal gambling operations called "policy gambling." In policy, as with Harlem's numbers game, gam-blers placed bets on sets of numbers they hoped would be drawn from a wheel spun twice a day. Policy gambling was wildly popular in Black Chicago throughout the twentieth century, and Jones had a key role. Tax documents and Senate testimony evidenced that Jones herself amassed 20 percent of the profits from the family's extremely lucrative illegal gambling opera-tions.[2] But unlike her sons, Jones was never the face of policy gambling in Chicago.

Jones's absence in this picture reflects the hypervisibility of her position as both a leader of Chicago's policy gambling industry and a Black woman navigating the politics of respectability.[3] Evelyn Brooks Higginbotham first coined the term "politics of respectability" to refer to African Americans' promotion of temperance, cleanliness of person and property, thrift, polite manners, and sexual purity.[4] Because of respectability's focus on domestic-ity as the central terrain of uplift, Jones brought an inventive approach to economic success, refashioning normative ideas about Black womanhood and respectability.[5] This book explores the various ways in which Black women did these things as a result of their work in policy gambling. Black women policy workers had to navigate the conspicuousness of their gender within Chicago's informal economy and their visibility before an aggressive Chicago Police Department from without.

In straddling roles as both matriarch of the family policy business and well-known philanthropist, Jones demonstrates the double consciousness Black women used to create an evolving politics of respectability in policy gambling and beyond. *Dream Books and Gamblers: Black Women's Work in Chicago's Policy Game* charts African American women's labors in Chicago's informal policy economy, from its upper-class echelons of policy owners or "queens" to its lowest rungs of policy writers, clerks, and pickup workers. At the same time, I investigate how these women navigated constant persecution by the Chicago Police Department. To do this work, I center on stories like Jones's—stories of Black women's lives and claims to agency in a hostile legal and business environment.

Bridgett M. Davis offers a similar retelling in her memoir, *The World According to Fannie Davis*. Davis chronicles the success of her mother, Fannie, as a numbers banker in Detroit in the 1960s and '70s, a job she took up after she and her husband left Alabama and moved to Detroit as part of the second wave of the Great Migration. She was one of thousands of Black women involved in the informal economy when formal opportunities offered in Detroit were less than acceptable. Fannie found little success in the Detroit automotive industry and refused to do "day work" as a maid in a white home, to clean offices, or to work in a low-rung factory—the three jobs employing 75 percent of Detroit's Black women at the time.[6] Instead, Fannie turned to numbers, with which she built a life for herself, her husband, and her four children. As Davis writes, "Mama was clear that the only way she'd have more than what this country intended for her was to work for herself in a business she controlled that depended on Black clientele. Determined to find a better way, she didn't have to look that far."[7] Bridgett credits her mother's gift at numbers for providing her with the finer things of her childhood and describes her mother's grit, innovation, love for her community, and passion for numeracy as she reconstructs the world of Detroit numbers running.

Illegal lotteries like numbers thrived in African American urban communities during the twentieth century but went by various appellations. "Numbers" was popular in Harlem and Washington, D.C., while "policy" dominated Chicago and "digits" prevailed in Pittsburgh.[8] Because all of these forms of gambling were illegal, one would expect them to have operated outside the bounds of urban feminine respectability. Yet illegal lotteries and the material culture associated with them persisted as spiritual, capital, and cultural resources for African American women like Jones and Davis. Money earned from gambling labor was used to support families, build Black institutions, and access emerging Black respectability during the first wave of the Great Migration. Although policy has been portrayed through the lens of masculinity and located in exclusively male spaces, in African American districts in northern American cities like Detroit, New York, Chicago, Washington, and Pittsburgh, women and their domains were integral to gambling.

The chronology of African American women's participation in gambling labor in Chicago begins and ends with two waves of the Great Migration, what historians refer to as the mass movement of African Americans out of the South into northern and western urban settings.[9] Most women who made the journey northward to Chicago were born in the Gulf South; the women were between twenty and forty years old; they were wives and mothers, sometimes migrating without their children; rarely single; and typically possessed between a sixth- and ninth-grade education.[10] They found a dynamic but complex landscape of labor and segregation. Joe Trotter instructs readers in his book *Workers on Arrival*:

> Expanding employment opportunities in the urban industrial economy opened an exciting and hopeful new chapter in the history of the black working class. While large numbers of black men and women would continue to work as general laborers and domestic servants in private households as well as a growing number of trade and transportation enterprises, manufacturing employment gradually emerged at the dynamic center of the new black workforce.[11]

Trotter tempers this optimism by saying that Black women continued to work largely in household service occupations and that their movement into manufacturing industries was gradual.[12] Darlene Clark Hine stresses that Black women faced greater economic discrimination and had fewer employment opportunities than Black men; while Chicago's occupational structure offered them much, Black women's work was the least desirable and the least remunerative for all migrants.[13] Hine offers these statistics of Chicago's labor-scape: "As late as 1930 a little over 3,000 black women, or 15 percent of the black female labor force in Chicago, were unskilled and semi-skilled factory operatives. Thus over 80 percent of all employed black women continued to work as personal servants and domestics."[14]

African Americans also confronted harsh segregation in housing in the city.[15] Before the Great Migration, most African Americans lived in sections of Chicago's South Side and through parts of the West Side alongside whites, and whites viewed them, for the most part, as innocuous. Prior to the migration, there was a really small number of people who were living in the North who did not pose a threat.[16] That would soon change. In 1890 approximately 15,000 African Americans lived in Chicago. By 1900, after the first exodus of African Americans from the South in 1890, Chicago's African American population had doubled.[17] By 1915 the Black population of Chicago had increased to over 50,000. But it could not expand past the bounds of a narrow slice of land south of the city's business district and west of Lake Michigan; an almost completely African American enclave on the South Side housed most of Chicago's Black population.[18] As Chicago's Black population more than doubled, crowding forced them over invisible boundaries into adjoining white neighborhoods, where they were met with threats and violence.[19] The rising tensions came to a head on July 27, 1919, when angry whites stoned and drowned a young African American named Eugene Williams at a Lake Michigan beach, igniting four days of unrest. The violence confirmed that the urban landscape brimmed with racial animosity, housing was woefully inadequate, jobs scarce, and segregation strict. But migrants kept coming. By 1920 the Black population in the narrow South Side swelled to 180,000.[20]

Between 1940 and 1960, the Second Great Migration, Chicago's Black population skyrocketed from 277,731 to 812,637.[21] Living and working conditions even before the Second Great Migration were terrible; the arrival of hundreds of thousands of migrants between these decades made conditions considerably worse.[22] As Black Chicago's population increased, access to land and jobs did not, and these realities were particularly harsh for Black women. When work opportunities were few and finances were low, the informal economy emerged as an attractive option, and like previous generations who had faced the decision to move north or stay in the South during the years of the Great Migration, Black Chicago's women had to decide whether or not to participate in informal labor like policy gambling.[23] This book proves that policy gambling could, of necessity, offer Black women routes to family and institution building as well as a form of respectability. As a result of policy's attractiveness, Black women occupied every rank of policy gambling's employ.

In Chicago's policy operations, bettors placed their money on one or more sets of numbers they hoped would be picked in a drawing of twelve numbers placed in capsules on a wheel. Station operators spun the wheels

FIGURE 1. Policy game tickets, March 1955. (Chicago Tribune Historical Photos/TCA)

twice a day—for a morning drawing and an evening drawing. Shane White and his colleagues explain the variations that number selection took: "Gamblers bet on various possible combinations, the most common being the first three numbers drawn; for example, a gambler could take a 'gig' on say, 7-10-11 being the first three numbers drawn (this was according to local dream books, the gig for 'William,' on which there was a plunge after comedian Will Rogers's death in August 1935)."[24] Patrons received lucky numbers through a variety of means and submitted their "best" picks to policy writers, individuals who canvassed neighborhoods soliciting bets for the daily drawings. Some gamblers paid for private consultations with African American women spiritualists, diviners, or mediums, who many believed had special knowledge of winning digits. Other gaming patrons received numbers during church services at storefront and mainline churches where women distributed lucky numbers between hymns. As Black female spiritualists handed out lucky numbers at church, a family-oriented institution in Black Chicago, Black women revised notions of gender and respectability.[25] Not only did policy gambling allow them access to respectability, but they were also integral to a sacred and secular practice that has been portrayed in terms of masculinity and male space.

After station operators drew the winning numbers, policy writers like Fannie Davis dispersed into their neighborhoods to pass out winnings and solicit another round of plays, making queens such as Harriett Jones thousands of dollars every day. At the top of policy gambling's hierarchy sat "kings" and "queens," extremely wealthy men and women who backed policy wheels or bankrolled the wheels, who were at times both the best-known people in the city and the most crooked.[26] Various appellations were assigned to the king millionaires: "digit barons," "numbers bankers," "sportsmen," "digitarians," and "1-2-3-4 Guys," though "king" was the most common.[27] The overwhelming popularity of kings often rendered Black women's success at policy gambling invisible and unrecognizable, but there were also women who took the crown. The most famous policy queen was undoubtedly Madame Stephanie St. Clair of Harlem, known as the "Queen of Policy" or "Madame Queen."[28] St. Clair used her social status and larger-than-life public persona to amass wealth while also drawing attention to the socioeconomic and political issues plaguing her community.[29] As a result, she put her reputation in harm's way.

Not all queens leveraged the limelight as St. Clair did. Chicago's policy queens, in contrast, may not have been queens in the sense of owning and operating a policy enterprise or being involved in the daily functions of the game, but through innovative strategies of respectability they earned veneration. Chicago's queens, especially Harriett Jones, positioned themselves as silent partners in wheels, protecting their respectability, solidifying their position as the backbone of the family enterprise, and using their money to launch several successful formal businesses in Black Chicago to cloak their informal economic success.

Black women all over policy's employ used similar strategies to protect their reputations and maintain respectability. This was particularly necessary because of the dangerous visibility of policy work and Chicago's legal assault against policy gambling. *Dream Books and Gamblers* catalogs the wide-ranging experiences of African American women associated with Chicago's policy operations between 1890 and 1968. Policy opened avenues otherwise unavailable to these women in the formal economy, but these were avenues that sat at the precarious intersection of women's visibility inside the industry and their surveillance by law enforcement from without. These two kinds of vision, though different, are closely intertwined. Black women challenged the visibility of policy gambling while they challenged the sexist and racially motivated surveillance the legal system imposed on them. As the stories of the women in this book show, Black women worked to leverage the visibility of policy labor and constant policing to their advantage.

Black women challenged both the visibility of policy work—for example, some queens placed themselves in the background of their family's policy work—and the scrutiny that the legal system imposed on them; for instance, some women challenged their sentences in court cases. Black women involved in policy in Chicago were continuously balancing these lines of vision as they sought to make a living and build a life for themselves and their families. The work of policy that made their feminine presence conspicuous, along with the heightened vigilance police directed at Black Chicago, meant that policy women were constantly navigating these two very different modes of vision. But where they chose to position themselves along these types of scrutiny varied according to class, the extent to which they embraced domesticity, and their historical contingency.

Defining the Informal Economy

Although both the Municipal Court of Chicago and the Illinois Criminal Code defined policy as illegal, it was central to the structure of everyday life in Black Chicago, where participation in the formal economy was tenuous and unstable, at times even backbreaking. Many "legitimate" industries and cultural enterprises—for example, African American women's clubs and philanthropic efforts, funeral parlors, and barbershops—were underwritten by illicit gaming, shedding crucial light on policy's consumers and workers and thus demonstrating the reach of African American women's capitalistic influence.

Policy gambling also helps us understand how Black Chicagoans understood risk and play in their communities. Novelist Richard Wright, himself a migrant from Mississippi to Chicago, said of the disappointments he found in Chicago, a world he encountered without the possibilities of "play": "[They] repressed all the dreams and desire that the Chicago streets, the newspapers, the movies were evoking in me. I was going through a second childhood; a new sense of the limit of the possible was being born in me. What could I dream of that had the barest possibility of coming true? I could think of nothing."[30] Wright came to these realizations most acutely as a door-to-door insurance salesman of fraudulent insurance policies; he found it baffling that men and women signed up for them. Inexplicable to Wright, too, might have been the thousands of gamblers who continued to turn to play despite its risks and few rewards. Unlike Wright, Harlem and Black Chicago saw opportunities for play; they took play very seriously because of its potential rewards and respite from the harsh realities described by Wright.[31] Policy and numbers play offered a salve to urban uncertainty.[32] Numbers runners and policy writers like Fannie Davis and the women you'll meet in the pages that follow offered this hope and aspiration by offering policy as a way to manage the ambivalences and uncertainties of life in the Black metropolis.[33] Due to their visibility as women in a male-dominated industry and to heightened police surveillance, Black women brought an inventive approach to economic success, entrepreneurship, self-protection, claims to public space, and defining or refashioning normative ideas about womanhood and respectability.

Due to the "everydayness" of segregation—racism in both housing and the job market—labor and leisure away from state surveillance gained traction in Black working-class culture in places like Harlem, Detroit, and, the focus of this book, Chicago. Past scholarship on Chicago's informal economy does not delineate a binary of formal/informal economy but rather, as St. Clair Drake and Horace Cayton do in *Black Metropolis* (1945), a binary of legitimate/illegitimate. This is a trend set by W.E.B. Du Bois in his 1898 study of Philadelphia, *The Philadelphia Negro*, where he wedded work and morals. His study focused on vice and the conceptualization of a submerged underclass, which he used as a framing device to think through the relationship between vice and Black neighborhoods.[34] Subsequent sociologists have also used vice and pathology to frame Black communities. Indeed, *Black Metropolis* retained this analytical category in its characterization of policy gambling as a "cult" and a "business under a cloud."[35]

To understand the political economy of Black communities and women's integral performance in them in the early twentieth century, we must better understand the many parallel illicit industries like sex work and policy gambling, or "the numbers," as more than merely illegal activity.[36] In Black Chicago, what came to be known as "Bronzeville" by the 1920s, there existed an economic system that stemmed from the migrations of the twentieth century and brought about a world of policy wheels, dream books, kings and queens, and wealth as a dynamic response to capitalism's racism and consequent limited opportunities in segregated northern cities. As Black urbanization intensified during World War II and its aftermath, the notion of an African American consumer market gained greater currency.[37] The mainstream market and the state saw the profitability of policy and seized on it, transforming it into state lotteries across the country.[38] So instead of a theory of racial compensation and other morally tinged ideas about crime and vice as one might get in Du Bois's *The Philadelphia Negro* or Drake and Cayton's *Black Metropolis*, we need to examine policy as a racial and gendered expression of capitalism; such examinations hold the potential to challenge long-held assumptions about race, gender, and work.[39]

Current historical and sociological literature theorizes gender and urban informal labor markets in innovative ways, and the literature on the informal economy is voluminous,[40] as are the myriad ways in which scholars reference the informal economy; the terms "informal," "parallel," "shadow," "alternative," "illegal," "shady," "illicit," and "Black market" appear as frequently as "underground."[41] Generally the informal economy is understood as any economic activity hidden from state regulation.[42] Women's work in this sector included peddling policy slips, selling hot foods, delivering medicine, child care, hair care, and prostitution. Their turn toward informal labor showed Black women's desire for social mobility and a desire to mitigate the pressure of paying for food and rent with insufficient wages earned in formal economic enterprises.[43] Thus, the turn toward informal labor instructs us as much about the informal economy as the formal, but, more importantly, it offers powerful insight into the desires of African American women.

Black labor (both formal and informal) impacted urban labor markets, city landscapes, and the struggle for race, gender, and class equality while under strict police surveillance. I situate Black women's labor practices within the troubling history of police surveillance of Black communities. Histories of Chicago policing are indispensable to examining policy women and how legal structures viewed women who engaged in policy gambling.[44] Policy work prompted a sense of being watched in most spheres of African American women's lives. This resulted in a lot of tension in their lives but also an uncommon sense of freedom. In arguing that policy work was both precarious and advantageous, demanding African American women's visibility in ways they sought to invert, this book contributes to a new wave of scholarship initiated by Victoria Wolcott and LaShawn Harris. Their scholarship has recentered discussions of the informal economy—policy in Detroit and numbers gambling in Harlem—on the extent to which it facilitated rather than merely restricted Black female respectability.[45] My work integrates Chicago into this new and unfolding paradigm of policy and gender scholarship. Policy, and, most importantly, Black women's labors within the industry, was an essential part of Black Chicago's development and is only beginning to gain scholarly recognition. We must stretch what has become a standard historiographical claim that policy gambling was a site of male wealth as well as a masculine space of civic philanthropy and entrepreneurship, evidenced by works like Drake and Cayton's 1945 classic, *Black Metropolis*. In contrast, the new exploration of Black women policy workers, including my own, demonstrates that women were also key players in this sphere.

Organization

Attention to African American women's visibility in Black Chicago's informal economy guides my analysis of both the racialized and gendered tensions of policy gambling and the resultant altered notions of womanhood and respectability. Poor and middle-class Black women related to marriage, motherhood, and work through the lens of policy gambling, and that relationship dramatically altered definitions of late nineteenth- and early twentieth-century Black womanhood and respectability.[46] In the subsequent chapters, my discussion of the many womanhoods of policy queens and writers adds to the existing frameworks in which we typically talk about Black women, labors, and the politics of respectability. The first chapter, "'The Best Job I Ever Had,'" situates these discussions within the labor history and geographies of policy gambling in Black Chicago. The remaining chapters provide a chronological, biographical, and thematic examination of the lives and labors of Black women policy workers.

The second chapter, "Chicago's First Policy Queens," explains the complicated rise to fame of two policy queens in turn-of-the-century Chicago. The first of these women was Eudora Johnson Binga, wife of Jesse Binga (who built America's first Black-owned and -operated bank) and sister to Chicago's first African American policy king, John "Mushmouth" Johnson. Binga used her fortune to develop a reputation as a philanthropic "race woman." She did this by edging out Elizabeth Slaughter, Mushmouth's lover and a successful small business owner, for a multimillion-dollar inheritance. Using appellate court records, newspapers, and archival documents, I examine the dual biographies of Binga and Slaughter, both migrants to late nineteenth-century Black Chicago at a time when class structures were simultaneously flexible and precarious. Both women sought to use policy to access the protective trappings of emerging Black respectability politics with tenuous results. In an unprecedented fashion, these women navigated the single life, including cohabitation with lovers, husbands, friends, and stern mothers.

The third chapter, "Chicago's Most Famous Policy Queen," narrows to a biographical study of Bronzeville's most famous but elusive policy queen, Harriett Jones, mother of the famed Jones brothers. Using primary sources from the Kefauver Committee to Investigate Organized Crime in Interstate Commerce, the Illinois Writers Project's "Negro in Illinois" Papers, and arrest records from the Cook County Court Archives, chapter 3 speaks to the varying dangers faced by policy queens. Women sought and crafted protection using strategies to defend their respectability and maintain lucrative businesses. Mrs. Jones used a silent partner strategy, unlike her policy queen predecessors. She showed that through a near-invisible but strong internal leadership of the Jones policy organization, she could keep her respectability intact while making millions of dollars off her thriving policy wheels.

Harriett Jones's biography starts with her birth in rural Tennessee and continues with her marriage to the powerful and famous head of the National Baptist Convention, Dr. Edward P. Jones, who died unexpectedly of an aneurysm, leaving her to fend for her three sons. Archival documents from the Kefauver Committee show how she remained at the helm of the Jones's policy operation, bringing in hundreds of thousands of dollars a year. Harriett demanded uncompromising honesty and thrift from her employees and sons. As the family took control of the most powerful policy wheels in Bronzeville, the "Jones boys" became a household name. The family was famous for its philanthropy, penchant for the good life, and run-ins with the police and the Italian mafia. Harriett, however, always kept herself out of the limelight in ways that were markedly different from those of her contemporaries. Her purposeful concealment kept her respectability intact. It was a masterful strategy but an approach that did not keep her children safe from an aggressive Italian mafia and police force.

Queens such as Slaughter, Binga, and Jones were the exceptions to policy's narrative, not the rule. Far more numerous were the men and women who used their last pennies to place bets on the various wheels. In 1937 sociologist Ernest Burgess estimated that as many as 350,000 bets were placed daily on policy, in direct violation of city and state anti-policy statutes.[47] Bronzeville's demand for winning numbers never relented. Policy inspired a world of derivative materials and markets, such as dream books, lucky oils, jinx-removal candles, and sprays along with mediumship and fortune-telling. Thus, the fourth chapter, "Dream Books, Fortune-Tellers, and Mediumship," examines the variety of mechanisms that patrons used to beat the odds and hit big numbers beyond the material world.[48] Among the most popular methods of divining winning numbers was the litany of dream books published during the period, which cross-referenced the content of dreams with lucky numbers. Those with purchasing power relied on material items such as candles, roots, or lucky powders as well. These items usually featured the images of African American women. Dream books were part of the commercialization of mediumship and supernaturalism that resulted from the decades-long migrations of African Americans. Mediums, who were often female, served as guides to interpreting and understanding dreams, beliefs, and symbols, and were used to select winning policy numbers. Dream books were written in the language of African American popular culture and delivered almost exclusively through the image of African American female "conjurers." Policy players' dream books acknowledged African American subjectivity. Authors of the books often commented directly on race as they interpreted events in the waking world and offered solace, hope, or laughter to those wagering bets daily. Some believed that "supernatural traditions were integral" to dealing with and overcoming limited employment and economic hardship, as well as race, class, and gender discrimination.[49] Inspired by the work of Harris, *Dream Books and Gamblers: Black Women's Work in Chicago's Policy Game* opens up the previously mysterious world to readers and connects the shadowy underworld to Black women's everyday lives.

Chapter 4 relies on archival documentation from Horace Cayton, St. Clair Drake, and Lucy Smith Collier, and newspaper articles from the *Chicago Defender* to locate African American women's success in these tertiary businesses and roles that were bolstered by the success of policy. Patrons consulted spiritualists and children for direction in policy; policy customers

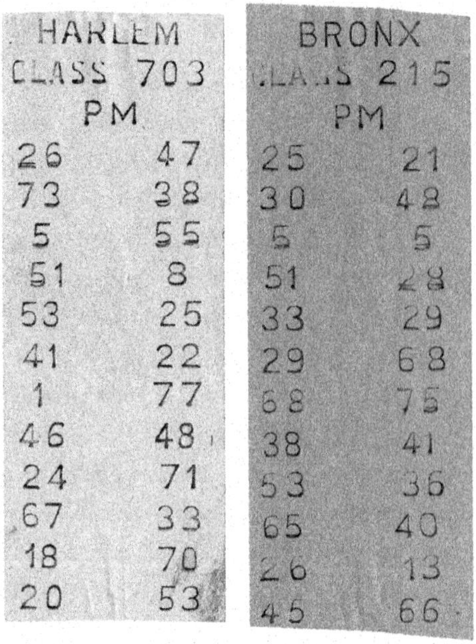

FIGURE 2. Policy tickets, 1938. (Hanna Holborn Gray Special Collections Research Center, University of Chicago Library)

received lucky numbers through private consultations, from dream books, on street corners, and by attending and leading religious services at storefront churches.[50] This section of the book further enhances historical understandings of the spatial web of policy, engaging those tertiary businesses and the spiritual world as extensions of women's domestic sphere and integral components of the success of policy.

The fifth chapter, "What Arrest Records Reveal," is a portrait of the women who were arrested for gambling, its promotion, and keeping gambling houses. I draw on arrest records, police reports, and warrants from the Cook County Circuit Court Archives to survey over two hundred cases in which African American women were apprehended for gambling-related charges. Arrest records shed further light on the "average" African American woman policy worker on the South Side of Chicago during this era, from their migration patterns and marital status, to their occupations, employment status within the industry, and encounters with law enforcement. These records are separated into three distinct chronological periods: 1925–1931, 1950–1955, and 1967–1968. According to police data, the women arrested between 1925 and 1931 were married, worked as housewives or maids, and were detained for selling policy tickets (a violation of Chicago

Municipal Code 408, chapter 28), or they were stopped for possession of policy paraphernalia (a violation of Chicago Municipal Code 413, section 2, chapter 38). Women arrested between 1950 and 1955 showed a shift in marital status and occupation, and the arrest slips lend insight into migration patterns: for the first time, it seems, some women arrested were native to Illinois. Those who had migrated tended to have been born in the upper South, hailing from Tennessee and Arkansas. The average age of this demographic was thirty-two years, and although most were married, there was also a higher number of single women reported by the police during this period. Typical occupations of this group included housewife, waitress, machine operator, policy clerk, and policy writer. Most were arrested for selling policy slips, possessing policy-related paraphernalia, or keeping a policy house.

I find that Chicago mayor Martin Kennelly initiated an assault on policy gambling in the late 1940s. As he intensified police raids in African American neighborhoods, Kennelly's police force brought in an average of one thousand women per year on policy charges, a trend that continued through Mayor Richard J. Daley's election and term beginning in late 1955. Police surveillance was a constant in the lives of African American women policy workers.

Using arrest records and criminal proceedings, chapter 6, "Legal Strategies for Policy Women," examines arrest rates and Chicago Municipal Court and Illinois Appellate Court/Supreme Court records of non-conviction for policy gambling violations. I also examine the Fourth Amendment's exclusion and exclusionary rule to scrutinize policy's role in the Chicago police's reliance on search and seizure laws to make policy-related arrests. The unusual combination of frequent arrests and few convictions created a "quasi-criminal" status for Black women that had a range of adverse social consequences both within and outside the policy gambling industry.

As stated above, policy existed and was regarded as a feasible option for an overwhelming number of African American women who found the formal economy lacking. Policy enabled women to improve their lives and leave inheritances for their children, as Harriett Jones did for the Jones Brothers Department Store and Eudora Johnson did for her family, although they were rare exceptions. *Dream Books and Gamblers* encourages a reevaluation of the methods African American women used to open new economic vistas, demanding that we move past contributory roles for

Black women in the formal and informal economy and view their labors as central to the economic vitality of Bronzeville. The multiple women who emerged from the archives whose stories are featured in this monograph pushed me to consider how Black women were the critical fulcrum around which womanhood and capitalism within racist and sexist contexts pivoted. Women's labors in policy gambling supports Treva B. Lindsey's assertion that "the range of African-American women's experiences and perspectives during this era refuted any notion of a monolithic, singular 'Black woman's experiences.'"[51] This book offers a gendered analysis of the variety of Black women's participation in the policy industry. It focuses on African American women actors, their anxieties, and how they used policy gambling to make a better life for themselves. To more fully understand their labors in Chicago and other urban centers, and to embrace the full scope of African American womanhood, we must understand their own self-articulation as more than mere contributors in Chicago's policy era.

Chicago's policy women—wives, queens, runners, gamblers, and conjurers—capitalized on their tenuous relationship to the economy as well as the men in their lives. In doing so, they came to realize otherwise previously unheard of possibilities. Welcome to my glimpse of their world.

1

"The Best Job I Ever Had"

Policy took off in Chicago in the 1880s and 1890s, where it was run by "Policy Sam" Young and John "Mushmouth" Johnson.[1] Johnson was backed by politicians and men who had "political pull," which ensured that the game went on "without interference on the part of Chief [Joseph] Kipley and the police."[2] By 1901 the city's major newspapers expressed chagrin that policy was running rampant "all over the city."[3] The *Tribune* tracked the game from Lakeview Avenue south to Sixty-Third Street, and from Western Avenue east to Lake Michigan, dotting the city with four thousand "policy shops" bustling with writers, clerks, pickup men for the morning and afternoon drawings for the 146,000 bets taken, and winnings delivered daily on the South, West, and North sides of the city.[4] But the locations of these "dens" of untoward economic activity were difficult for police to track due to their frequent relocation to elude monitoring.[5] Such evasive tactics worked because "policy shops, drawing money chiefly from the pockets of the poorest, honeycomb[ed] the entire city."[6]

Policy began in New York in the antebellum era and died off in the early years of the twentieth century to be replaced by a new game based on the New York Clearing House numbers. Matthew Vaz explains:

> The numbers game, first appearing in Harlem in the early 1920s, relied on an uncontrollable, and agreed-upon, daily published figure to generate a win-

ning three-digit number. Originally, the game used the three digits before
the decimal point in the published totals of the New York Clearing House
(a respected financial institution). The game later shifted reliance on local
racetracks to generate figures. If the Aqueduct Racetrack published a daily
intake total of $142,549.75 then the winning number for the day was 549
and any New Yorker could verify this outcome by looking at the right spot
in the newspaper, while feeling confident that the outcome was not rigged.[7]

Chicago, though, was different in that Chicago's gamblers could pick their
favorite numerical combinations for various drawings during the day—putting a "policy" on their favorite picks.[8] Chicago started and ended with this
distinct feature of insuring one's picks: "For a small sum, usually a fraction
of the cost of a lottery ticket, individuals could insure or take a policy on a
number with a broker or agent."[9]

One of the reasons these establishments survived as attractive labor options for Black men and women is because vice establishments did business
without interference from law enforcement, with some of them patronized
by policemen.[10] Early on in New York, police were taking thousands of
dollars in bribes to leave policy shops unmolested.[11] A similar connection
between police corruption and enforcement of gambling laws characterized
the policy game in Chicago. Will Cooley informs readers that Chicago has
a long tradition of tolerating vice as long as it remained in the Black Belt:
"City officials had tolerated vice in the Levee District until 1912, when reformers successfully closed it down. However, gambling, prostitution, and
drug dealing simply moved into other areas of the city, especially the Black
Belt, with the approval of law enforcement."[12] Cooley cites a 1917 *Chicago
Tribune* article that described the dozen disreputable houses operating
openly within a few hundred yards of the Twenty-Second Street police
station.[13] According to Simon Balto, police corruption and inefficiency were
particularly acute in Chicago, earning the Chicago Police Department a
reputation as the "most demoralized, graft-ridden and inefficient among our
larger cities."[14] Nathan Thompson, author of an informal history of policy
kings and numbers racketeers, crafts a list of police officers and politicians
who took bribes from gambling bosses like Policy Sam, Giveadam Jones,
and Henry Teenan.[15]

But payoffs between gambling kings and queens, politicians, and the
police could not always guarantee Black control over Chicago policy gambling. With the repeal of Prohibition, white gangsters who had prospered

in the illegal alcohol trade scrambled for new sources of revenue, and the numbers business, Matthew Vaz comments, seemed like an easy target.[16] In 1930, in particularly brutal fashion, Black bosses of policy gambling lost control of the game to the Italian organized crime syndicate known as "the Outfit." White gangsters murdered Black policy king Walter J. Kelly in 1939. The Jones brothers and their mother, whose story is the focus of chapter 3, gave up their gambling enterprises after Outfit associates kidnapped the eldest brother, Ed, in 1946 and held him for ransom. The Joneses fled to Mexico City and left their businesses to Ted Roe, who by 1950 was the last independent Black policy king left in Chicago. Two assassins shot Roe on August 4, 1952, and the *Chicago Defender* reported that the Outfit had "dethroned the last king of a rapidly vanishing policy empire."[17] The fatal blow to Black control of policy gambling arrived in 1974, when Illinois launched the Illinois State Lottery. Activists and public officials like Brenetta Howell Barrett and Senator Lewis A. H. Caldwell testified in favor of local control of gambling, but ultimately state lottery expansionists prevailed.[18]

Black Women's Quotidian Life in Policy Gambling

Policy was a complex operation—a true human resources feat that created, by necessity, its own infrastructure. For example, Queen Florine Stephens employed nearly sixty policy runners in her operation, most of whom were women—specifically, women who loved their jobs.[19] Policy employees called the game "a godsend" or "the best job [they] ever had."[20]

African American women of Chicago relied on policy gambling as a source of economic and social security. The industry afforded the opportunity to ameliorate their poverty, ascend the social ladder, and establish stability within their homes. At the same time, however, the mobility and evasiveness required by policy work undermined the sense of security that attracted African American women to its employ in the first place. This was particularly evident after Chicago authorities began to crack down on the game in the late 1940s. Against the backdrop of heightened police scrutiny, gendered webs emerged around policy that connected the public and domestic arenas where women employed by policy worked and lived. I map those webs by following the daily habits of African American women policy workers to illustrate how policy work demanded women's visibility. The experiences of women policy workers diverged along class lines as well as in response to the type of work they performed in the industry. They shared notions of domesticity, working to establish the home as both a sanctuary as well as a place of work. Similarly, their social lives took on multiple and at times contradictory meanings. Finally, they were subject to divergent reputations in the eyes of the public; the press reported them either as denigrated "policy workers" or glorified "women of fame."

Policy's diverse occupations contributed to vastly different gendered experiences in Bronzeville. I highlight what women shared and didn't as writers, clerks, runners, and queens. Their narratives reflect the universal importance of making money, strengthening their relationships with one another across time and space, as well as the extent to which their line of work made them vulnerable to law enforcement. At times this instability and scrutiny put them in competition or at odds with one another. The quotidian fabric of policy procedures—how to place a bet, how to pick up money, where to drop money, how to spin a wheel, what a station looked and felt like—contrasted with more sobering tensions faced by Black working women. Arrest and the possibility of jail time were lived realities for these women, who even in the worst times had to ensure there would be dinner on the table. The rhythms and realities of policy work unfolded across Chicago's dynamic landscape, providing a gendered geography of Black women's working and domestic spaces. The paths traced by policy writing, clerking, and running often penetrated both public and private spheres, rendering Black women's domestic spaces exposed to aggressive police and public intrusion especially after 1945.

Policy as Women's Work

African American women were fundamental to policy operations from the beginning as ordinary laborers and in the quickly ascending elite of policy gambling. Their work in policy took many different forms. According to Gustav G. Carlson, a 1940 researcher of numbers, policy, and the Italian lottery in Detroit, Chicago, and Harlem, the writer, or runner, occupied the lowest position in the community.[21] Writers solicited bets for the drawings that took place twice a day at wheels located at policy stations. Policy clerks, on the other hand, ran operations at policy stations. They answered phones, printed policy slips, orchestrated the spinning of the policy wheel, and tabulated winnings. In other regions of the country, these labors were divided into separate designations such as cashiers and checkers, and women often filled both categories.[22] Policy clerks took slips containing bets to check the tickets for winners after the drawing had been completed.[23] As cashiers, they were accountants of the wheels, assembling stacks of money to disseminate at collection stations across the city.[24] They were stationed at offices or "policy houses," places of congregation where the writers, pickup men, and other individuals would "loaf and discourse upon the perennial topic of numbers."[25] These were not female-sanctioned spaces, according to early twentieth-century gender norms.[26] Women, therefore, adopted pseudo-feminine roles in the policy industry, taking on its secretarial aspects. For example, they prepared all matters—printing, stocking, and accounting—before the wheels were spun. As clerks, they tabulated every bet taken by writers throughout the city and made proper entries in the books of the house.[27]

Drawings were a chaotic symphony of noise, people, and movement, as Lewis A. Caldwell describes:

> Everything is quiet except for the jingling of money and whir of adding machines in the cage. One of the announcers secures from the locked storeroom, which is behind the cage, a small keg which has an opening in the center. From a box he empties the seventy-eight numbers or "pills" to be dropped into the keg under the supervision of someone in the audience. This same person then draws from the keg or drum the twelve numbers which constitute the drawing. The drum is thoroughly shaken after each number is selected. . . . As the last number is announced, the second guard, who has set up the numbers in the special press as they were being called, rushes to a small front room in which there is an electrically operated press. The cylinder is inserted and policy slips are printed. . . . Writers and pickup men have formed lines at the four windows of the office-cage where they are paid off for all winning combinations appearing in their books. Another line is filing past the press where each individual writer receives a "block" of slips, which he distributes to his customers.[28]

The entire drawing ceremony took on a stock exchange environment, "with men rushing back and forth, numbers being called, and the general loud talking and excitement."[29] Women were involved in inserting rolls of papers into the presses that printed policy slips at the rate of three hundred per minute.[30] Drawings were heavily guarded by armed men. A wheel manager, or executive officer—who was sometimes a woman—oversaw these operations. But this person was seldom the owner of the business, which illustrates the hierarchical nature of policy gambling employment, because the manager had to report to the king or queen.

The most dangerous work was employment as "pickup men," who ran money back to the houses, to clerks, and to wheel operators. Very few women held these roles and, at most, a select few managed the men in these positions. Everyone associated with the house was dependent on pickup men:

> The function of the pick-up man is to collect the bets of all the writers within a given area and it is he who carries the bets to the house. In some organizations the pick-up man is the only contact that the writer has with the house for which he writes. In such cases, the writer does not even know where the house is located. In most instances, however, he knows the whereabouts of the house and will frequently carry his own take to the house.[31]

Policy writers depended on pickup men, who were often their only point of contact with the house. This served to be both advantageous as well as precarious for women. First, the lack of visibility required of them in comparison with the pickup man afforded them more cover from the police. Little connection with the house would hinder law enforcement's ability to track them to the house's illegal activity. On the other hand, it also meant little protection if they were arrested. Without ever having seen the house or individuals in upper management, women arrested for writing had little valuable knowledge to wager with police to obtain collateral for plea bargains or other deals. Women's relationship to the house and pickup men helps us reconsider the visibility of their labor in this particular sector of the informal economy.

Most women employed in the policy industry worked tirelessly among the hundreds of other writers at the bottom of the policy operation. And, unfortunately, some faced arrests or fines, and several even faced jail time. Police harassment was constant but not necessarily a deterrent. One woman reflected in 1940, "The police were taking us down in droves, but Joe had a bondsman and lawyers, so we never stayed long. Twenty-five dollars each was the usual fee. Many times, the women were 'sprung' before the wagon came to take us to the station. I saw the inside of a police station just once in five years."[32] A 1941 *Defender* article by Dianna Briggs confirmed this report: nearly a hundred people were apprehended in a policy raid. The defendants packed a State Street criminal court for nearly a week, but only two emerged with convictions or fines—twenty-five dollars each for Miss Lillian Nelson and Willie Mack—everyone else was discharged.[33]

Writers had to avoid detection while making themselves available to their audience. Avoidance was an expression of the conspicuousness of their work and was also key to the economic survival of a house or station. On each slip was printed the name of the wheel, which made its location obvious to police, certainly, but also to potential customers. Therefore, little contact with writers seemed an obvious tactic to employ to evade detection. As Caldwell reported, "For the sake of expediency the pick-up men, who must also return the results, never left their machines [automobiles] but nonchalantly toss[ed] the packets of slips onto the street in front of the stations where anyone might see them."[34] Employees of the policy wheel had to be nimble enough to avoid discovery but visible and accessible to those interested in placing bets on a daily or even twice-daily basis. It was a difficult balance. The community rose to help. Robert Roy, a columnist for the *Chicago Defender*, offered this advice in his 1960 column "Behind the Scenes":

> Attention operators of the???? [*sic*] (Cyclone) policy wheel: CHECK ONE OF YOUR DRIVERS who insists on leaving "slips" in window of a certain Drexel Boulevard address—THERE'S ALWAYS chance that cops might enter the apartment lobby and pick up the slips and wait around to catch the pick-up man at a later hour.—YOU SHOULD ADVISE the fellow (a new man it seems) to return later if no one answers bell in apartment where he is to deliver the policy slips.—YOUR "SCENES" EDITOR could catch the pickup man easily if such an assignment was part of his duty.[35]

However careless, runners and pickup men were the arteries of the operation, serving as the lines between taking bets and delivering the winnings. Pickup men were vital at money-drop stations, which were always in danger of being hit by raiding police parties or thieves. After two days of surveillance, police arrested two women managing a policy money-drop or collection station on Michigan Avenue that, uncharacteristic of most women's roles with collection stations, handled impressive dollar amounts. Under the operation of Miss Celeste White, the drop station funneled about twelve thousand dollars per day into the Windy-City-Subway-Big Town policy wheel's coffers. Between ten and fifteen runners dropped money off at the collection station on an average day, each leaving between five hundred to a thousand dollars.[36] White's arrest was a triumph for the Chicago police in the late 1960s.

Salaries for positions within the policy organization differed regionally. In Chicago the weekly salaries paid for each type of job in 1937 were as follows:

Station Manager—20% of business
Station Checkers—$45.00/week
Field Checkers—$40.00/week
Pick-up men—$35.00/week
Guards—$25.00/week
Writers—20% of business secured.[37]

An interviewee for the Council of Federated Church Records commented that despite their position at the lowest rank of this pay scale, "there are many girls who work in policy stations and make between fifteen and twenty-five dollars a week and they seem to be satisfied with their jobs."[38] In Detroit, another popular policy gambling center, the pay scale in 1940 was slightly better and had its own unique hierarchy:

Station Manager/Executive—$50–$200/week
Operator—unknown
Checkers—$10.00/week
Clerks—unknown
Cashiers—unknown
Pickup men—10% of money from territory
Writers—20% of independent earnings from territory.[39]

The differences in pay between Chicago and Detroit stand out, but the similarities—that policy writers made the least amount of money—are important to studying African American women's roles in the policy gambling industry. The fact that policy writers were the lowest paid meant it was not uncommon for women policy writers to seek additional labor from within policy as checkers, clerks, and cashiers when permitted in order to augment their meager and often unpredictable salaries. The number of policy writers employed by a single organization varied; according to Carlson, the average was three hundred to five hundred writers.[40] Larger organizations, like the Jones brothers' operation (discussed at greater length in chapter 3), employed thousands to cover as much ground as possible.

Rarely, if ever, did policy queens manage their own wheels, which can be read as a strategy to navigate their visibility in the industry and respectability politics. Policy queens Irene Coleman, Leslie Williams, and Ann Roane owned but did not manage their wheels. Coleman and Williams co-owned the Belmont and Old Reliable policy wheels, which had formerly been owned by Irene's father, the late Buddy Coleman. Roane, whose wealth came from her ex-husband, Detroit policy king Irving Roane (whom she had divorced in 1939 before moving to Chicago), partnered in ownership with Matt Bivins in the Alabama/Georgia, Jackpot, and Whirlaway wheels.[41] All women policy bank owners remained in the background, leaving the daily operations to male managers.[42] Operating in the queen's and king's absence, "the position of the manager is an important one and he is paid accordingly,"[43] Carlson noted. Most important for these policy queens, their managers provided the necessary safeguard for them to maintain distance while profiting immensely from policy gambling, confirming a strategy of visibility that kept their feminine status intact.

For policy to work as a cultural resource for Black women, policy workers had to either hide or leverage their visibility in the industry and before law enforcement in such a way as to wrestle it away from its being cast as a criminal menace. Policy work's appearance in government statistics of gainful employment and on census forms, despite its illegality, shows Black women legitimating their informal work. There are several instances in the census that raise the interesting point that some women identified themselves as policy employees to census enumerators. Given the illegality of the game, as well as the possibility of increased and continued surveillance over their bodies and their domestic and labor spaces and communities, it is puzzling that some women were open about their occupation. Unlike prostitution, policy work was not relegated to the shadows but appears in government statistics of gainful employment; census takers recorded "policy clerk" and "policy writer" as "gainful employment."[44] In the 1930 and 1940 censuses, several women identified themselves as policy employees, either policy writers or policy clerks. Throughout my research I was unable to confirm women's fear of repercussions or that they were afraid that their exposure jeopardized their legal freedom or put them on law enforcers' radar. Instead, the records indicate that African American women were employed at all levels and in all applications of the industry—as policy writers, clerks, runners, station managers, and managing pickup men. Most had been born in the Gulf South, were between twenty and forty years old, rarely single, and typically possessed between a sixth- and ninth-grade education.[45]

Dangerous and demeaning formal labor means that for many women policy was the best alternative. A woman who had recently migrated to Chicago from Oklahoma confirmed this when she explained:

> I left Oklahoma with my two children, two and three years old, in 1921 after saving money from my maid's job. My husband was glad to get rid of us. Two days after being in Chicago I got a dishwashing job in a north side restaurant. In 1925 a doctor told me to stop that work because the soap was injuring my hands. I had to do something in order to feed my children, so got a job writing policy. I was given instruction for a week before I got a book. In less than a month I was writing $20.00 a day, and keeping five for my share. From then until 1930 I made good money. . . . It was the best job I ever had. . . . In 1928 there were 800 writers working for my boss and about half of them were women.[46]

Her reflections suggest that policy writing was economically viable employment. But some policy workers found the pay inadequate and juggled policy with other professions.[47] Carlson noted that in the 1940s, many writers worked informally while on the clock: "The milkman may pick up bets left by his customers with the empty bottles; the janitor in some large office building may make the duty of emptying wastebaskets the occasion for taking bets in the various offices. Boot-Blacks, elevator boys, and red caps also write numbers as a lucrative side-line."[48] Census data also confirms that policy wasn't adequate as a single source of income. When women listed "writer" or "policy clerk" as their primary occupation, they also checked the "other source of employment" box on the census form. During the Great Depression, many turned to policy when relief efforts or other occupations fell short. Such was the experience of Mrs. G. W. Neighbors, an upper-middle-class African American woman. In a 1938 interview, she told policy reformers, "I know a lady whose husband was ill and I heard her tell in a grocery store all about how policy had helped them get work and there was no relief then and she turned to policy."[49]

Policy writing was a highly public job and one that required a woman to move frequently to avoid arrest and suspicion. One could be arrested for merely carrying policy slips or policy paraphernalia or having them in their apartment.[50] Some writers went door-to-door, while others received bets at stations.[51] On average a woman lived less than half a mile from the closest policy station between 1930 and 1949.[52] Door-to-door writers, Carlson noted, reminded people of salesmen: "If his [a writer's] sole occupation is writing numbers he is assigned to a definite area which he canvasses daily going from house to house like any ordinary salesman. His activity is so similar to that of the collectors for the Metropolitan Life Insurance Company that the insurance salesmen are commonly referred to in the community as 'Metro-policy' men."[53] That life insurance salesmen were referred to as "policy men" indicates how popular and visible policy writers were in Bronzeville. It also suggests how revolutionary women policy writers were. Among the chief assets of the women writers Carlson recalled from his youth were "nerve and integrity—the former being necessary to take the rap if caught by the police and the latter in enabling to build up a large clientele."[54] Their grit can be viewed as a transgression of strict gender roles.

Carlson confirmed the ever-pervasive feature of the writer, locating them across masculine and feminine spaces: "[The policy writer] is a ubiquitous element in the community and is encountered in practically every place where people congregate—in hotels, stores, barber-shops, pool rooms, and even in church parlors."[55] Yet women executed strategic networking and canvassing skills to build up geographies of bet taking and solicitation to make their profits for the day by abiding to routes that kept their femininity intact. They also kept their families together. Bridgett M. Davis stressed that because of policy gambling, her mother, Fannie, "wasn't forced to leave her children at home with just each other, while she went to work for low pay. Every day when we came home from school, my mother was there. In fact, my siblings and I never had babysitters."[56] Navigating the boundaries of gendered labor in this way, women maintained kinship networks while utilizing those networks for profit. Solicitations took place near the kitchen sink, clotheslines, the beauty shop, and along sidewalk play spaces.[57]

Social Status and Standing

Status meant everything for the queens of the industry. One member of the Garnet Girls Club, a popular charity and social club whose most famous members were related to Harriett Jones, Chicago's most notorious policy queen, commented, "You know Chicago thinks so much about how much

... a person has. There are people here who don't accept anybody unless
they have family background, schooling, looks, and money."[58] The barrier
between policy queens and policy employees had to be firm; queens, especially unmarried ones, could show no sign of dependency on others for
their wealth. It was the protective barrier that allowed Irene Coleman and
Leslie Williams to enjoy an exciting yet competitive public life, rubbing
shoulders with Bronzeville's finest social set in the most visible fashion
while downplaying the nature of their incomes.

If queens did not socialize with their employees, they often interacted
with each other, and the public devoured it. In 1938 and 1940, for example,
Coleman and Williams attended the First Mid-West Horse Show at the
American Giants' Park.[59] I. E. Kelly (a lesser-known policy king), William
"Big" Russell, policy king McKissack Jones, and James J. Gentry also enjoyed the show. A 1940 *Jet* magazine article reported that Leslie Williams
and her father, Buddy Coleman, enjoyed the anniversary party of the Royalites, an elite social club with a reputation for welcoming the "nation's most
style-conscious ladies" and the "best-dressed group of club women in the
city."[60] The same article described a lavish social affair hosted at the home
of Royalite Miss Audrey Hinton, saying that the gathering and its hostess
were "the last word in fun. . . . Miss Hinton, who evidences her exquisite
taste not only in her surroundings but in a smart personal wardrobe, has
recently had the rooms decorated to resemble a beautiful miniature tavern
on the one side, and a home like game room on the other."[61] The Royalites
were the darlings of *Jet*'s society pages well into the 1960s. Williams's attendance at Royalite events was a marker of her acceptance into the most elite
social circles. These details enthralled readers, offering them just enough
glitz for admirers and plenty for those who may have been watching to see
if or when the queen would fall from grace.

Policy queen Ann Roane adopted a decidedly different strategy to pro-
cure fame. Her marriage to Detroit policy king Irving Roane was a brief but
highly public affair. When the marriage ended, she received a large sum of
money, nearly "$11,140 in the divorce settlement."[62] A few months later,
Irving Roane was indicted along with John Roxborough, a noted Detroit
policy king and manager of the world-famous boxer Joe Louis, on charges
of "a graft conspiracy for the protection of the alleged $10,000,000-a-year
numbers and policy racket." Also named in the indictment were eight African American police officers and seventy-six white police officers.[63] Irving

Roane pled guilty and was ordered to pay fifteen hundred dollars.[64] His ex-wife, Ann, managed to avoid the courtroom altogether, subsequently moving to Chicago and remarrying in 1941. Al Monroe, of the *Chicago Defender*, mockingly referred to Ann's considerable wealth, undermining her husband in a column that announced her second marriage: "Thus where there was a fine car now there is a finer car in the Armstead household." He continued: "Do you know? That Ann Roane, bride of William Armstead[,] is the divorced wife of Irving Roane, one of Detroit's 'well heeled' guys. Flash! And that she isn't exactly walking on her toes either."[65]

Ann lived a life of opulence and enjoyed policy's profits ostentatiously. By 1943 she set up residence at the DuSable Hotel.[66] She began new business ventures in Bronzeville, using the winnings from her wheels and her policy contacts. In 1943 she joined forces with Harriett Jones, the Jones brothers, and the Joneses' family attorney, Aaron Payne, to launch her own branch of the Jones/Payne Hawthorn Mellody Farms milk distributorship at 3562 Cottage Grove Avenue.[67] Other women followed Roane's lead by opening or operating legitimate businesses while raking in thousands from policy wheels. For example, Lillian Daniels profited greatly by permitting gambling in her funeral home. She grossed between fifteen hundred and two thousand dollars daily at her funeral parlor at 6642 Ingleside Avenue.[68] Both Roane and Daniels deployed employees and legitimate businesses as barriers between themselves and possible injuries to their reputations through association with policy gambling.

All three queens—Irene Coleman, Leslie Williams, and Ann Roane—were indicted for policy gambling in June 1942. After a three-day trial, twenty-six alleged policy wheel owners went free in a criminal court before Judge John Sbarbaro.[69] Although they were charged with conspiracy, Sbarbaro ruled that the state had not produced sufficient evidence to prove that a conspiracy existed. The trial pitted the testimonies of policy operators and writers against those of the wheel owners. The trial ended when Robert Marcus, a white bondsman, took the stand and denied that any of the owners attempted to bail out their employees who had been arrested. He thereby refuted any culpability on behalf of the policy kings and queens, leaving the lesser rank-and-file employees vulnerable—and visible. Writers and clerks such as Inez Wright, Maxine Gilliam, and Anna Rita Barnes took the stand to testify against policy kings and queens Coleman, Williams, and Roane. All three women took considerable risks in doing so. They must have wondered whether they would have a job at the trial's end. Queens were clearly in the most advantageous position.

Public Opinion

The dualities of policy gambling were so prolific that public opinion even differed on women's status in the game. This was due in part to the continually shifting reputation of policy writers and clerks in the *Chicago Defender* and *Ebony* magazine.[70] One such example was Mrs. Helen French. French worked as a policy writer for Ben Johnson, a policy king and owner of a dry cleaning establishment. Johnson was found guilty of tarnishing French's name by distributing five thousand printed handbills that branded her a thief: "This woman, Mrs. Helen French[,] is a thief and a robber. She stole $40 in 'hit' money from me. Let all of us policy station owners ban together against this sort of thing. You furnish me the names of those who have stole[n] from you and I'll do likewise."[71] French was awarded five thousand dollars in a libel suit in a 1938 circuit court. Her case demonstrates the informal economy worker's ability and savviness to use the legal system to their advantage. French's appearance in court and subsequent success shows the court's tacit approval of her informal economic labors. It seemed the law stood by her, keeping her respectability intact.

On the other hand, the law could also disqualify policy gambling as a means of fiscal security and social standing. In 1941 the *Defender* reported on a convincing young woman who wrote the State Division of Placement and Unemployment Compensation to solicit unemployment compensation benefits. The *Defender* reported that it was the woman's "policy to write policy and to write policy only."[72] When she became unemployed, the article reported, the woman filed a claim under the Illinois unemployment compensation law requiring persons who drew benefits to be able to work and to be available for work. They must also register for the Illinois State Employment Service and must accept any suitable work offered. But the young woman refused to accept any work other than policy because "in no other line of work could she make as much money as she could be making writing policy."[73] Officials said the law could not coerce her to accept work in a gambling house, since that would force her to violate the law. This young woman was willing to go to great lengths to write policy for a living and considered it worth her time and the state's efforts to compensate her for lost wages. But the state did not have to comply when policy was in the mix. The penalty for violating Chicago's policy laws ranged from small fines to short periods of incarceration. By being willing to risk their freedom and openly admit their connections to the policy racket, women opened themselves up to encounters with the carceral state.

Public scrutiny of policy women was severe, as evidenced by a 1952 article in *Ebony* with a subtitle that blared: "Police find that 'female of the species is often more deadly than the male in gambling, dope and other crimes.'"[74] It continues: "They operate independently of male accomplices and even murder does not faze these skirted hoodlums." The article starts in on gambling, saying, "Most bigtime vice queens have found gambling the most lucrative, least dangerous and most accepted racket [where] women raked in the biggest profits." Articles like this show that within the African American community, Black policy women appeared unwholesome. But women worked to reclaim their status as mothers and entrepreneurs. Was policy a cultural resource or a criminal menace? Although the question was raised by city officials and newspapers such as the *Chicago Tribune* and the *Chicago Defender*, the answer always depended on who was asking. Many of Chicago's sociologists, urban reformers, preachers, women's clubs, and local government officials linked policy to urban pathology and urban decay.[75] This is not how those who played it saw things. The game slips that littered Bronzeville's sidewalks and alleyways daily are indicative of a viable fiscal endeavor: a testament to a functioning, albeit informal and illicit, economy.[76] Bronzeville's lack of social services, financial institutions, commercial investment, and development, alongside ubiquitous segregation, gave rise to informal parallel institutions, many of which operated in the gray areas between legitimacy and criminal behavior. As I show in this book, African American women read this complex landscape of segregation, respectability, and sexism and mapped their bets through the informal economy. As a result, they encountered risk and, at times, paid a great price.

Disdain for policy certainly was not universal, as interviews from the 1938 Council of Federated Church Records indicate. For example, Mrs. Henry Mae Mitchell was a woman on relief, trying to get a job with the Works Progress Administration, and a member of the prominent Olivet Baptist Church. She "thought that policy is all right, gives Negroes more work than others, she says."[77] Mrs. G. W. Neighbors, wife of a famous *Defender* photographer, did not look down on people who played policy. She noted that "everyone has an opinion on policy but they aren't molested with door-to-door sales of policy."[78] At the same time, however, she insisted that the barrier between her immediate family and policy should remain firm: "I wouldn't want my daughter to work in a policy station."[79]

Radically, some wives' comments revealed a preference for social striving via vice, regardless of what their husbands thought. For example, Mrs. Pearl Managree agreed to sit down for an interview in 1938 at her home, "a very nice four-room apartment." Christopher Van Buren, the interviewer, noticed immediately that the "lawns are in very good condition, and the streets are very clean. On entering the court-way building, I noticed that the building was in very good condition."[80] Van Buren asked how the Managrees "made it," financially, in Chicago. According to Mr. Managree, his wife was highly influential, but he relayed that she was not as staunch as he in her opposition to gambling, drinking, or carousing: "My wife tells me sometimes now that maybe I would be better off today had I done some of these things but however I get along fine. I have a few friends and am making a little money." His conclusions intimate that his wife may have wanted more for the couple and saw vice as a legitimate means to obtain it. But in an effort to recover appearances, he quickly asserted, "I do not play policy and I don't think any of my family plays. I would like to see the entire game stamped out. I think it is the worst thing in most communities today." He further maintained the very real barrier between the couple's legitimate class status and vice by stating emphatically, "I do not think there is a policy station in this block."[81] His navigation of the formal and informal economy evidently worked, because the Managrees were favorites of the *Chicago Defender*'s society pages; they appeared regularly in its "Around and About Chicago" column, and the paper praised Mrs. Managree for her work as a sponsor of the Women's Civic League Style Review.[82] Their case is an illustration that social status, vice, gender, and the necessary barrier between these elements were powerful forces in the alchemy of Bronzeville's status seekers and keepers.

Policy queens, operators, cashiers, checkers, clerks, and writers derived new formulas for working in this industry through their own innovation and creativity. Helen French, policy writer, used a libel case to keep her reputation intact. Irene Coleman; Leslie Williams; Ann Roane; Lillian Daniels, with her funeral home policy operation; and Celeste White, who managed a sophisticated money-drop system, all erected sophisticated facades to keep their reputations and finances in order. Their success stories offered clerks, writers, and runners the hope of social mobility, security, and domestic sanctuary through the policy industry. Some stories, however, offered only narratives of loss when lower-level policy workers clashed with queens. Through women's aggregate labors, however, policy proved to be a lucrative and solid option for women until the late 1960s. The ability to work a short distance from home, the rhythm of the clerking and writing bets, and the popularity that came with canvassing their own neighborhoods made the work attractive and conducive to African American women's lived realities.

However advantageous working out of the home was, its conspicuousness was problematic for women who sought to maintain domestic security due to the threat of arrest or violence. Furthermore, they regularly faced the need to find a balance between maintaining a home and a successful workplace. Policy's advantages and disadvantages, however, required the visibility of Black women in the city, making them vulnerable to police intrusion, violence, and economic risk. As a result, they experienced Bronzeville in geographic and surveillance modes unfamiliar to others; theirs was a unique Black working experience defined by the contours of their visibility as laborers in the shadow economy. It made policy gambling appealing, but it also placed policy women in a dangerous and unreliable position. For some, however, it was worth the risk.

2

Chicago's First Policy Queens

The population of African Americans in Chicago increased from 3,600 residents in 1870 to 6,480 in 1880.[1] By 1885 the ranks swelled to 10,376, and by 1890 the population had risen to 14,852 yet still accounted for only 1.3 percent of the city's total population.[2] Despite the small population, whites were pushing Black populations into an all-Black corridor along Lake Michigan southward from the central business district. Prosperous African Americans had begun to rent and buy property in South Side areas as early as the 1870s, and this southward trend accelerated through the remainder of the century.[3] By 1900, when more migrants were pouring into the city, 80 percent of the Black population lived on the South Side.[4] In order to cope, "respectable African Americans attempted to forge a virtuous community life in urban spaces frequently seen as odious by outsiders."[5] In the midst of this dramatic demographic shift for Chicago, the Black elite traversed city streets alongside the reputable middle and lower classes. According to Christopher Robert Reed, members of the Black elite and respectable middle class "moved as two ships passing in a fog-laden night. They glided past, often oblivious to one another's presence, and wished to stay that way so as to avoid the possibility of a social collision."[6] Respectability had its own spatial dynamics and structure based on an emerging, albeit unstable, three-tiered class system. The top class of this structure consisted of relatively few members, with middle-level "respectables" moving upward at a fast pace and a working class stuck at the bottom. The three classes mixed on the street, but the elite clambered for mechanisms to separate them socially to keep their status intact, lest controversy erupt.

To achieve upper-class status and secure it was quite a feat when definitions of class were unstable. A chance encounter on the sidewalk, where a policy- or sex-related transaction could occur, could tarnish one's reputation in a moment. Proximity to policy gambling threatened disrepute, especially for African American women of the upper class in South Side Chicago, and yet two women, Elizabeth Slaughter and Eudora Johnson—both linked to Chicago's most infamous Black policy king, John "Mushmouth" Johnson—managed to join their ranks.

John V. Johnson, nicknamed "Mushmouth" for his penchant for swearing, rose to fame and fortune after a short career as a Pullman porter and saloon proprietor, becoming Chicago's most legendary policy king until his death in 1907. Mushmouth's financial means laid the course for his family's future trajectory. The family migrated to Chicago in the late nineteenth century, when the African American population in that city was small.[7] Mushmouth took a job in a saloon upon his arrival in Chicago in 1873, quickly gaining fame among the partying set. The road to riches was difficult, and his first job established the emerging family patriarch as a hard type. He was known as a pioneer in the field of craps and policy games, credited with having made half a million dollars in 1903.[8] In several stories appearing between 1901 and 1903, the *Chicago Daily Tribune* listed Mushmouth as lieutenant to policy king "Patsy King."[9] The paper reported, "Johnson is so high in the regard of the boss that he is given free rein in the operation of the bungaloo games and in promoting policy in general among the colored population."[10] Soon Mushmouth eclipsed King as the leader of the policy underground. With the Black Belt's informal economy solidly in his control, Mushmouth purchased a house at 5830 Wabash Avenue, establishing him as a member of Black Chicago's elite.[11] He thrived within the informal economy while he "supported his family's aspirations" and, by extension, all of Black Chicago's.[12] He reportedly paid the tuition for his cousin Cecelia Johnson to attend the University of Chicago. Mushmouth's brother Elijah used the gambling proprietor's legacy to open the Dreamland Ballroom, which would eventually become the famous Dreamland Café.

Battling a serious illness for several years off and on between 1904 and his death in 1907, Mushmouth died with $250,000 to his name, "eight pieces of real estate, a handful of notes owed to him from various people, and three warehouse receipts for five barrels of Anderson Club Whiskey."[13] Unfortunately, he left no will. Articles in the *Chicago Defender* and the *Broad Ax* depict surviving members of the family vying for their portions of the fortune.[14] Mushmouth's surviving brother, Elijah, and sisters, Eudora and Louisa Ray, fought over the inheritance after their mother, Ellen, died.[15] Even before Ellen passed, Eudora took the lead in a public battle against Mushmouth's lover, Elizabeth B. Slaughter, a well-known milliner.[16] The court documents and newspaper articles evidenced that Eudora, as his eldest sister, saw the inheritance as hers—and was willing to go to great lengths to obtain it.[17] In doing so, she risked publicly tarnishing her name against that of Slaughter, a successful and reputable female entrepreneur. Every Chicago paper was quick to pick up the story, and eventually a good part of the estate, roughly $150,000 or more, went to Eudora.[18] But this was hardly the last time the papers would focus on Slaughter or Eudora.

This chapter explores the history of policy queens through the lens of the two women competing for Mushmouth's fortune—Elizabeth Slaughter and Eudora Johnson (later Binga). They were the subject of nearly every Chicago parlor—Black or white—throughout the late nineteenth and early twentieth centuries. Their lives help us understand the different trajectories of Black womanhood before the Great Migration.[19] Their different paths were defined by the emerging definition of "policy queen" during this time. Their lives provide vital glimpses into what it meant to be a woman rising in social status on Chicago's South Side, what the small number of women in a similar position could hope to attain, and how precarious that position was when one was visibly associated with policy gambling.

Their biographies demonstrate that the Great Migration offered an unprecedented point of entry for women into higher classes and opportunity to acquire new social capital. Both women fit the assertion that Black Chicagoans possessed a "high level of vigor, competitiveness, and restlessness. As a group in flux and full of ambition, it was freed of many of life's obligations."[20] Such a characterization of the population as driven and competitive reflects the women's wealth, education, and a high degree of marriageability. But their relation to Mushmouth and his involvement with policy complicated such status. The women's strategies for procuring the title of policy queen reflected this; they took advantage of opportunities when they could and used whatever means necessary to secure respectability. They succeeded. Both achieved high standing among the Black Chicago movers and shakers; Reed listed Eudora Johnson as claiming influence from none other than Fannie Barrier Williams—a relationship that might also have put her within Ida B. Wells-Barnett's orbit.[21] As policy queens, both Slaughter and Eudora used policy to access the protective trappings of emerging Black respectability, reinforce ideas about racial uplift, and financially support Black Chicago's socioeconomic and cultural institutions.

The two women's stories lend insight into how as Chicago's first policy queens they navigated policy's troubling visibility by making space for philanthropy as well as criminal activity. They genuinely believed in both as ways to live their best lives. Employing their business expertise and wealth, Slaughter and Eudora subverted gender norms about Black women expounding competing notions about the sexual politics of respectability to reach the highest social class. Both women relied on their highly visible and much advertised proximity to policy to access and redefine the protective trappings of Black respectability that were emerging during the early twentieth century. Slaughter's and Eudora's ties to Mushmouth propound a definition of "policy queen" that challenges conventional and recent scholars' use of the term, one that confirms the two women's construction of the role. As Chicago's first policy queens, they show us what they valued in Chicago's informal economy and indicate that their ties to it did not compromise their social status. Slaughter and Eudora paved the way for other policy queens who rose to prominence during the Great Depression, like Harriett Jones, mother of the Jones brothers, but, as their biographies show, through divergent sexual and entrepreneurial politics. Their involvement in Black women's clubs, choice of husbands, ostentatious living, and extensive travel, which were thought of as pure frivolity by some, are essential to understand a particular Black womanhood in turn-of-the-century Chicago.

Policy Queen: Businesswoman

On the eve of the first wave of the Great Migration, Elizabeth Slaughter moved from Louisville, Kentucky, to Chicago to attend the Armour Institute (since renamed as the Illinois Institute of Technology). The details of her age and what year she enrolled are not known, but she was at least sixteen years old, as that was the cutoff age to enroll in courses at Armour's Department of Domestic Arts, specializing in millinery, and she graduated sometime in the late 1890s.[22] The department sought to familiarize students with both technical and specialized training, "the former being intended for those who desire professional training."[23] After several courses in the study of color and textiles, framing, design, and manufacture, Slaughter was permitted to "work for the Order Department, by which means experience is gained in making and trimming articles of millinery for the trade."[24]

Within a decade of Slaughter's graduation, she had a well-established business in Louisville. Louisville papers described her store as "admirably located, and she enjoys the patronage of the hat buying contingency of Louisville's 50,000 colored population. Her parlors are equipped with every appointment usually found in first class millinery emporiums."[25] In 1899 Washington, D.C.'s *Colored American* declared that Slaughter was "Womanhood's True Type" and "praised her 'extraordinary business ability,'" which exhibited the three pillars of womanhood: femininity, Blackness, and economic expertise.[26] The article's author stressed that Slaughter served an interracial clientele: "[Her shop is] well and neatly furnished, and she keeps on hand a line of goods that will please the best class of patrons among both races. I regard her work of great interest from the fact that she is one of the first among colored ladies who have made an effort along this line."[27] Her hiring practices showed a commitment to racial justice, as the *Colored American* pointed out: "Many girls who cannot find employment in places kept by white people, are here given the opportunity to equip themselves for a broad field of usefulness."[28]

Slaughter's reputation as a businesswoman was well established by the turn of the century, and using her Louisville experience, she set her sights on launching a business in Chicago. In 1903 she opened Green-Lilly Millinery at 128 East Thirtieth Street nestled in among the shops, clubs, theaters, and restaurants in Black Chicago's thriving commercial district known as the Stroll.[29] The *Broad Ax* praised her as "an expert in making all kinds of art or fancy needle work, and many of the ladies of fashion residing in the aristocratic parts of this city, gladly pay her the highest prices for her creations in this line."[30] As in Louisville, she never wavered in her commitment to employing fellow Black women: the *Broad Ax* reported that "she . . . hired local African-American female employees, making a name for herself among the race."[31]

FIGURE 3. Miss E. B. Slaughter. (G. F. Richings, *Evidences of Progress among Colored People*. Philadelphia: G. S. Ferguson, 1902. Courtesy of the Wilson Special Collections Library, University of North Carolina, Chapel Hill).

Her commitment to racial equity landed her a prominent spot in G. F. Richings's 1902 edition of *Evidences of Progress among Colored People*, an encyclopedia featuring leading Black citizens from all regions of the United States. Richings wrote this book because he wanted to counteract the misplaced white assertion that African Americans had not made progress since emancipation, and with regard to his African American audience, Richings hoped the book would "stimulate a greater interest in these institutions and thereby help to bring the race up to a higher educational and social level."[32] The book's sketch of Elizabeth Slaughter lauded her as a formidable competitor among white milliners, a reputation "that in itself will at least have a tendency to make white women engaged in such business treat their colored customers with more consideration."[33] The review held her up as a model representative of both her race and class, concluding, "I am sure that the better class of colored ladies are proud."[34] She set the civil rights standard for subsequent policy queens to follow.

Her millinery shop, licensure, and credentials positioned her to influence Black Chicagoans. Slaughter's business endeavors are also a fascinating demonstration of Black women's adornment politics and her desire to assert leadership in her community.[35] Her shops were places where African American women adorned their bodies in ways that reflected individual style, allowed for agency, and challenged white assumptions about Black womanhood and respectability. Tanisha Ford argues that sartorial practices like this provided opportunities for women to express their thoughts on upward social mobility and freedom.[36] Slaughter parlayed her success as a businesswoman into a geographic mobility that she enjoyed as she traveled in and out of Chicago for the next few years, returning to Louisville briefly for a time and then returning to Chicago in 1903.

Her remarkable fluidity as a member of Chicago's Black business world exhibited the tendency of many upwardly mobile migrants to relocate periodically between the South and North during the first wave of the Great Migration without sacrificing their businesses. The *Broad Ax* made frequent mention of Slaughter's comings and goings in its "Chips" social column. In 1905 she made the front page of the *Broad Ax* for prioritizing her commitment to her shop over chaperoning a squirrel-hunting and fishing trip for a women's club: "Lizzie Slaughter was unable to accompany the young ladies of St. Thomas' Guild to Waukesha on the account of an unexpected increase in her millinery business."[37] Clearly, Slaughter balanced business with the social demands of "the Girls Friendly Society of St. Thomas Episcopal Church," membership in which was a marker of high-society life.[38] As she bounced between Louisville and Chicago, she hosted friends from Lexington and vacationed with the elite in the aristocratic hideaway of Benton Harbor, Michigan. She finally settled in Chicago when she took up residence with an aunt at 3544 Dearborn Street.[39] All subsequent mentions of her in the *Broad Ax*'s "Chips" column refer to her at this Dearborn Street address.

It was "while she was building her business" that Slaughter began an unconventional—for the early twentieth century—liaison with "Mushmouth,"

Chicago's famed African American policy king.[40] On February 20, 1904, the "Chips" column on the front page of the *Broad Ax* reported that "Col. Mushmouth Johnson, so it is rumored, will in the near future lead Miss Lizzie Slaughter, who is quite pretty and very popular, to the altar in St. Thomas Church, and that she will become the Colonel's lovable and blushing bride."[41] For reasons unknown, the wedding was delayed. Unfortunately, Mushmouth fell ill in the spring of 1907 and died the following fall. His illness took a significant physical toll on Slaughter, and she was "seriously indisposed" for a week in June 1907.[42] A year later, in May 1908, the *Broad Ax* reported that she was confined to her home with a nervous breakdown for weeks.[43]

Shortly after, Slaughter sued Mushmouth's sister Eudora for ten thousand dollars in a libel and slander case.[44] Court records show that on September 7, 1907, in the presence and "hearing of certain persons," Eudora

> falsely and maliciously spoke and published of and concerning the plaintiff these other false, scandalous, malicious and defamatory words following, that is to say: "She" (meaning the plaintiff) "is my brother's" (meaning the defendant's brother), "kept woman;" "she" (meaning the plaintiff) "is a dirty, low, vulgar woman;" "she" (meaning the plaintiff) "is a woman without principle or character;" "she" (meaning the plaintiff) "is nothing but a dirty little whore;" "she"(meaning the plaintiff) "is my brother's mistress."[45]

The same court record stated that on September 30, 1907, Eudora spoke and published the following concerning Slaughter:

> Lizzie is nothing but a harlot, she is a kept woman, she is kept by my brother, she is my brother's kept woman, he has been intimate with her for five years, she has been sleeping with my brother, she is not and never will be married to my brother, but she has been intimate with him, she is a prostitute, she is a low woman, she is kept by my brother, she is a dissipated woman, and has been kept by my brother, my brother keeps her, she has acted the whore, she is my brother's mistress, she is a loose, low woman, she is a dissipated, low, vulgar woman, she is the cause of our family being unhappy.[46]

If the testimony is accurate, Eudora employed racist stereotypes and assumptions about Black women and their sexuality to make her case. She invoked the historically rooted enslaved Jezebel stereotype of "whore" to refute Slaughter's status as a respectable businesswoman. Eudora's comments invoked the legacy of long-lived racism and sexism that would have given her an advantage before an all-white jury.[47] However, Slaughter won in 1908. So powerful was Slaughter's standing as an entrepreneur and so-cialite that she survived this sexual scandal that made headlines across the city. She also might have been leaving a legacy of a competing notion about sexuality and sexual impropriety that was decades ahead for Black Chicago. It is clear from the trial that aspects of her relationship with Mushmouth were ambiguous, perhaps too progressive for early twentieth-century Chicago. It's also clear that the sexual scandal did not tarnish her reputation.

Slaughter maintained her place in Black Chicago's elite society post-trial. The *Broad Ax* reported in the year of the case that Slaughter and her lawyer, Edward H. Morris, attended functions together.[48] Well known in gambling circles, Morris became known as the "defendant attorney for the gambling fraternity."[49] According to "Chips," Slaughter spent summers at the Morris vacation home in Benton Harbor, Michigan, and entertained female friends at her Dearborn address.[50] The Morris-Slaughter association and the coverage of Slaughter's day-to-day doings in the *Broad Ax* demonstrate that in 1908, whatever Eudora's indictments were, the damage had not been permanent.

Slaughter pushed a complimentary narrative of policy queendom in newspapers, drawing attention to her business prowess through advertisements for the Green-Lilly Millinery Company in April 1911. The shop "invit[ed patrons] to their millinery display of ladies, misses' and children's hats. Latest styles. Prices reasonable."[51]

Her own beauty, too, was a component of Slaughter's policy queen reputation. In August 1912 she was a contender in a beauty contest at a street fair in Black Chicago. Jesse Binga, who had married Eudora earlier that year, had organized a carnival for the last two weeks of August. The *Broad Ax* ran advertisements for the carnival and its beauty contest for five weeks leading up to the contest. Slaughter's name appeared steadily in third place among the contestants although far behind the winner, Miss Hattie Holiday, who "accepted the honor with that Queenly modesty that she is noted for and her subjects fell at her feet with praise and acclaimed her the most popular also the most beautiful among the many that contested for the honor."[52] Despite her loss to Holiday, Slaughter gained recognition as one of Black Chicago's most beautiful and rich.

Policy's wealth seemed firmly in her grasp. But in 1913 the Illinois Appellate Court overturned the 1908 libel verdict. According to the court, "The [1908] case was, however, tried by both parties upon the theory that whether or not the words spoken charged the plaintiff simply with being or having been guilty of fornication with Johnson, or charged her with committing or having committed fornication promiscuously, were questions of fact for the jury."[53] Eudora also presented evidence that Slaughter had solicited the services of a midwife, a Mrs. Strue, on two or more occasions for abortion services, but the court refused to enter into evidence Eudora's accusation that Slaughter sought out an abortion. The court reasoned that "the indictment was manifestly incompetent as evidence and the offer of it as such was improper."[54] Eudora's strategies reflect her own architecture of policy queendom and what she felt was disallowed in queenly etiquette.

Slaughter defended herself by showing that she and Mushmouth had entered into a marriage engagement in 1902 with plans to wed later. Her attorney, Edward Morris, the same one she had employed in her first case, further demonstrated that Eudora and her mother had made every possible attempt to thwart the marriage. The court reported:

> In his opening statement to the jury, counsel for plaintiff was permitted to state that a marriage engagement existed between the plaintiff [Slaughter] and Johnson [Mushmouth]; that the defendant [Eudora] and her mother objected to and sought to prevent their marriage; that during his lifetime Johnson, out of his abundant means, supported the defendant and her mother and provided them with all the necessities and luxuries of life; that up to the time Johnson became acquainted with and courted the plaintiff all of his property stood in the name of the defendant, and that thereafter when defendant and her mother objected to his marriage with the plaintiff, Johnson insisted that the defendant should turn over to him all the property belonging to him.[55]

The appellate court concluded that this was where the circuit court decision in 1908 went wrong—these facts, "if true," had no bearing on the case except to influence the jury to award Slaughter a substantial portion of Mushmouth's estate because his sister and mother were doing their best to make sure she inherited nothing. The court saw it as "reparation of the alleged wrong inflicted upon her by the defendant in opposing her marriage to Johnson."[56] The appellate court concluded that the previous jury's award was so grossly excessive "as to necessitate a reversal of the judgment."[57] It further ruled that there had been no change in the relations between Slaughter and Mushmouth from 1902 to 1907, when the slander was levied, except such as was induced by his illness. Eudora, the appellate court reasoned, showed that illicit relations existed between the two from 1902 to 1905 and that such relations would have continued had Mushmouth not become ill. Eudora's case was that Mushmouth and Slaughter had no intention to marry; she insisted that they had planned, instead, to remain in an illegitimate relationship. Thus the appellate court overturned the 1908 verdict in favor of Eudora, who by 1913 was a married woman, to Jesse Binga no less, and was now a woman of substantial financial means and cultural capital. Her new husband took credit for the win: "I made them go in and settle that for $5,000. Then I told [Morris] after I was married 'If you ever do anything toward defamation of my wife I will give you plenty.'"[58]

But Slaughter did not fall very far following the court's reversal, and she went on to lead a fortunate life. The 1913 appellate court decision damaged neither Slaughter's own prospects for marriage or business success nor her ability to garner coverage in Chicago's papers. In 1916 Slaughter married "businessman and Bahamian native" Terrevous La Fayette Douglas.[59] News of the wedding appeared boldly on the front page of the *Broad Ax*. The *Broad Ax* column merits quoting at length to demonstrate the lavishness of the event, even if the ceremony itself was simple:

> Wednesday evening, at 6:30 o'clock, Miss Elizabeth Slaughter was united in marriage to Mr. T. La Fayette Douglas, the plain and very simple wedding ceremony was performed by Rev. Father John Sheridan Morris, the faithful and hard working Pastor of St. Monica's Roman Catholic Church, at his parsonage, 3623 South Wabash Ave.[60]

It is worth noting that the couple were wed in the Bingas' church.[61] The bride in her wedding dress was described in extravagance:

> The bride looked ever so charming and very beautiful as she has always been blessed with a great abundance of grace and beauty and with much love and sympathy for all those whom she comes in contact with. Her wedding gown consisted of imported white crape [*sic*] cloth, trimmed in real heavy Duchess lace, pearl banding draped at the bottom in silk net, pearl edging. The bridal veil, real rich lace touched with pearls. Jewels, pearl necklace; she carried a bouquet of roses and lilies of the valley.[62]

And the column listed the members of Black Chicago's elite among the nearly five hundred guests who attended "the more than homelike wedding reception."[63]

Mrs. Towels Mitchell, Mrs. James Fielding, Mrs. Thomas M. Grant, Mrs. Edward Hill, Mrs. Benjamin Johnson, Mrs. Delie Young, Mrs. Maggie Jefferson, Mrs. Mamie Marshall, Mrs. Robert Miller, Mrs. Maud Eaves, Mrs. Florence Brent and Mrs. Dejunius Ogburn and several other ladies actively assisted Mrs. Williams to administer to comforts of the many friends who were in evidence on that more than happy occasion and the choice refreshments were served during the reception in a most lavish manner.[64]

The guest list and description indicate that Slaughter married in finery in the Morrises' home—among the finest homes Black Chicago had to offer—with Mrs. Morris as the matron of honor and guests of the highest class. Gifts, too, were lavishly given: "Both the contracting parties being well known, popular and highly respected, they received a big wagon load of useful and extremely costly and beautiful presents."[65] The Douglases moved to Evanston and opened the South American Art Novelty Store.[66]

Policy Queen: Dutiful Wife

Policy threatened disrepute for Black women of the upper class, yet Slaughter and Eudora managed to balance both rank and policy ties. Both used policy to reckon and navigate respectability. Eudora's tenure as Black Chicago's next policy queen raised adoration to new heights until her tragic death in 1933. How did she do it?

After Mushmouth's death, Eudora maintained her own social distance from the middle and lower working classes. "Mushmouth," some attest, "never claimed respectability."[67] Eudora, by necessity, had to proceed differently. She began to activate those distinctions by advancing herself through philanthropic and social clubs and demanding to be seen as the respectable woman she was. Archival records, newspapers, and university records show that Eudora and her cousin Cecelia were involved in several social organizations that were foundational, albeit controversial, elements of Black Chicago's beginning. Eudora's established position in social networks, not business networks like Slaughter, elevated the character of the neighborhood and altered the way elite women operated within Black Chicago for decades. She also laid out an alternative path to Slaughter's emphasis on business for future policy queens.

For example, between October 1911 and August 1912, mere months before the Illinois Appellate Court overturned the verdict in Slaughter's libel and slander case against Eudora, Eudora's name appeared nearly weekly in the *Broad Ax*'s "Chips" column. In a veritable popularity contest, "Chips" and the paper as a whole used Slaughter and Eudora to carve out a certain variety of Black femininity for social-aspiring women in early twentieth-century Black Chicago.

In early 1910 Eudora began to run in more elite social circles, appearing regularly with "Chicago's only Afro-American Banker," Jesse Binga. Binga had a reputation for being a hard worker and having raised himself to prominence. He left Detroit at a young age to wander about the West, where he entered the Pullman service. Eventually he worked on a line between Utah and Montana. According to a 1927 *Crisis* retrospective, he made his first significant business deal by investing in twenty plots of land taken from a Native American reservation in Idaho; he made a fortune in real estate and moved to Chicago on the eve of the World's Columbian Exposition in 1893.[68] Here, too, he made gains in real estate. At a time when thousands of migrants were looking for housing in Black Chicago, he quickly became known for making white residential areas accessible to upwardly mobile African Americans.[69]

Binga had been a railroad porter, proving himself a shrewd businessman by his acquisition and sale of western lands in the 1890s and profitable huckstering on Chicago's streets at the time of the World's Fair. Once established in Chicago, Binga acquired real estate along State Street and charged exploitative rents to fellow African Americans. His holdings were so extensive that an entire block on State Street from Forty-Seventh to Forty-Eighth carried his imprint as "The Binga Block." Operating from his first major office at 3331 South State Street, he acquired and sold property throughout the South Side, extending his reach even into all-white neighborhoods. In 1908 Binga established the first of his two banks in Chicago, located on the southeast corner of State and Thirty-Sixth.[70] In 1926 the *Broad Ax* made explicit the importance of his career:

> That we have the brawn, brain and intellectual acumen to wield the banner of success along the higher and honorable lines of business is exemplified and set forth in the brilliant career of Mr. Jesse Binga, real estate dealer and banker and one of the first citizens of our race and the city of Chicago at large. His rapid and steady rise to fame and commercial leadership has been both permanent and spectacular.[71]

Binga and Eudora's courtship featured prominently in the papers, supporting Reed's assertion that "Binga's entrepreneurial exuberance combined public spectacle with economic advancement aimed at sustaining self-reliance."[72] Eudora had a hand in this strategy as well, planning lavish celebrations like Binga's "Box Party" at the Seventh Regiment Armory, but her handiwork received little credit in the press.[73] Instead, papers such as the *Broad Ax* credited Binga with the event and focused instead on Eudora's appearance. For example, at a New Year's Eve charity benefit a year later, Eudora appeared "attired in an embroidered white satin, fillet [sic] lace, diamond necklace, and sable furs" with her cousin Cecelia, similarly dressed, and "honored members of the white race," Dr. Mozee, a dentist and Cecelia's future husband, and Mr. Shank, a millionaire.[74] Attendance at events like these signaled that Eudora and her cousin were members of the elite, even the elite's innermost circle, but it also illustrates that Black women socialites with wealth from the underground economy were incredibly conspicuous. For example, "Chips" ran a story in October 1911 advertising that Eudora had purchased a "brand new electric car, which cost $3,000."[75] Eudora balanced stories of her opulence with stories that highlighted her membership in reputable social organizations. For example, the *Broad Ax* reported that she was a member of "The Choral Study Club,"[76] which celebrated its thirty-fourth anniversary in December 1911 with a concert at the Institutional AME Church.[77]

Aligning herself with dynamic institutions like the Choral Study Club signaled to an incredibly discriminating community Eudora's ascension as a woman of wealth and someone who knew how to use that wealth responsibly. Most importantly, however, it marked her as a suitable mate for Jesse Binga, since status in early twentieth-century Chicago was based on the manner in which one lived.[78] But not everyone was convinced that Eudora possessed the right pedigree. Gerri Major, a society columnist who married Jesse Binga's cousin H. Binga Dismond, had this blunt assessment: "Miss Eudora Johnson was not a young woman at the time of her marriage to Mr. Binga. She looked like a caricature of a 'big, fat, black mammy,' but she was the first black person I ever knew to stay at the Plaza in New York. . . . Mr. Binga was a distinguished looking gentlemen [sic]. I would not say that he married Miss Dora for her money, but $200,000 in those days was an awful lot of money. Mr. Binga could have chosen anyone he wanted."[79] Major's comments reflect Eudora's successful navigation of her potentially damning association with policy gambling, or policy's visible stain. She was seen at the Plaza Hotel in New York—this gave her some cachet, enough to convince Major that she was "worth" something. Major's comments also show us that some of the Black Belt elite saw Eudora's money as tainted but, more importantly, that Binga didn't care.[80] In historian Margaret Garb's opinion, "Binga's marriage to Eudora Johnson revealed the blurring of moralizing distinctions between respectable and unsavory Chicagoans."[81] Eudora's marriage blurred the lines of the three-tiered class system; Eudora made it possible for women leading the informal economy to access via inheritance the riches and protection of policy gambling.

The *Broad Ax* predicted that the Johnson-Binga wedding would be known as "one of the swellest and one of the most elaborate weddings ever held among the Afro-Americans in Chicago."[82] The couple married in February 1912.[83] The paper devoted over half of its front page to coverage of the wedding day. In a blatant display of the couple's opulence and connections, the paper made it obvious that no expense was spared and no detail overlooked. The headline signposted that the party was "the most elaborate and the most fashionable in the history of the Afro-American race in the Middle West, or in another section of the country." The paper listed "many rare and very expensive presents received by the bride and groom" that ranged from pearls from a sibling to table linens from Johnson's in-laws, the Reverend and Mrs. Binga, a real estate mogul from Detroit. The article provided just enough detail so that others could mimic the affair (for example, it named the businesses that provided the catering, cakes, and flowers) but not enough so that the wedding could be completely replicated (there were no hints about the bride's dress, for example, which had been imported from Paris and was "the highest embodiment of the modiste's art").[84] Some sixty wedding guests, a mixture of Black Belt elite and those ascending class ranks, attended the ceremony and reception in the newlyweds' Vernon Avenue home.[85] The guest list included eminent doctors, lawyers, newspaper editors, and businessmen. But, according to Gerri Major, "While the Bingas' wedding was a society event, you could tell from the people who were not there, just how society it was. . . . Miss Dora did not belong to black society and that was that."[86] Don Hayner agrees, concluding in his biography of Jesse Binga, "Despite her extensive charitable work, particularly with elderly residents of the Black Belt, Eudora and her mother lived on the fringe of the aristocratic society of the so-called old settlers—the black elite who had been in the city for years; they never seemed fully accepted."[87] Her associations with policy notwithstanding, Eudora fit all the criteria of the newly emerging upper class: she was married to

Chicago's most successful businessman, possessed some college education, was extremely wealthy, and was invited to all the right dances or threw them herself. Marrying Eudora provided Binga with old-settler clout, which he lacked but was on its way out, imbued Eudora's name with respectability, and positioned both of them—"permanently," the *Broad Ax* notes—within the social elite.[88] Furthermore, the marriage provided Binga with the capital to continue his venture as one of the most enterprising African Americans in Chicago. According to popular talk making its rounds, the most obvious source of income was Eudora's inheritance from the Johnson family fortune in gambling.[89]

The couple was the royalty of Black Chicago. Through Eudora's philanthropic associations they garnered respect for their work with various charities and churches, including the Phyllis Wheatley Club, Sisters of the Good Shepherd, Sisters of the Blessed Sacrament, and other prominent Catholic societies.[90] They founded the "Old Folks Home" and contributed to the YMCA.[91] They established scholarships for students to attend the University of Chicago, Fisk University, and the Chicago Musical College.[92] Eudora's nephew Fenton Johnson became a leading figure among the city's intellectuals in the Black Chicago Renaissance with her help, proving historians' point that policy underwrote the arts.[93] Eudora and Jesse Binga funded the *Champion*, a literary magazine for Fenton's publications. Fenton would also become one of the elite by joining the Appomattox Club, a political organization that had been established by Black politicians in 1900.[94]

The couple was also notorious for their visible and highly advertised grand-scale living, which became a requirement for all future policy queens. Their much-celebrated Christmas parties were yearly obsessions. "Never before in the history of the West has there gathered under one roof such a galaxy of social lights," wrote the *Defender* of their 1919 Christmas party. The men wore faultless evening attire, while the women were, without exception, "veritable dreams wearing the finest creations from the smartest shops."[95] The *Broad Ax* termed the Christmas party "the most unique and most brilliant social function so far held by the wealthy property-holding people residing in Chicago."[96]

Eudora, like many women in the upper class, saw club membership as a way to leverage her own visibility to become better known within exclusive circles and invert her conspicuous association with policy gambling, something that all women associated with policy gambling had to do. In

1925 she became president of the Bachelor Girls Club, which was a social fraternity that functioned like another highly visible group, the Garnet Girls Bridge Club.[97] Although not one of the elite social clubs of Chicago, the Garnet Girls ranked "definitely above the 'general run' of women's clubs."[98] Eudora found that policy wealth did not exclude her from membership or leadership.

Clubs like the Garnet Girls and the Bachelor Girls indicated the range of club options for Black women and how they understood class, femininity, and respectability. Some Black women used club connections to carve out reputations for themselves in Black Chicago's highly competitive church circles. One young Garnet Girl, who had achieved mobility within both the NAACP and the Chicago Urban League, used her connections with the Garnets to gain status in the fashionable Congregational Church of the Good Shepherd. She explained her strategy cunningly: "I am a new member of Good Shepard [sic], and I plan to get down to work and do something soon. I shall join a club and become active. I want to become acquainted with the members and the pastor. I want to be known."[99] Her strategy worked: four months later she got the Garnets to contribute to a community center fund, and they helped her daughter win a local popularity contest. When asked what the club meant to her, she responded, "The Garnet Girls' Bridge Club came in and helped [my daughter] win. The girls are like that about everything they do. My club has meant much to me, and I feel that I have done my best for the club."[100]

Eudora took on club life with the same vigor and gained many returns to solidify her social status, especially her work with Fannie Barrier Williams and the Phyllis Wheatley Home. Organized in 1896, the Phyllis Wheatley Women's Club provided homes for young African American women who had come to Chicago for employment.[101] The home provided "wholesome home surroundings for colored girls and women who are strangers in the city . . . to house them until they find safe and comfortable quarters."[102] This organization supported the home, which provided safe, clean, and inexpensive housing for young black women.[103] Fannie Barrier Williams served in a number of positions, including on the club's board of directors and as the corresponding secretary of the home's board of directors. Here she must have worked in concert with Eudora. In 1927 the *Intercollegian Wonder Book* listed Eudora as a lifetime member of the Phyllis Wheatley Home and listed Jesse Binga as the banker for the club.[104]

Eudora's matrix of policy queen elitism included many variables: wealth, philanthropy, club membership, and life on a grand scale. As a result, Eudora connected wealth earned from the informal economy to the formal economy, a trend that later policy queens such as Harriett Jones would adopt. She also emerged as a leader in all of these efforts during a tumultuous time in Black Chicago. She and her husband survived World War I, the outbreak of influenza, the 1919 Chicago Race Massacre, and several bombings of their home at 5922 South Park, an all-white area.[105] According to historian Robert Howard, "Binga and Eudora stood their ground through all this turmoil and refused to move," hiring security guards to watch their home twenty-four hours a day.[106] They seemed unstoppable.

End of Eudora's Reign

In 1929, with the onset of the Depression, Eudora and Jesse Binga were riding high—Binga's bank had nearly $1.5 million in deposits, and he built the "Binga Arcade" the same year. It was a five-story building of imposing design, with office space and a dance hall on the roof. But on July 31, 1930, the bank was shut down by the state examiner. Banks were closing across the country, and a wave of controversy swallowed the couple.[107]

Edward H. Morris, who had served as Elizabeth Slaughter's counsel in the defamation lawsuit in 1908, was appointed as receiver for the Binga State Bank in 1930. He said in a petition dated July 31, 1931, "It would appear that said Jesse Binga owned certain real estate and interest in real estate, when in truth and in fact, the said Jesse Binga placed the money of said Binga State Bank in said real estate transactions and took title in himself."[108] In his official capacity as bank receiver, Morris concluded that the Binga State Bank had been conducted in an "illegal, fraudulent, and unsafe manner," with Jesse Binga managing and controlling bank property as if it were his own.[109] Old tensions emerged with a fury. Binga blamed Morris for having a vendetta against him dating back twenty-five years concerning "trouble over defamation of character, some subterfuge. . . . We have always been at enmity."[110] Slaughter and Eudora's decades-old feud reemerged.

On March 5, 1931, Binga was arrested on charges of embezzlement. Unable to post the $55,000 bond, he was locked in the county jail for six weeks. His first trial began in 1932 and was a public spectacle. It "lasted a week [and] featured the prosecution's presentation of boxes and boxes of evidence and a multitude of witnesses. It ended in his acquittal, but the prosecution proceeded to charge Binga with embezzlement."[111] In the second trial, the prosecution persuaded Inez Cantey, Binga's personal secretary, to turn state's evidence. Cantey took the stand, testifying for two full days. Her most damning statement, according to Robert Howard, was that the misappropriation of bank funds was done only with Mr. Binga's permission.[112] Significantly, in March 1933, just before the second trial, Eudora died of a cerebral hemorrhage.[113] Some claim her death was caused by the stress of the trial. The court charged onward, and eventually State of Illinois found Jesse Binga guilty of embezzling $32,500 for his personal use.

As the judge read his sentence on June 10, 1933, Binga cried out, "They're persecuting me. They have killed my wife and now they're trying to kill me. I've lost all I owned; now they're persecuting me. Stop this thing or I'll go mad!"[114] Sympathetically, the *Chicago Defender* stated, "He was being persecuted. No doubt he was. Not by the authorities, but by those whom he had befriended and who deserted him in his hour of tribulation."[115]

After several unsuccessful appeals for almost two years, Binga began serving his ten-year sentence in Joliet State Penitentiary in 1935. Through the combined efforts of religious leaders, famed defense attorney Clarence Darrow, attorney George Griffin, and many others, he was granted release in 1938. Father Joseph Eckert of St. Anselm Catholic Church agreed to supervise him while on parole, employing him as a handyman and usher for fifteen dollars a week.[116] Three years later, in April 1941, at age seventy-six, Binga received a full pardon from the governor.[117] He spent his final years living quietly with his nephew until his death in 1950.[118] According to Chicagoan Dempsey Travis, "Binga remained a figure of controversy to Black Chicago. Some said he was simply a crook. Others said he was merely a creative businessman who ended up taking too many risks and that without the Depression he might have continued as Black Chicago's foremost businessman. Others said he was a victim of circumstances brought down by a white system."[119]

The *Defender* counted Eudora among the few who had supported Binga, standing "by him in his hour of greatest need."[120] The paper likewise credited her with his success: "His wife died of a broken heart on April 1 of this year. It was originally her fortune which she inherited from her brother, upon which the Binga bank was founded."[121] Mrs. Eliza Chilton Johnson, a participant in St. Clair Drake's Church Federation Interviews in 1938, when asked what she thought of Mrs. Binga, replied, "This woman took a gamble with Binga and lost it all."[122]

Policy's Crown

Some women ascended the ranks of society in Black Chicago from the 1890s onward through the policy wheel. Slaughter's track record as a businesswoman and Eudora's unique combination of socialite and philanthropic work once married to Binga laid out possible avenues toward success. Both Slaughter's and Eudora's bids for power are illustrative of the fluctuating dynamics of gender and race that made an emerging Black Chicago such an electrifying and transformative space from the 1890s to 1930. Between 1908 and 1913, when the crown was still up for grabs, each of these two women enjoyed popularity in the Black press while running in prominent social circles, but Eudora's trajectory eclipsed Slaughter's at the most crucial point. The key to understanding their particular embodiments of policy queen in turn-of-the-century Chicago—and in particular what Eudora brought to her marriage to Binga—is not only their reliance on the informal economy as a source of their wealth but also their strategic navigation of its visibility. Slaughter and Eudora engaged in considerable risk taking as Eudora's marriage to Binga proves, but, consequently, they blazed the trail for a particular kind of Black womanhood that included club life, education, charitable giving, and, significantly, gambling. It set the standard for queens to come and noted future generations of wealth seekers that no matter the means, investment in Black Chicagoan socioeconomic and cultural institutions was expected, if not required, to hold on to the title of policy's royal set. This combination safeguarded most policy queens from public scrutiny, earning them reputations for generosity, gift giving, and benevolence.[123]

3

Chicago's Most Famous Policy Queen

Chicago's most famous policy queen was Mrs. Harriett Jones, wife of Dr. Rev. Edward P. Jones and mother of three. She was widowed in 1924, leaving her with the care of three young men on the eve of the Great Depression. Instead of sliding into poverty, however, Harriett led the family into unparalleled wealth, first as the queen of multiple policy wheels raking in profits for twenty years and then, when her policy empire fell subject to white encroachment, as the matriarch of thriving international textile and automobile industries for the next thirty years. Harriett Jones's path to affluence emerges as a startling and troubling exception to a narrative of poverty and loss in Bronzeville.[1] Harriett's life challenges conventional ideas about Black working women in Chicago and recasts definitions of being a policy queen. While her sons, the Jones brothers, became notorious for their economic influence, Harriett was rarely associated with their success. The press relegated her to the background, which appears to be by Harriett's design. To outsiders, she hovered like a phantom over her sons' success, obscuring her own visible success in the policy gambling world. But records from the Kefauver Committee, a special commission of the U.S. Senate that existed from 1950 to 1951 to investigate organized crime, reveal her as the architect of the Jones policy empire. Furthermore, as a policy queen she reveals how policy played a crucial role in her family's strategies during the Great Depression regardless of respectable status. Certainly policy's fame and fortune did not guarantee a secure future for Harriett and her family, but her biography uncovers how her turn to the informal economy solidified more certain futures for her sons, daughters-in-law, and grandchildren.

In contrast to her life as a multimillion-dollar policy queen, Harriett's beginnings were decidedly modest. Her parents were Jordan Wynn and Harriott Harris. Her father was born in 1841 in the not-yet-formed state of Texas.[2] He was twenty-five years old when Union troops rode into Texas on June 19, 1865, and announced that the Civil War was over; a quarter million African Americans found freedom after toiling for two and a half years following the Emancipation Proclamation.[3] Wynn joined many African Americans after the Civil War in scaling the country to reclaim lost loved ones and reunite with family.

Harriett's mother, Harriott Harris, was born on William Houston Harris's plantation in 1852 in Wilson County, Tennessee.[4] After she and Jordan Wynn married in 1872, they settled in Greenville, Mississippi, where Wynn set up as a farmer and Harris found work as a housekeeper. Next to nothing is known about Harriett Jones's childhood. She first appears on record when she married Dr. Edward P. Jones in 1896, whose upbringing was distinctly different from her own.[5]

Whereas Harriett descended from working-class Mississippians, Edward Sr.'s lineage consisted of high-profile clergymen.[6] He attended Alcorn College and Natchez College, graduating as valedictorian in each class. In 1894 Edward Sr. was ordained into the ministry. However, his acumen for entrepreneurship and finance was already evident when, early in his tenure as minister, he raised funds and built an impressive six-million-dollar modern church in Vicksburg. He was also elected recording secretary of the Baptist State Convention, an event that Patrick H. Thompson's *History of Negro Baptists in Mississippi* concluded "needed no comment; suffice it to say that the energy and ability of Rev. E. P. Jones have won for him an honorable name and predict for him a bright future."[7]

Edward Sr.'s ambition in fund-raising nearly matched his ambitions to climb the social ladder. He flexed his financial and networking muscles in the arenas of business, fraternal societies, lodges, international travel, and state and national politics but never the informal economy. He joined the Colored Odd Fellows Society, a prominent Black fraternal organization. A mutual aid society, it was the perfect match for his church-charity experience and social ambitions. He relied on the Odd Fellows to solidify the family's connections to Black Vicksburg's most elite.[8]

Edward Sr.'s extensive networking activities left Harriett to take care of matters in their home and church office at 1413 First North Street in Vicksburg. She hired a domestic worker to help tend to her sons and perform secretarial duties for the church newspaper. But Harriett was careful to never ask her domestic laborers to do cleaning or washing.[9] Her demeanor and devotion, which aligned with gendered expectations for the respectable middle class, were integral to the success of their marriage and Edward Sr.'s seemingly endless ambition, and the wider Black Vicksburg community took notice. W. E. Mollison featured both Edward Sr.'s and Harriett's portraits prominently in the 1908 edition of *Leading Afro-Americans of Vicksburg, Mississippi*. Harriett was one of the few women featured in the edition. Edward Sr. also conceded that Harriett was the backbone of his triumphs: "Whatever success [I have] attained is due to the devotion and wholesome advice given by [my] wife."[10]

Edward Sr.'s high-ranking connections and Harriett's counsel laid the groundwork for the family's migration to Chicago, where decades later Harriett would set up their policy empire. The flashpoint was when he found himself in Chicago as a delegate at-large to the Republican National Convention in both 1908 and 1912, which he attended as one of Mississippi's leading Republicans. Edward Sr.'s charisma and flamboyance earned him the nickname "Mississippi Jones."[11]

Evidently, after such forays north, Edward Sr.'s sermons became more radical, much to the alarm of white Vicksburg. His sermons in church had one theme: to find a better life and leave town as soon as possible.[12] Prominent white people of Vicksburg discovered how hard he was pushing members of his congregation to move north and pressured him to promptly leave town with his entire family. Yet doing so was not as simple as buying a train ticket to Illinois.[13] In an age of unrelenting segregation, Black passengers would be asked about their place of employment and whether they had permission from supervisors to leave. Some cities even passed laws barring out-migration. Thus, in order to travel, African Americans had to make careful plans.[14] Isabel Wilkerson confirms that plans and directives to leave were frequently the subjects of conversation as Black migrants planned their escape by quoting one Alabama woman: "In our homes, in our churches, wherever two or three are gathered together, there is a discussion of what is best to do. Must we remain in the South or go elsewhere? Where can we go to feel that security which other people feel? Is it best to go in great numbers or only in several families? These and many things are discussed over and over."[15] Accordingly, the Joneses' migration north took months of planning. In addition to the demands that Vicksburg's white elite put on the family, a horrific lynching occurred in the city in 1918 that spurred increased out-migration. Residents recalled how "every Black person in Vicksburg knew was what going on that night—Black men especially. Many of them would disappear for a few days after a lynching."[16] Former Illinois state representative Corneal Davis spoke about the terror of his family's exodus northward to Chicago from rural Mississippi around the same time:

> All of my people had already left Mississippi because just before then there was a boy in Vicksburg that I used to play with who was named Hamilton, and one day they picked him up because some white woman said she had been raped or something, and they took that boy who was completely innocent, and they hung him up on a tree, and that's when the Black people all started leaving Vicksburg because they wasn't ever hanging Black people like that in Vicksburg before then, and so my mother, she sent me this newspaper with the article in it about the boy that had been hanged, and she knew I knew him, and so in her letter she said "Son, we are leaving."[17]

In response to the rapidly deteriorating conditions in the town, the Joneses' "move took place three or four months ahead of schedule."[18] They left for Chicago by train several days after the lynching, traveling with their three boys and sitting "in the Black coach, of course, and it was crowded and unbelievably dirty."[19] A travel companion, legendary jazz bassist and photographer Milt Hinton, commented that "it smelled like rotten food and it was noisy. It was hard to fall asleep and the trip seemed like it went on for days. We got to Chicago sometime late the next day. . . . It was October or November and it was pretty cold in Chicago. My mother had brought a coat to the station for me and put it on me the moment we arrived."[20] Like most African American migrants, after reaching Chicago, the Jones family headed immediately to the South Side and would eventually take up residence at Thirty-Sixth Street and Vincennes Avenue.[21]

Edward Sr. relied on his connections to get a job as pastor of Mt. Zion Church in Evanston, Illinois, where he also became head of the National

Baptist Convention. The latter was a contentious appointment, considering that Edward Sr. was involved in the convention's highly publicized and controversial split with the Baptist Convention in 1915.[22] By 1916, newspapers reported that he had been able to sway members amid the controversy: "Many . . . who did not unite with the Jones faction in Chicago have now announced their intentions to unite with the Jones faction."[23]

Edward Sr. exhibited his acumen at resolving church disputes with bravado when controversy over the convention split reemerged at the South Side's Salem Baptist Church, at Thirtieth and LaSalle streets. Its then current minister summoned police to the church when he anticipated trouble with former deacons who voted for his resignation. The deacons called for Edward Sr., who "hurried to the rescue. He withdrew the forces opposed to the pastor of Salem and held meetings Monday evening at the Community Center, 3201 Wabash Avenue, and at the Odd Fellows' hall Wednesday and Friday evenings."[24] He advised the deacons to "file an injunction against Salem's pastor restraining him from handling financial affairs of the church or acting in any way as its pastor."[25] They did so, serving the pastor with the papers as he was crossing the street to the church. Armed men in support of the pastor greeted Jones's supporters on Sunday morning; Edward Sr. was absent. The *Defender* journalist was sure that "his life, in all probability, would have been taken" had he come on the scene.[26] Edward Sr. reemerged at the evening service with a bodyguard of police officers and his followers, declaring his intention to take full charge of Salem. With his fame, he elevated the church to higher heights and fuller pews, transforming Salem into "one of the largest in the North from a congregation of less than 300."[27] He managed to leverage this tense and violent situation into extensive press coverage, his leadership and bravado on full display, an indication of the ways he synonymized the Jones name with success and spectacle in Chicago circles. Edward Sr. was often described as a great orator and a mastermind. In line with how other policy kings were viewed, the minister was considered either devilishly conniving or fully trustworthy.

Harriett and the couple's three boys—Edward Jr., George, and McKissack—lived in Edward Sr.'s shadow but enjoyed the security and prosperity it provided. They resided in a respectable neighborhood on Chicago's South Side, and the sons attended prestigious schools, including Hyde Park High School, the University of Chicago, and Howard University.[28] Her husband's inclination to flamboyancy, ambition, and incendiary oratory made the family famous throughout the South Side. But in 1924 everything changed when Edward Sr. died suddenly of apoplexy (now known as a stroke).[29] The older sons moved back home. Harriett and her sons had important choices to make. Policy gambling emerged as the family's strategy to ameliorate poverty.

The historical record does not provide information about the choices the family made in light of Edward Sr.'s death nor the contents of his will. It was alleged that the insurance money from his death that Harriett received, an unknown lump sum, played a key role in launching the Joneses' entrepreneurial success.[30] But even before their father's death, the sons had begun dabbling in a number of businesses both formal and informal, one of them being a taxicab business.[31]

Another successful business venture for the Joneses was a tailor shop at 4312 Indiana Avenue, and rumor had it that they launched their first policy station out of the shop's back entrance.[32] From the outset, the Jones brothers printed handbills advertising their station and passed them out to friends and associates, resulting in immediate success.[33] Harriett, too, was involved. In his testimony before the Kefauver Committee, Edward Jr. noted this:

> MR. [RUDOLPH] HALLEY: Did you have any other partners?
> MR. JONES: No.
> MR. HALLEY: Just you and your two brothers?
> MR. JONES: That is right.
> MR. HALLEY: And your mother was with you?
> MR. JONES: Yes, sir.[34]

By 1942 Harriett had the highest income in the household—thousands more than her sons. She brought in $241,000 that year ($4.1 million in today's money), making the family's total assets $1,145, 958 ($18.8 million today).[35] She went from the well-to-do wife of a Mississippi Baptist preacher and a postwar migrant to a millionaire policy queen.

The crucial determiner of the fate of the Jones family was not Edward Sr.'s death but Harriett's alleged investment of his life insurance policy in her and her sons' business dealings. Despite the fact that policy gambling was illegal and considered unrespectable by many, Harriett wholeheartedly threw her money behind policy as a way to ensure the family's economic success. She might have been positioning herself for this role even before Edward Sr.'s death. And, as documents from the Kefauver Committee prove, a vital part of that formula was the degree to which she remained invisible as the one directing the financial maneuvers but revealed herself as the devoted mother and matronly policy queen giving wholesome advice. Harriett's business decisions were not about avoiding public assistance and the shame that accompanied it but about accumulating wealth and the subversive mechanisms of policy that could be used to financially support Black Chicago. Harriet was invisible as financial director but visible giving matronly advice to her sons—inverting the precarious spotlight of policy gambling but accentuating the domestic politics of respectability.

The three young Jones men became Chicago's most notorious policy wheel owners, known for the family's numerous policy wheels that raked in millions of dollars every week. At the height of policy, they owned twelve of the thirty-eight most lucrative policy wheels operating on the South Side.[36] According to Chicago resident Dempsey Travis, no operation compared to that of the Joneses:

> Their headquarters at 4724 Michigan Avenue employed as many as 250 people, a number which does not include several hundred working their stations and runners. At the height of the Jones brothers' career they grossed $250,000 a day. An efficiency expert once said that the Jones' wheels operated like clockwork, as efficient and as well run as many of the marble-lined banks and brokerage houses on LaSalle Street, and many times more profitable.[37]

The trio of brothers—fondly referred to as the "Jones Brothers" by the *Chicago Defender*—lived lavishly. "In addition to a villa in Paris, a summer home in Peoria, and a villa in Mexico City on Compe 73, they owned four hotels: the Vienna Bathhouse, the Grove, the Garfield, and the Alpha."[38] In 1927 the Jones brothers were the first African Americans to own a piece of real estate in the commercial district in the heart of Bronzeville at 436 East Forty-Seventh Street, where they opened the world's only African American–owned department store.[39] This Ben Franklin store furnished the community with more than 125 full-time jobs.[40] The Jones brothers built on its success, opening the Jones Brothers Finer Food Mart, at 303 East Forty-Third Street, which featured "a state of the art meat department and free delivery."[41] Through their wide-ranging spheres of influence, the Jones brothers helped create a community that thrived at a particularly crucial time in the history and formation of Black Chicago. Robert E. Weems Jr. and Jason P. Chambers write that policy kings like the Jones brothers, with Harriett at the helm, "reinvested portions of their profits back into the community, employed its members, and served as the source of loans to entrepreneurs when traditional banks proved unwilling to do so."[42] Harriett was every bit as much a part of this, too. The Jones family did all of that as the World War I–era Great Migration dramatically enhanced the potential profits associated with policy.[43]

The Great Depression and Irresistible Lure of Policy

The population of Black Chicago continued to grow during the worst years of the Depression.[44] A steady stream of migrants became regular players of the numbers game, undeterred by the high level of unemployment in the Great Depression. One resident recalled, "There was a great depression on and people were hungry. And if they could make a [winning paying from wagering a] dime or a nickel off this thing, they made it."[45] Many turned to policy gambling because formal economic mechanisms and relief programs were inadequate. The Jones family found that sustained migration and hardships caused by the Great Depression were, for them, a lucrative road to wealth.

African Americans received even less aid for daily necessities than whites, proving that the country's relief systems were rife with bias and humiliation.[46] For example, in 1938, nearly a decade into the Depression, South Side resident Mrs. Henry Mae Mitchell explained how relief was a consistent barrier to her family's ability to find permanent residence: "I have on several occasions found places to move in, but I was rejected on the basis of my being on relief. It is hard to rent a place if you are on a relief." Mitchell was also eager to join employment with the Works Progress Administration, but for "some reason her white relief worker refused" to get her a position there. Mitchell relayed the humiliation and anger she felt at being unable to clothe herself or her child:

> I am barefooted now and so is my child, and that damned old relief worker lies like hell about my clothes. She says that she turned in a requisition for some clothes, but I know that is a lie because I have a friend who gets shoes every three months and I can't get them every year without going to the Alderman and having him call the relief station for me.

Interviewer E. R. Saunders, whose race was not noted in his writing, interrupted—"Is your worker colored or white?"—to which Mitchell responded:

> She is a white woman and it's hard to get any consideration from her. . . . Every time I ask my worker for a job she tells me that she is doing the best that she can, but she is a damn liar. If she would give me a job, I would move out of this building because I stay sick all the time here.[47]

Mitchell's statements had the resonance of a testimony offered from a witness stand. She deftly and swiftly dismissed the stereotypes of African Americans (particularly women) on the relief rolls, whom onlookers frequently deemed irresponsible, insolent, and morally backward.[48] Mitchell was well aware that the country's system of relief—to which she, like any other American, was entitled—was rigged when it came to color. It was staggering how far discriminatory practices spread; approximately 18 percent of Chicagoans receiving some form of poverty relief were Black, despite the group being only about 8 percent of Chicago's population.[49] Little wonder many turned to policy gambling when relief and job security were hard to find.

Jobs were so scarce that one Black Chicagoan likened landing a job to winning the lottery:

> There wasn't anything like jobs. You didn't even have to worry about trying to find jobs because there weren't no jobs to be found. The best thing you could do was go down there to the post office and get those applications, fill them out, and that was it. You had to wait, and some people got lucky and got hired at times. So, during that time, I was just more or less just hustling.[50]

"Blacks," so the expression went, "were first hired" (because they were cheap) "and first fired" (because they were Black).[51] In Depression-era Black Chicago, "over one half of the Negroes employable were out of work, for they were the first to lose their jobs and the last to secure new employment, even in work created in governmental bodies."[52] Most women worked in domestic labor, where, according to Joe Trotter, they "occupied the cellar of the gender- and racially divided workforce."[53] Domestic work was particularly grueling; "employers devalued African American women's labor through low pay, lack of benefits, and the perpetuation of aspects of the old 'master-servant' relationship governing domestic work."[54] For those fortunate enough to find employment outside of domestic work, wages were abysmal. Mrs. Odessa Evans, who worked in "a girl's place at a hotel on the North Side," remarked, "It is a shame the way those poor girls have to work. They only get fifty-two fifty a month. At least that's what they're supposed to be getting. They used to get sixty dollars a month. During the Depression they were cut down to forty-five. Now they are supposed to have gone back up. Those poor girls."[55] When they gained industrial jobs, "they endured special racial and gender limits" inside the factory gates, characterized by both lower pay than their white counterparts and hazardous conditions.[56] Because of such poor pay and discrimination during the Great Depression, many turned to policy gambling—a lucrative consequence for policy queens. But oftentimes those illegally occupied in policy were deemed ineligible to receive government aid.

Many residents of the South Side turned to policy gambling to relieve or distract themselves from the burden of poverty, a trend that upset many but made the Jones family rich. In addition to this reason why the Joneses were so successful, Christopher Reed points out, is that the power and influence of the Church—and its critique of gambling—had significantly declined since the early part of the century when ministers issued their disapproval of policy with a more authoritative voice.[57] The Depression rendered such critiques hollow. Famous Pentecostal preacher Lucy Smith Collier, whose staff of female workers fed as many as ninety people a day for nearly six months during the Depression, noted, "I don't hold it against the people if they play policy numbers, so long as they don't deny themselves the necessities of life. I know that this is often unavoidable. . . . What else can the people do? Conditions here are not good."[58] Collier, who daily saw the grinding poverty of her congregants, concluded that "the lure of the overwhelming chance of 'hitting a winning number' through playing policy became too popular to resist."[59] Nor did the Illinois Relief Commission's statement on policy gambling—"persons cannot be accepted for relief when it is known they are illegally occupied"—thwart the pastime's popularity, leaving the commission at a loss as to whom to fund. The divisional director of the Chicago Relief Administration confessed as much: "It has been impossible to stop the paying of policy by relief recipients. . . . However, when a client is found to be engaged in the operation of a policy wheel or as a solicitor his income is budgeted."[60] This made life more difficult for men like "Mr. G":

> Since Mr. G is no longer able to sell his socks, he is wholly dependent on his earnings from writing policy. Mrs. G. stated that he makes an average

of $5.00 a week at this work. After a conference with the senior supervisor concerning Mr. G's employment it was decided that relief could be issued and that $20.00 was to be deducted as income from the family budget.[61]

Lewis A. H. Caldwell, author of "The Policy Game in Chicago" and future Illinois state senator, acknowledged that "a majority of the investigators in the relief offices admit quite frankly that they do not record information pertaining to the playing of policy among their clients unless there is undeniable evidence that sizable income is made."[62] Caldwell also recalled that policy served a social function as well as a financial one for "bored women and frustrated, unemployed men."[63] The Jones family saw dollar signs and a lucrative opportunity in such hardships.

Policy's ubiquity was a source of frustration for municipal officials. In a 1931 speech, Democratic mayor Anton Cermak said that policy "is played by 95 per cent of Colored people over 14 years old and operators will take bets as low as five cents."[64] But Cermak's intent was more sinister than his comment suggests. Nathan Thompson quotes Cermak as saying, "If Blacks switched their allegiance to the Democratic Party, the action by my police department would be stopped."[65] Incensed, the *Chicago Defender* responded with a scathing editorial defending the virtue of Black Chicago, proclaiming, "Policy is not a game of universal indulgence."[66] Moreover, the *Defender* chastised the mayor for insulting everyone in Black Chicago: "His insult is given to the membership of every church in Chicago, pulpit and pew alike, to every home of honor and intelligence and to tens of thousands of citizens who respect the law and are obedient to it."[67]

Cermak's comments would not have been lost on the Joneses, who had links to church pulpits but also capitalized on the problems Cermak identified. Themselves Democrats, the Joneses relied on Chicago police and Cermak to curb white encroachment on their policy wheels. In exchange for protection from police prosecution, Cermak relied on the Joneses for help in mobilizing Bronzeville voters for the 1932 presidential election. Jones and Cermak, according to Weems and Chambers, agreed that if Edward Jr. used his influence to increase the number of Black Democratic voters in Bronzeville, he would be given the right to control all Black gambling operations in Chicago, free of police interference.[68] After Cermak's assassination in early 1933, Edward Kelly became Chicago's interim mayor and agreed to honor the agreement that Cermak made with Edward Jr.: the Joneses controlled Black gambling activity in Chicago with impunity.[69]

Perhaps mindful of her family's tenuous relationships with police and the mayor and the potentially lucrative nature of the situation, Harriett insisted "that the wheel run legitimately and that no cheating of customers be tolerated. The winning numbers were always legit and people came to trust the wheel that was run by the three preacher's kids."[70] Her "wholesome advice" proved sound because the money kept pouring in, even from unexpected places. In January 1942 the family received more than four hundred thousand dollars from the federal government in excess income taxes: "A belated Santa Claus visited the homes of the Jones Brothers, policy operators, this week and left [a] stocking filled with $435,111 with a bright colored card from Uncle Sam."[71] Harriett enjoyed her portion of this largesse, an estimated $4,900, and the *Chicago Defender* printed her name in the story.[72]

With her name in print testifying to her submitting more than necessary to the federal government, Harriett's noble economic intentions were fully visible in her family's policy operations. Testimony from her sons and from the family's operations man, Theodore Roe, before the Kefauver Committee proves, crucially, that Harriett was indispensable to the family's policy fortunes and furthermore that she shared equally, getting 20 percent of all profits.[73] Roe, in his testimony to Senator Estes Kefauver of Tennessee, named Harriett Jones an equal partner in the Maine-Ohio-Idaho policy wheel—their most lucrative wheel—and confirmed that she received 20 percent of the profits like everyone else.[74] The committee's zeal was impressive; it held hearings and investigations in fourteen cities and heard testimony from more than six hundred witnesses.[75] After Roe and Edward Jr. confessed to their policy operations in testimony before the committee, they were arrested and charged with misdemeanors. The committee found that they "unlawfully and willfully conspired together with Harriette [*sic*] Jones, Ed Jones and Clifford Davis and divers[*sic*] other persons whose names are unknown to this affiant with fraudulent and malicious intent and unlawfully, wrongfully and wickedly to sell and offer what are commonly called lottery policy."[76] Conspiracy was a misdemeanor and would yield more jail time, whereas the charge of operating policy carried a one-year sentence.

Harriett was in Mexico at the time of the committee hearings, and it is unknown why State Attorney John S. Boyle chose not to pursue her arrest.[77] According to Edward Jr., in an interview with the *Chicago Defender*, Harriett was always involved in the business's highest levels of decision-making, comparing her to the "supreme court" that solved disputes between the brothers.[78] All differences of opinion were settled by her final word. Harriett's position as a policy queen was at times invisible and informal, but according to her sons, behind the scenes she was prominent, even authoritative. She was indeed the backbone of the family enterprise.

Jones's Publicity and Philanthropy

When the money was consistently coming in from the policy wheels, Harriett turned her resources toward the community to craft a public image of her liking. To acquire respectable social standing, Harriett fostered a spirit of reinvestment in Black Chicago, but even as a leader in legitimate businesses Harriett took on an invisible role. The family's most important contribution to the community was the aforementioned Ben Franklin store on Forty-Seventh Street.[79] The *Defender* continued its praise of the Jones brothers, not their mother, when it lauded the store as a "magnificent achievement in the history of the Race," a place where African Americans could shop in a store owned and operated by African Americans, "manned from top to bottom by Race generalship."[80] Nothing was spared in the celebration of its grand opening. The "royal family"—Edward Jr. and his wife, Lydia Jones; George and his wife, Pauline Jones; McKissack and his wife, Jean Jones; and their "beloved mother," Harriett—arrived for the opening to astonishing fanfare.[81] Harriett called it a "day of dreams, come true," commenting, "I am very happy and proud of my boys and I am praying for their continued success."[82] Among the throngs to attend the opening were the "world's greatest tapdancer," Bill "Bojangles" Robinson; the Reverend C. H. Cobb, "Mayor of Bronzeville"; heavyweight champion Joe Louis; and more.[83] Louis remarked, "I am glad that they have opened the store and I am sure it will be a fine thing: I wish them much success."[84] The editor and owner of the *Defender*, Robert S. Abbott, proffered a sobering account of the festivities a few days later, saying, "The Jones boys' store must not fail. The key to its success lies in the hands of some 300,000 Negroes in Chicago."[85] If the Jones brothers, who, according to Abbot, had opened the store in "honesty, perseverance, and organization," were going to succeed, it would only be with the support of the community. The patronage of the store by members of the community would ensure its success.

At the same time, the Jones family's financial investments in Bronzeville, like the store, served as a down payment on community support and sanction for their policy business as well as protection from the police. It was a strategy that worked. Over and over again the *Defender* praised the Jones brothers' flawless ambition as an example to young men, particularly young migrants. In a story leading up to the Ben Franklin store opening, the *Defender* described the trio: "Coming here from Mississippi, these boys, sons of a Baptist minister, worked as cab drivers, railroad employees, and finally became businessmen. They acquired good educations, were frugal, and made plans for the future. They made good, and after the death of their father, Rev. Edward P. Jones, they have supported their mother, to whom all three are deeply devoted."[86] Aside from the striking irony of the Jones brothers' use of policy gambling to make frugal decisions, the most glaring omission in the *Defender*'s account is the absence of Harriett's efforts from this masculine rags to riches story. Harriett moved to respect the gendered conventions of respectability by adopting a less prominent role in a business enterprise—even when those enterprises were on the legitimate side. As matriarch and entrepreneur, she did not fit into the plotline even though she was both the fiscal and social architect of the narrative. Or perhaps leaving her out was deliberate. Perhaps the paper colluded with Harriett's desire to protect her reputation, and her sons' desire to protect their mother, embracing what historian Darlene Clark Hine identified as a "culture of dissemblance."[87] Omitting her name suggests Harriett's wish to protect the sanctity of her family.

Club membership also served as a way for Harriett to secure the protection needed for her suspect reputation as a policy queen. She found her fit in Bronzeville's vibrant club life when she joined the previously mentioned Garnet Girls Bridge Club, whose members were willing to overlook concerns about gambling and vice in exchange for the Jones family's financial contributions and Harriett's popularity. The Garnet Girls Club, an upper-middle-class organization, and clubs in general, served as a veneer over those women with suspect policy reputation.

The club was founded in 1929 and received a state charter in 1933.[88] Examining the Garnet Girls' opinions on status, vice, and philanthropy illustrates the vital role of club life for Black women and how they understood class, femininity, and respectability. The compiler of the records for St. Clair Drake's 1938 study of Federated Churches identified occupation, income, and education as by far the most important criteria in determining membership and the Garnet Girls' overall class position. The compiler located them solidly in the upper middle class but not actually members of the upper class for several reasons. The record starts by citing the dances to which the girls were invited, all of which were attended by "lower upper class and middle class persons." There was a distinct lack of invitations to upper-class dances.[89] In addition, the compiler stated that upper-class clubwomen did not work and that their husbands were either professional men or very successful businessmen. In comparison, nearly all the Garnet Girls listed in the files were employed in occupations ranging from beautician, to shopper and buyer, to stenographer and seamstress. The compiler also described the women as "on the defensive in relation to formal education." One woman remarked, "I am sorry that I was unable to go farther in school. It is impossible for everybody to get a good formal education, so I have tried to make the best of it with what I have. I wish that I could go back to school. Everybody wants to know what school you attend, and it is embarrassing when you feel as I do about school."[90]

The compiler judged the club's place on the social ladder by taking cues from the Garnet Girls' associations with people "of the lower upper class, with the mother of the 'Jones Boys,' famous business men and policy kings who have recently been mobile from the middle-respectable to the upper-shady."[91] The latter term connoted people like the Joneses who, although richer than established members of the upper class, were excluded from that tier of society because their source of wealth was disreputable or nouveau.[92] Upper-shady women, thus, deployed lavish lifestyles to counter suspicion and defy the rival classes:

> The women's lives, like the men's, are centered on conspicuous consumption—display of the most lavish kind. This set is organized around a cult of clothes. Nothing but the right labels at the right prices will do. Both the men and the women know how to buy and wear clothes—and with taste rather than garishness. Clothes are both an end in themselves and an adjunct to the social ritual of this *café au lait* society.[93]

James C. Davis, author of *Commerce in Color*, points out that "the 'Gentlemen Racketeers' pursued a dual strategy of emulating the consumption practices of the upper class insofar as was possible while also seeking to undermine the prestige of the upper class by becoming, themselves, the class to which other[s] aspired."[94] The Great Depression and policy's ascendancy threw notions of class and respectability into disarray. Quickly,

Bronzeville's most outstanding community members were those of the "fast set." Cayton and Drake maintained that people like Harriett Jones were anxious about what the "true" upper class thought of them. And according to Davis, policy kings and queens "recognized that ostentatious display and conspicuous consumption could only go so far toward generating the respectability attached to the upper class, all of whom were considered 'Race men.' To acquire this standing, they had begun conspicuously displaying wealth in the service of civic- and race-oriented activities."[95] According to Drake and Cayton, while their motives for undertaking these activities "appear[ed] to be highly mixed, . . . undoubtedly one motive was their hope that such activities will wipe away the stain of policy."[96]

The members' own understandings of the club's position and the Joneses' affiliation reflected alternative class and gender dynamics. Economic crisis diminished the abilities of social clubs like the Garnet Girls to distinguish themselves from upper-class shady people like Harriett, throwing their reputations into jeopardy. Still, women aspired to obtain a middle-class respectability to an upper-class shady lifestyle. One woman commented at an upper-class dance "while slightly intoxicated":

> I'm going to be a great woman. I don't mean just something ordinary. I have contacts in the North Side that most people can't get. I learn and observe things every day that other women have no way of seeing. I'm gonna be great some day! A lot of people won't accept me, but some day I'm going to make them all take notice. . . . You just watch me! Everybody is going to come to me some day.[97]

This young woman yearned for fame, fortune, and respect—three things that Harriett possessed in complex and contradictory ways. Therefore, Harriett Jones shows us that policy queens weren't shut out from respectability; they navigated their visible policy wealth to include respectable standards.

However, St. Clair Drake's interviews with the clubwomen also show the Garnet Girls' conflicted relationship with Harriett and her daughter-in-law Jean Starr Jones during the 1930s.[98] Policy was a subject that club members had difficulty discussing because of its association with the Jones women:

> There was a flurry of discussion on "policy" with some disagreement as to whether it should be sanctioned, a subject which was no doubt perplexing to these women, being on one hand active church workers and "civic minded" and

on the other hand being closely associated with the mother of the "Jones Boys" and having had the boys' foster sister as one of their most popular members.[99]

It is uncertain who the foster sister was, but Harriett's daughters-in-law all appeared prominently in Garnet Club event press releases.

Throughout the Garnet Club records, there is also a tension between social striving, philanthropic responsibility, and living the good life. The compiler stated that "one of the most striking things about this group is their attitude toward 'charity' and their emphasis upon 'doing something worthwhile,' helping 'less fortunate people,' doing 'whatever we are able,' or feeling 'the responsibility of doing something for others.'"[100] The compiler admitted that this rhetoric was characteristic of club life in Black Chicago but stressed that the Garnet Girls distinguished between being a charity club and a social group: "Since we have been giving to charity, we have become a recognized group. Clubs just don't seem to accomplish much when they are just social clubs. We don't want to be called a charity club. We are a *social* group, but we feel keenly the responsibility of doing for others."[101] The Garnet Girls were aware of the primacy of their social aspirations, but they also recognized that a successful charity event required publicity, and the Joneses brought plenty of press wherever they went. The club leveraged this attention in its yearly philanthropic events that centered on fashion; the Jones women appeared prominently in several Garnet Club fashion show charity events throughout the late 1930s. Lydia, Pauline, and Jean (along with a granddaughter called Little Harriett) modeled sportswear, evening gowns, and beachwear for the Garnet Club Style Show in January 1938, for example. They were featured in photographic spreads. In 1938 Lydia Jones designed the program for the event and raised nearly twelve hundred dollars for charity.[102] The clubwomen also performed the same event at the Savoy in 1941 to benefit the Monumental Baptist Church, with Little Harriett in a miniature wedding gown.[103] The association with the Jones women worked. The *Defender* described the Garnet Girls as having "a wide reputation as criterions of dress and fashion, [they] were stately."[104] The reciprocity between the Garnet Girls and the Jones family worked to the advantage of both: the women's club used the family's economic status to advance the organization while the Joneses used the club to wipe away policy's stain.

Harriett had philanthropic interests of her own outside the club circle but maintained her strategy of silent partnership. She always avoided the flash of the camera. In 1947, as she had done in previous years, she donated a thousand dollars to Provident Hospital but did not appear in the public relations photograph; Harriett's attorney Aaron Payne presented the check to Dr. Homer V. Wilburn, medical director of the hospital.[105]

Harriett's presence in the Garnet Girls, but, more importantly, her remarkable absence from public life, challenges Drake and Cayton's assumption about policy's stain. LaShawn Harris and Victoria Wolcott both furnish crucial evidence from Harlem and Detroit, respectively, along with the theoretical tools to counter the narrative of policy queens' failed attempts at respectability. Harriett—Chicago's most famous policy queen— was a vital actor in this emerging narrative. Her highly visible membership in the Garnet Girls served as a mechanism to manipulate class position and gender expectations for women at the heads of policy gambling families.

Harriett's success also helped her progeny manage class and gender norms. Her sons all married and set themselves up to enjoy a good and thrilling life. Edward Jr.'s first wife was a woman named Flossie, the mother of his oldest son, Edward Peter Jones, born in 1921.[106] But she died the following year at age twenty-three.[107] Edward Jr. then married his more notorious wife, internationally renowned Harlem Cotton Club dancer Lydia, in 1929. Lydia had been roommates in Paris with a countess and they remained close throughout their lives. Edward and Lydia spent extensive periods of time in Europe visiting the countess and spending time in their villa in France.[108] They also attended a reception thrown by *Defender* editor Robert Abbott in honor of the countess when she came to Chicago in 1935.[109] McKissack married famous model and dancer Jean Starr, but he died in an automobile accident in 1944 before the couple had any children.[110] George married Pauline, had several children, and traveled widely.[111]

The women who married into the Jones family benefited from the family's financial success and, perhaps taking instruction from their mother-in-law, each of them was named as a benefactress in the policy wheel business—none more so than Lydia. Lydia split Edward's share of the profits equally with him and invested it in her own policy station.[112] White encroachment on the gambling industry during the late 1930s would be impossible to withstand, and the family's policy empire started to unravel.

The Takeover

Harriett's travels suggest she foresaw this unraveling. Harriett and Edward Jr. made two trips out of the country in the 1930s, one to France in 1939 and another to Mexico City.[113] These trips were scouting missions during which Harriett and her sons charted out new territory for settlement and the family's next business venture. In a serial retrospective on Edward Jr., the *Defender* made the case that in the late 1930s he had given up the policy business and moved his immediate family to Paris.[114] The family had certainly endured several notable setbacks. In 1940 the federal government charged the Jones brothers with evading nearly two million dollars in income taxes from 1933 to 1938. Edward Jr. took the blame for the family, spending twenty-two months in prison in 1940, and the tax debt was settled for slightly less than half a million dollars.[115] While in prison, Jones was said to have given his secrets to white mob boss Anthony J. Accardo, paving the way for the mob to muscle its way into the policy operation by 1946.[116] Edward Jr. was kidnapped that same year.[117] Chicago police captain Milton Deas Jr. remembered the night when the mob kidnapped one of the boys: "In order to convince those Jones boys that they had to leave, they kidnapped one of them, and the night that they kidnapped him, my mother heard their car when it turned on Forty-sixth!"—"white gangsters" had run the Jones brothers out of town.[118] According to the Kefauver Committee Report, George Jones negotiated with the kidnappers, and the family left Chicago about a week later, "although [they continued] to draw sums approximating $200,000 a year from the operations of the wheel."[119] In a rare moment, Harriett broke her silent partner strategy and offered this comment to the press: "Why shouldn't we leave? My boys have made the money they need, and I don't like the way they're being pushed around."[120] McKissack's deadly car accident, Edward's imprisonment, and then his kidnapping for a ransom of one hundred thousand dollars prompted the Joneses' move to Mexico City, leaving the wheels in charge of their partners, Theodore Roe and Charles Davis.[121]

The Joneses were able to retain control of their policy wheels through 1948 and used the daily profits of seventy-five thousand dollars to launch several businesses in Mexico City, including an automobile store and a clothing store.[122] Chicago media kept track of the Joneses while they were making millions. For example, in 1952 *Jet* magazine added Lydia Jones to its list of "Wives of Negro Millionaires." *Jet* also credited Edward Jr. and Lydia with running a flourishing downtown store, the Casa Jacquar, which "features expensive hand-painted and hand-blocked cottons, silks, imported woolens, skirts and blouses."[123] The Joneses continued their extravagant lifestyle with the purchase of a fifteen-room mansion, and Lydia was said to have a "change of three mink coats and with her husband, owns three cars, one of them a limousine."[124] Someone close to the family described the Joneses' opulence in Mexico City: "They had three beautiful ocean-front homes, all three right next to each other. Ed had one, George had one and their mother had the one in the middle."[125] It was a perfect descriptor for Harriett's verve and resilience as a leader of the Joneses' Mexico City industry, which supported the family for the next thirty years into the late twentieth century.

Most of the stories in the *Chicago Defender* about the policy era during the Great Depression lauded the philanthropy of the Jones brothers, but very few directly mentioned Harriett and her activities. If we read against the grain of these articles, however, we can catch a glimpse of her legacy as Chicago's most famous policy queen. Her silent partner strategy protected her public reputation while helping the family avoid jail time and safeguarding her sons from their rivals. Al Monroe, who wrote most of the stories about the Joneses for the *Defender*, penned what amounted to a love letter to them in 1962 after learning Edward Jr. had been hospitalized. In his column "So They Say," Monroe swiftly cast aside any doubts about the integrity of the Jones brothers, advising his readers to focus less on the "take" the Joneses received from policy and more on the "give," the millions they donated over the span of twenty years while "they ruled the roost in policy." Instead of disparaging the illegitimate business of policy, he emphasized the thousands of jobs they provided at their milk business, Food Mart, and Ben Franklin store. He lauded their efforts to stabilize rent, lend money, and provide food—doing more for Bronzeville during the Great Depression than public relief efforts ever could. Yet even Monroe conceded that "they took millions from the gambling public on Chicago's Southside."[126] LeRoy Martin, the former police superintendent under Mayor Harold Washington, reluctantly admitted:

> Had it not been for Policy—and as an ex-police officer I don't want to ever give a criminal credit for anything!—but a lot of people would have starved had it not been for Policy. . . . It was a way of pumping money into the

economy. . . . But they [the Jones brothers] fed a lot of families because it was the Depression, and, as you and I both know, if white people are out of work, the Black man would be even worse off.[127]

Harriett gained considerably in her exploitation of thousands at the Jones policy wheels. She had taken many risks and when the risks became too great, she made calculated choices to find alternative returns. When policy ceased to reap rewards, she made an extraordinary choice to leave Chicago for Mexico City. She didn't just live in Mexico City; she and the family *thrived* in Mexico City for the next thirty years. Harriett died at her home there in 1971. She was ninety-five years old. *Jet* remembered her in death in much the same way she had been depicted throughout her life: by listing the accomplishments of her sons and her daughters-in-law.[128] While Harriett was never flaunted in the Jones spotlight, the handiwork and craftswomanship of the Jones lifestyle belonged to her. Harriett's high standards for how the family ran their policy wheels set their policy industry apart from all others, even if the papers would never remember her for it.

Harriett's story helps us reformulate the story of policy queens and what they left to their children by way of the informal economy. Only six years after Edward Sr.'s death, Harriett became the matriarch of Chicago's leading policy wheels—worth nearly twenty-five million dollars—and by 1947 she occupied the apex of several businesses in Mexico City. Yet so little is known about her personally, and she is given minimal credit for establishing the prosperous futures of Bronzeville's famed entrepreneurs, the Jones brothers, her daughters-in-law, and multiple grandchildren. Through her own labor, handiwork she perhaps kept from her husband, Harriett made the Jones name synonymous with success, high standards, and an immense policy gambling fortune. She is a crucial exception to Black Chicago's Depression narrative. Her remarkable prosperity reveals the agency she exercised in a difficult social and economic climate, and her hard work left behind a legacy of unmatched affluence for future generations of Joneses.

4

Dream Books, Fortune-Tellers, and Mediumship

While the structure of gambling in both Harlem and Chicago made it impossible—or at the very least difficult—for patrons to fix the picks for each day, or "game the system," patrons went to great lengths to obtain hot, guaranteed-to-hit numbers before their neighbors did.[1] Gamblers in Chicago, Detroit, and Harlem demanded unfettered contact to the day's and drawings' best—that is, winning—numbers. By the early twentieth century, Harlem's winning numbers were based on pari-mutuel numbers printed in the daily newspapers. With no control over them, patrons were forced to accept the results: "So far as ordinary gamblers were concerned, [these numbers] were impossible to 'fix'."[2] In Black Chicago, however, policy had always offered its patrons their choice of numbers. Policy bettors placed their money on one or more numbers they hoped would be picked in a drawing of twelve numbers that had been placed in capsules on individually owned and operated wheels. Patrons could purchase slips from numerous wheels all over the city. Gratification was quick; station operators spun the wheels twice a day for a morning drawing and an evening drawing. The options were many, but patrons still exhibited a love of competition and getting their hottest or luckiest numbers before others. Patrons received lucky numbers through a variety of means and submitted their "best" picks to policy writers, highly visible individuals who canvassed neighborhoods soliciting bets for the daily drawings.

The resulting esotericism and competitive attitude led Chicago sociologists Drake and Cayton to lament policy gambling as a "cult."[3] Describing the people's obsession with getting the best numbers, they aggrieved, "Just any number will not do for a 'gig.' People want 'hot' numbers."[4] The mechanism policy customers employed to pick "hot" numbers relied heavily on access to the expertise of Black mediums, sometimes called fortune-tellers, diviners, or spiritualists.[5] Gamblers and policy operators held the expertise of Black mediums in high regard. Bridgett M. Davis explains that mediums had visions and "could see into things, witness the future"; her mother held these "women, always women, in high regard."[6] Policy customers received lucky numbers through private consultations with women mediums who ran séances out of their apartments and homes along the South Side, by attending public religious services at Chicago's many storefront and Spiritualist churches and by purchasing various items such as dream books, candles, roots, or lucky powders from curio catalogs. Such spiritualist commerce was built on a rich tradition of African American women's mediumship and work, predicated on consumers' access to, high esteem for, and the visibility of Black female mediums. Bronzeville relied on Black female mediumship and its commercialization to bridge the harsh segregation of this world with messages from beyond. As a result, Black women found power and profit.

In addition to labor as mediums (the focus of this chapter), women found work in a variety of other highly visible and at times formal spin-off industries related to policy gambling. Women worked policy wheel repair, a business cornered by Robert Wilcox, or printing wheel and paper manufacture, dominated by Ed White; the Benvenuti brothers' Victory Paper Company; and W. A. Johns Paper Company at Twenty-Second Street and Union.[7] The *Chicago Defender* tried to carve out a niche in the printing business by printing the winning numbers for at least twelve different policy wheels in its cartoon "Old Dan the Numbers Man."[8] The Jones brothers, too, used their policy gambling largesse to make gains in secondary ventures such as a specialty store at 120 East Fifty-Fifth Street or the Jones Brothers Finer Food Mart at 305 East Forty-Third Street, which offered a state-of-the-art meat department and free delivery. Their bookkeeper was Maude Craig, wife of Jones policy collector Charlie Craig.[9] In 1943 Ed Jones and attorney Aaron Payne launched the Jones/Payne Hawthorn Mellody Farms milk distributorship at 70 East Fifty-First Street. Many women found employment as route managers, in sales, or as drivers, and helped, according to Nathan Thompson, supply fresh milk daily to nearly every school in Bronzeville.[10] Later Ed Jones Jr. joined with policy queen Ann Roane to set up the Hawthorn Milk Store at 3562 Cottage Grove Avenue.[11] A list of Ed Jones's most important business associates reveals the numerous industries embroiled in and profiting because of Bronzeville's love of policy gambling: Brinks Express Company, Drexel National Bank and Safe Deposit Company, Drovers Trust and Savings Bank and Safe Deposit Company, Miner and East Incorporated, and the Utility Machine and Engraving Company.[12] The Joneses also held Black mediums in high regard, as they too employed mediums to attract more customers. Thompson claims that Ed Jones brought a spiritualist into the fold to "hype 'can't miss numbers.' This Spiritualist would 'interpret' symbols in dreams and translate them into can't miss numbers."[13]

The Joneses' and gamblers' reliance on mediums reveals mediums' popularity and the tensions of African American women's work in the economic outgrowths of Chicago's policy industry, especially its dynamic spiritual and secular realms. Mediums experienced similar tensions of visibility that other women who worked within policy gambling were subjected to, including policing, arrest, and charges. To begin with, their work was often associated with "the occult," a term that means hidden. Mediums needed that invisibility; they needed anonymity because their activity was illegal, therefore their work as individual consultants and within organized religion reflects that desire to remain hidden. Yet at the same time, mediums also needed visibility for business, just as policy writers being known around the neighborhood meant a larger clientele. Like other women working in the policy industry, mediums directed the visibility of their work in creative ways to widen their spheres of influence and profit. Thus, mediums found ingenious ways to advertise, peddle goods, and make names for themselves. Bronzeville's divination women must be positioned as an integral part of the local policy industry. The mediums' work, always both spiritual and secular, pushed traditional gender roles. African American women's work as diviners reveals the inextricable nature of their relationship to the divine, capitalistic, and carceral structures that sought to subdue them. African American women diviners and their eager patrons sought to make Black women more powerful and present in Bronzeville's spiritual realm, which offered them a way to "navigate the unfamiliar and potentially threatening social terrain of anonymous urban life."[14]

Divination and the Law

Black women's wide-ranging influence in both the capitalist and spiritualist arenas of Bronzeville subjected them to legal and extralegal forms of anti-Black racism. Historian Jamie Pietruska tells readers in her book *Looking Forward* that "fortune-tellers regularly encountered discursive and legal mechanisms designed to control their labor."[15] This took multiple forms, from "direct criminal prohibitions" to "zoning restrictions, licensing requirements, or heightened tax liability."[16] Cases against diviners often involved determining whether or not they sincerely believed they had the gift of foresight or whether they were practicing a legitimate religion such as Spiritualism.[17] Pietruska explains:

> As fortune-tellers reimagined their practices, so too did state courts, which reshaped the regulation of fortune-telling through a series of early twentieth-century decisions that centered not on the empirical question of whether one was reading palms, cards, or tea leaves but on the epistemological question of whether one was genuinely attempting to foretell the future or merely pretending.[18]

My focus in this chapter is on three cases from Chicago that illustrate how the city distinguished between the capacity to foretell and the act of foretelling. These cases also exhibit how African American women divination laborers navigated policy's visibility.

Chicago's 1905 municipal code prohibited "Fortune-telling, Etc., Advertising of Prohibited; Fraud Prohibited in Connection with Fortune-telling, etc., and in connection with Meetings Held in the Name of Spiritualism."[19] The code located mediums within the fraudulent, "crafty science" that was designed to take property from customers.[20] In section 1549 of the 1907 code, the prohibitions against fortune-telling became more specific. Banned was all fortune-telling connected to leisure activities, gambling specifically; violators were subject to a fine of twenty-five to one hundred dollars for each offense.[21] The 1907 Chicago ordinance made it a misdemeanor to

> obtain money or property from another by fraudulent devices and practices in the name of or by means of spirit mediumship, palmistry, card reading, astrology, or like crafty science, or fortune-telling of any kind . . . [or to] hold or give any public or private meeting, gather, circle, or séance of any kind in the name of spiritualism, or of any other religious body, cult or denomination, and therein practice or permit to be practiced fraud or deception of any kind.[22]

Municipal authorities wanted to distinguish Spiritualism from fraud, confirming Jeremy Patrick's assertion that American courts were far more solicitous toward spiritualists that were deemed sincere and that they never came down uniformly hard on fortune-tellers.[23] Mediums used this ambiguity to their advantage as they sought to navigate the visibility of fortune-telling and the protections of Spiritualism.

Two opinions written by different judges on the Appellate Court of Illinois in 1911 and 1912 illustrate this solicitous attitude toward spiritualists and a hesitancy to ban all fortune-telling.[24] In *Chicago v. Payne*, James Payne, a professed spiritualist medium, was charged with violating the 1907 ordinance. The court noted that he had done no more than hold a séance, stating, "For the purposes of this case Spiritualism may be defined as a belief in the power of some departed spirits to communicate with the living by means of mediums. . . . We do not think that the common council of the city of Chicago . . . intended to declare such belief unfounded and make the act . . . a misdemeanor."[25] The complaint against Payne was quashed and he was free to go. *Chicago v. Westergren* involved Mrs. Rosa Westergren, a self-identified medium, who had handed a prediction to an undercover police officer for fifty cents, leading to a conviction and fine. The court reversed the conviction, concluding that the officer had never actually been deceived or defrauded:

> We are not disposed, nor is it here necessary, to attempt any discussion of spirit mediumship. We wish only to observe that in this age of marvelous advancement in science, when all the energies and abilities of learned and sincere men are devoted to study, experiment and research on these questions, we have not the temerity to mark limitations therein. However unreasonable such ideas may appear to many, it is certain . . . that a large number of people have faith and confidence in spirit mediumship and we are of the opinion that the belief therein and honest practice thereof without fraudulent means, tricks or devices cannot be held criminal.[26]

Litigants also challenged municipal authorities by arguing that municipalities lacked the legislative power to regulate fortune-telling. The earliest known invocation of this argument came in 1912 when the Supreme Court of Illinois ruled in *Chicago v. Ross* that the city lacked the power to make "spirit mediumship, palmistry, card reading, astrology, seership, or like crafty science or fortune-telling of any kind" a misdemeanor.[27] But for women profiting from patrons looking for lottery numbers, the state ruled on the side of cities. In the case of *Chicago v. Ross*, "state law had granted cities the right to prohibit fraud but the court ruled that this had to be read in the context of preceding language making the grant of power only to gambling and lotteries."[28] In aggregate, these three cases show that the Appellate Court of Illinois protected practitioners of Spiritualism and resisted moves by the City of Chicago to designate all fortune-telling a misdemeanor.

The City of Chicago, however, proved to be more aggressive toward practitioners of the crafty sciences, especially when gambling was involved. According to Christine Corocos, "Some prosecutors and police did not see such messages as legitimate spiritual guidance or acceptable religious prophecy. They still labeled such communications as 'fortune telling'" and therefore illegal.[29] Debates about the lawlessness of fortune-tellers often started at the moment of police intervention, angering paying customers in the process. Patrick references two cases from New York in which the argument was made that "it can be seen that fortune-telling was a practice in which witnesses rarely complained about the service they received in exchange for payment they provided."[30] Police held the view that the public was so duped that the police were required to take additional steps to secure the public's protection: "Specially trained police officers made 'daily rounds' to stem [fortune-telling] and that an added power of summary arrest was deemed necessary to make the process less burdensome on the police."[31] The State of New York went so far as to discuss an amendment to its fortune-telling ban to give police the power of summary arrest when they encountered fortune-telling, thus dispensing with the need to obtain an arrest warrant, because complaints were rarely made by the persons whose fortune was told.[32] Therefore, divining women connected to policy gambling were most at risk not from their customers but from police officers, facing police officers' raids and undercover sting operations.

Divining women responded to these tensions in creative ways and, when they could, used the ambiguous nature of fortune-telling's legality to their advantage. Some used accepted modes of spiritual expression, such as Spiritualism, to give a veneer of accepting the language and ideology of religious leaders, police, and court authorities, even while simultaneously adapting idioms that mocked and undermined established authorities. Others kept their divination labors veiled and secret. Pietruska emphasizes that "the history of policing and prosecution of fortune-tellers makes visible how contests over the production of future knowledge hinged on ideologies of gender, race, and class—as well as their submersion."[33] She suggests that racial ideologies and gender norms were central to the arrests as well as the appeal of fortune-tellers and that the appropriation of fortune-tellers' racial identities by white middle-class consumers and practitioners exposes more about the white middle class "than about fortune-tellers themselves."[34]

Mediums and Individual Consultations

Gamblers consistently sought out mediums in Chicago, who followed a long and complex tradition of occult and conjure that had begun on plantations before Emancipation. Mediums continued the tradition of African American women during the colonial and antebellum periods who practiced conjure and magic to serve enslaved communities.[35] With the Great Depression, conjurers and doctors gave way to religious scientists, doctors, and professors.[36] Such occupations shifted with the demands of the Great Migration as new forms of urban religiosity clashed with the old.[37] The rhythms of this modern African American religiosity mirror what policy women experienced as laborers.[38] Urban dwellers had newly emerging spiritual needs that African American women mediums scrambled to meet. At the same time, urban African American women faced changing economic realities they addressed by participating in the policy industry as diviners. In other words, the Great Migration facilitated an increase in both supply of and demand for mediumship.

Despite the possibility of arrest, the demand for mediums bore on. Census data between 1910 and 1940 shows that many African American women of Cook County listed their occupations as "medium," "minister," "spiritualist," "clairvoyant," or "fortune-teller," despite the city's municipal codes banning such practices.[39] Twenty women listed their occupations as such in the census from 1910 to 1940, fifteen worked on their own account, and thirteen listed themselves as the head of their household. Most of the women were unmarried, with fourteen of them listed as widowed, single, or divorced. Finally, the women were middle-aged, reporting an average age of 38.6 years old. None of the women were native to Illinois. All of the women reported their births as having occurred elsewhere, most of them in Southern states such as Alabama, Kentucky, and Louisiana.

Using advertisements, fortune-tellers constructed a range of professional personas.[40] For many of the women and men in this field, divination was both a ministry and a profession, and their titles reflected that. Experts such as "Professor Edward Lowe, Astro-Numerologist"; "Madame Williams, Your Friend and Adviser"; and "Doctor Pryor," with his "Japo Oriental Company"; and "King Solomon's Temple of Religious Science" invoked professional titles.[41] Epithets such as "'God sent healer,' 'clairvoyant,' and 'witch-doctor,' . . . [demonstrated] the variety and eclecticism of the new Conjurers in the urban context."[42] For example, Madame Fu Futtam, a candle shopkeeper in New York, was engaged in "spiritual and occult work as well as giving dream interpretations and lottery luck numbers to her clientele."[43] Likewise, the aforementioned Madame Williams advertised special meetings three evenings a week in Chicago and "advised thousands in their personal problems with complete satisfaction," guaranteeing them advice on all affairs in life, love, health, domestic, and financial conditions.[44] Knowing she could not thrive on philanthropy alone, she advertised "Lucky Numbers free—11 hits in 3 days."[45] There were many such spiritual advisers, several hundred in Bronzeville.[46]

Men, too, asserted professionalism through gendered categories. A fortune-teller who took the title of "professor" or "promised scientific expertise" laid claim to a masculine authority.[47] For example, so large was the aforementioned Professor Lowe's library that Drake and Cayton referred to it as "his own magnum opus."[48] His bookstall displayed the *Key to Numerology*, *Albertus Magnus*, *The Six and Seventh Book of Moses*, *White and Black Art for Man and Beast*, and the *Book of Forbidden Knowledge*.[49] Much as professionals line the walls of their offices with manuals and philosophical texts, Professor Lowe did the same at his storefront. In 1910 Professor White, a Chicago "Psychic and Scientific Palmist," offered readings for twenty-five and fifty cents.[50] In 1925 D. S. Brown of Chicago sold "Voodoo bags for success in hazard betting, card games, dice, and all games of chance."[51] In 1935 Doctor E. N. French of Chicago advertised something called the "Success Seal," said to be helpful "in business, to get work, in love and marriage, to win games, and to gain influence and power over all things."[52] He also offered a course, "'easy to learn; based on the Bible,' in the great art of giving readings, healings, and spiritual advice to others. $500 course for only $55.50. Send me $1.00 and I will send you first lesson at once. You can pay $1.00 weekly."[53] Doctor French accompanied the advertisement with a picture of a Black man in a suit and turban, merging the businessman with the Eastern supernatural practitioner.

Men and women touted their expertise as having been honed through study in the "Orient" or inherited from their ancestors in the South. Many clairvoyants peddled "Oriental" credentials. For example, Madame Harper claimed she had unsealed "the Cabala," which gave her understanding of all occult mysteries. The aforementioned Professor Lowe, an astro-numerologist, asserted that his "gift" came from his mother, that he had studied "the science of the Zodiac," and that Chicago's most intellectual circles recognized him and his work.[54] A 1924 notice in the *Chicago Defender* described "Edet Effiong, West African scientist and herbalist," as a "Mohammadan Native of Africa and Oriental Science," who provided "luck and advice . . . as to the whereabouts of lost friends or stolen articles, love, finance, etc., to those who desire it."[55] Effiong also claimed to have the ability to "cure all kinds of diseases, by Oriental Science."[56] To take advantage of the rapidly changing spiritual cosmologies of Bronzeville, many mediums knew that "with the allure of their professional credentials came a new emphasis on the ethnic and international backgrounds of practitioners."[57] Such professional and gendered credentials rested upon an ethnic or racial connection to the Orient and the South. Tammy Stone-Gordon argues that occult workers "utilized the classified advertisement to play freely with and often invert dominant notions of gender, race, class, age, ableness, and nation. . . . Immigrant status meant exotic knowledge rather than foreign threat."[58] Advertisements for specialists such as Lowe or Madame Harper hailing from India or Asia, possessing "Hindu" or "Oriental" secrets, were frequent in African American newspapers.[59]

Like other occupations in the policy industry, LaShawn Harris posits that "public acclaim was essential to African American female mediums and was directly linked to their client base, potential earnings, and reputations."[60] Advertisements for services regularly appeared in African American newspapers, popular magazines, and by telephone, telegraph, or radio.[61] The first advertisement for a female clairvoyant in the *Chicago Defender* debuted on Saturday, April 9, 1910:

> The Key of Mystery Solves All Troubles. If your life is dreary and your troubles have no end, write to the world's greatest clairvoyant[.] Madame M. Harper; 641 East Miami Street, Indianapolis, Ind. Is a friend in need; one who has unsealed "The Cabala;" one who thoroughly understands all Persian, Indian, Egyptian and Hindoo Occult Mysteries, Gives Luck. This True Born

Clairvoyant. Writes your horoscope for $1.00. Will gladly give any advice to you. Send stamped envelope for answer and write to this wonderful woman.[62]

Advertisements like this appear all over the *Chicago Defender*, reflecting Bronzeville's demand for African American mediums' services. According to Shane White, Stephen Garton, Stephen Robertson, and Graham White, "Droves of African Americans consulted various spiritual guides, desperate for the edge that would score them a hit in the numbers."[63] Fortune-tellers were predominantly, but not exclusively, female practitioners, and the majority of their clients were women, according to Pietruska.[64] As Pietruska demonstrates in her study of New York fortune-tellers, some marketed their services according to gender, with "a common phrase being, 'ladies, 50 cts.; gents, $1.'"[65] Part of the appeal of fortune-telling was its intimate and private nature, which also acted as a protective aegis from law enforcement. As Pietruska explains, "The site of exchange—in cities, most often a private residence that clients visited individually or in small groups—was not a visible public space like a saloon or brothel. The transactional and private nature of fortune-telling rendered it difficult to police."[66]

Mediums and Organized Religion

Mediums sometimes sought refuge in Spiritualist churches, which, according to Drake in his WPA-supported study "Churches and Voluntary Associations in the Chicago Negro Community," represented a "blending of the Protestant Evangelical worship service with certain items of the catholic ceremony."[67] Mediums provided "readings" and "messages," sometimes as communications from the afterlife.[68] Spiritualist worship relied on an emerging synergy of organized religion and spiritualist numbers diviners. For example, Drake notes that although rarer than shouting by the preacher, such actions as speaking in tongues, prophesying, healing, giving messages, and magical rites, including the blessing of handkerchiefs, money, and flowers, were important elements of ritual that were common to all churches.[69] Moreover, emphasizing the magical elements of religion was important to the lower-class congregants.[70] African American women spiritual leaders and diviners capitalized on this by making themselves integral to spiritualist forms of religion and worship, gaining ground in organized religion. In contrast to the old religious establishment in Chicago, the new sacred order was decidedly female and "fundamentally Protestant and explicitly Christian."[71] Wallace Best tells us that Spiritualist churches practiced a "new radically demonstrative brand of Pentecostalism," with "divine healing, psychic phenomena, and séances."[72] Furthermore, African American divination women were able to take their historical roots as "slave doctors" and work their skills into the newly found embrace of "emotional worship for the way it reflected 'African' and 'slave religion,'" something Chicago's Black Protestants had openly discouraged before the Great Migration.[73] Drake reported that all the Pentecostal, Holiness, and Spiritualist churches had ample opportunity for women to fill some types of positions, including the role of healer, mediums, and choristers.[74] Cook County's census data confirms this fact: eight African American women between 1910 and 1940 identified themselves as spiritualists while two identified themselves as ministers.[75] Spiritualist women joined the ranks of the many Black women who were largely responsible for making the church a vehicle that met the spiritual and secular needs of the Black community.[76]

But skepticism about Black women diviners abounded. In their sociological study of Black Chicago, Drake and Cayton sought to ascertain the degree to which these women were concerned with their patrons' religious salvation. Addressing them as "spiritual advisers" instead of "Spiritualist" pastors, Drake and Cayton cast their judgments readily and visibly.[77] Storefront churches carried a certain social and geographical connotation: upper- and middle-class Black Chicagoans associated them with Southern migrants, the poor, or those in "stages of insanity."[78] Female mediums pushed back against this disdain. As one spiritual adviser revealed:

> I have done good for a lot of people and they never forget what I do for them. When the spirit comes to me, whatever it tells me, whatever it tells me I do that. If it says pray, I do that. To give numbers is no sin because the people have to live, and to try to win a little money. That is no harm. Knowledge will have to come from God and no man can do the job if he is not in possession of that knowledge. That power I have. On many occasions God comes to me in a dream. That dream I will play in policy and catch it. Then, I invest the money wisely. That is all there is to it. But you have to live free from sin to do this.[79]

This individual identified herself as being invested in the salvation of her patrons—one must be free of sin to access the secret knowledge of the hottest numbers.[80] Harris notes the importance of this resistance: "Claiming to possess the gift of prophecy was significant for African American female mediums. It marked the distinction between true seers and spiritual fakers and brought public acclaim for some Black female mediums."[81] Harris quotes Madame Sally Broy, founder of the Righteous Supreme Temple in Chicago, who "claimed that she was 'born with a veil over her face' and that she 'received a power from God to cure any disease on earth. I am able to heal your condition without seeing any party or anything you wish to know about yourself or anyone else.'"[82] Harris also references the comments of Madame Fu Futtam, who "maintained that she was a true seer and claimed she 'possessed a gift for seeing visions and dreaming dreams. I have possessed it since I was very young. It is a heritage handed down from the ancient mystics.'"[83]

A variety of spiritualists used their gifts to make gains within organized religion, an arrangement that profited both the medium and the minister.[84] Ministers made fortunes by supplying their congregations with church service readings.[85] Drake and Cayton exposed a South Side preacher who "gained popularity by including a few numbers in his Sunday sermons."[86] Spiritualist churches, however, regularly employed mediums to distribute numbers, thus highlighting the visibility of mediums.[87] Victoria Wolcott described two mechanisms that Detroit church mediums used to receive and transmit lucky numbers during formal church services. One of them was the "hymn method." The hymn number called out would represent the lucky number to be played that day.[88] Another congregation relied on the medium's "test message" method. Prior to the service, assistants were expected to "move among the congregation selling little numbered cards for a quarter. When the time comes for the messages to be given[,] the medium calls out a number and the individual possessing that number either raises his hand or stands. When this is done the medium raises her eyes heavenward and gets a message from God for this individual."[89] Although Gustav Carlson did not specify the gender of the church assistants, he did so with the medium by using the pronoun "her." There would be no mistake—the medium was instantly recognizable at the front of the church.

In ecclesiastical contexts, then, women could find purchase in their feminine roles and as leaders, whether it was while sermonizing from the pulpit or in back rooms interpreting dreams. Black women mediated categories of gender through the spirit and games of chance. Therefore their daily survival tactics are nothing short of transformative; the lived realities of Black policy women reveal the significance of occult and games of chance to survival in a capitalist and racist world. Wolcott argues that for "Spiritualist mediums, participation in the underground economy and religious sects led to cultural authority and economic independence."[90] A young Black janitress explained the importance of spiritualism to Fred Moore, editor of the *New York Age*: "I certainly do believe in spiritualism. . . . I couldn't possibly live on the pay I get as a janitress, and what I win on the 'numbers' helps me to get along. . . . I am ahead of the 'numbers' game right now."[91] One migrant who arrived in Detroit in 1916 with her husband and three children confessed that her family would not have survived without a spiritualist woman she met on a streetcar who gave her a box of incense and a candle.[92]

The emergence of storefront churches (a combination of commerce and religion) also provided new opportunities for women. We can read African American women's opportunity from this combination, and we can also read women's transgression of public and private spheres. "Often run and always attended by women," storefront churches, Wolcott argues, "became social locations where women could exercise power and establish self-esteem through religious worship."[93] Usually Spiritualist, Holiness, or Pentecostal in nature, these small groups "operated out of individuals' homes and rented commercial spaces, allowed some practitioners to maintain sources of livelihood and to promote their skills as mediums, psychic readers, and spiritual healers."[94] Storefront churches "put communication with the spirit world at the core of their ministries."[95] Bridgett Davis explains that most of Detroit's Spiritualist religious establishments were run by women. But some "women weren't ministers, rather they worked solely as mediums within a church or by doing individual readings, again for a fee. These mediums were believed to have the power to either predict a number outright, or divine it by feeling a believer's 'vibrations,' which 'gave off' what number he or she should play."[96] Many mediums attended Chicago's First Church of Deliverance, where blessed flowers were sold with the promise of bringing the wearer "good luck or some blessing."[97] Davis said that during one Detroit church service, "congregants who wanted to receive numbers would stand and march single file past the medium, who'd be standing near the altar. She'd dip her hands in holy water, sprinkle the believer, and whisper a number in her ear. In another variation, the medium would lie in a coffin, and as people filed by, she'd give each one a number from 'the deceased'."[98] Women were the common denominator in many of these gatherings. Most of the mediums were female, legitimizing the notion that women had special access to the divine, whether in a storefront church or in private, using strategies such as dream books, powders, and talismans to discern the winning numbers.

Engaging in divination in storefront churches, "where neighbors congregated in a more democratic and less hierarchical setting than established churches," was one way for women to simultaneously engage with spirituality through feminine codes while also securing church profits.[99] Storefront churches were among the institutions that helped African American women withstand the staggering disorientation of migration and served as urban institutional bases for new spiritual traditions. Women's status as practitioners or symbols of divination illustrates the idea of their visibility and invisibility, but opportunities emerged when African American women wedded the supernatural with capitalism.

Gamblers' Own Strategies

African American mediums provided their customers with an edge and a sense of empowerment in both private consultations and in spiritualist or storefront churches.[100] However, some people did not visit spiritualists but instead relied on their own ingenuity. Gamblers who were reticent to visit mediums relied on a web of interpersonal relationships, services, goods, and "hunches"—something the gambler had a good feeling about—to increase their odds at the wheel. Everyday occurrences such as numbers found in "a girl friend's name, a street address" were sufficient as "'hunch' sources."[101] Other, rarer circumstances, a dead relative visiting one in a dream perhaps, warranted the necessary gamble. In 1945 a young African American mother explained her luck:

> I had lived in Chicago for four years when I began playing policy in 1930. At the laundry where I worked, the girls had played for years, but I never gave the game a thought 'til one night I dreamt of my mother who had been dead for thirty years. At work I mentioned the dream to Jessie, and she made me play a quarter on the "dead mother" row. Well, sir, as I'm living this minute, the gig fell out and I won $25. That started me off. My luck got so good, and since I was bothered with rheumatism I quit the laundry.[102]

Prodded by the dream of her long-deceased mother, the woman seized the rare opportunity to take control of her earthly circumstances. As another woman enthusiastically delineated the various strategies of Bronzeville's policy gamblers, both those who were lucky and those who were unlucky, she revealed her own theories for hitting winning numbers:

> Well, some play by hunches, dreams, or numbers on a car or transfer ticket. Some go to Spiritualists. They [lucky numbers] are obtained for the most part, though, from dreams and hunches. You watch the "book" your dream falls in most and play in that "book." Some people are lucky and some are not. Some people believe in burning different incenses for luck. They claim it gives them success. My dreams are good in the Harlem and the Bronx [wheels].[103]

Her confidence in her own ability to read her dreams was buttressed when her dreams proved reliable in predicting not one but two wheels. Many in Bronzeville were skeptical of the "assorted spiritualists, numerologists, and root doctors who gave out numbers with varying degrees of larceny and good faith."[104] Some just imitated mediums. For example, "one keen-sighted laundry operator found it good business to advertise weekly 'lucky' numbers on the side of his truck."[105]

Family members also relied on young children, an extension of the women's sphere, to access the winning numbers and to avert suspicion. Children consulted on dreams and worked as runners; according to *Ebony*, youngsters got to keep twenty-five cents of each dollar bet.[106] Drake and Cayton show that it was widely believed that children gave out the best numbers ("children are lucky you know, and are the best ones to give you winning gigs").[107] An observer from the 1930s likewise expressed the belief that children had special access to the divine: "[They] are more gifted with the powers of divination than their elders."[108] Many adults growing up in Bronzeville corroborated this assertion: "Adults would constantly come to children and say, 'Did you have any dreams last night?' They'd ask you and you would tell them your dream. *And you knew why*? If, indeed, that dream proved profitable, yeah. They might even reward you with an ice cream cone or something."[109] One daughter recalled helping her mother get a jump start on the day's best numbers:

> At an early age, I provided my mother with a lot of information. From my dreams. I was right on the money. So much, my uncle called from New York and he said he wanted a number. And that he would buy school clothes for

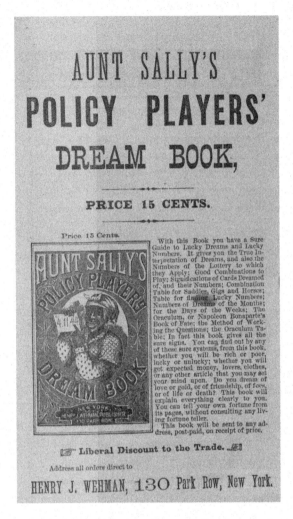

FIGURE 4. J. H. Harvey, *Wehman's Complete Dancing Master and Call Book Containing a Full and Complete Description of All the Modern Dances, Together with the Figures of the German*. H. J. Wehman, Publisher, New York, monographic, 1889. (Library of Congress)

me. Well, I needed school clothes, because we were on welfare. I gave him the number. He won a couple thousand dollars, and I never heard from him. But another lady who played the numbers, she won a couple more thousand dollars.[110]

As a result of such skepticism, or when gamblers couldn't reach mediums in person, they relied on a variety of stand-in mechanisms to pick their numbers, the most popular being dream books that featured images of African American mediums. Bronzeville's gamblers relied on dream books to locate winning numbers. The magic manuals often relied on stereotypical images of women from the Orient and the mammy archetype, racialized images of women of color.[111] When mediums weren't accessible or visiting a medium wasn't desirable, access to lucky numbers was funneled through women's visible depictions on the covers of dream books. Dream books were a commoditized strategy for bettors to seek the advice of these African American women without visiting taboo institutions.[112] The books preserved readers' moral character; reading books was more acceptable than visiting mediums, because gamblers did not encounter the women directly.

One of the most popular dream books, *Aunt Sally's Lucky Policy Player's Dream Book: A Study of Harmony in Numbers*, was first published by Wehman Brothers of New York in 1889.[113] Like hundreds of other typical dream books that were popular in early twentieth-century America, *Aunt Sally's* listed dream images in alphabetical order, with one, two, three, or four numbers beside each item in a row, specifically designed for the convenience of those who bet on policy. The cover illustration features a caricature of a Black woman—Aunt Sally—wearing a head scarf. Aunt Sally's face is shaded black with gray tufts of hair popping out from under her the scarf; her head scarf and sleeves contrast dramatically against her skin and her white short-sleeve top, its bright red with black polka dots drawing the viewer's eye down to the bend of her elbows and then up to her wrists. She points to a well-known combination of numbers—4.11.44—or what was commonly called the Washerwoman's Row, written on a piece of paper. Her eyes stare into those of the reader. But the racialized cartoon evokes a timeworn stereotypical image of the mammy archetype that overpowers Aunt Sally's assertive glare.

The cover designer framed Aunt Sally's image between two important phrases: "Policy-Players" floats at the top and "Dream Book" at the bottom of the cover. This purposeful design places a caricature of African American women at the center of policy gamblers' most popular strategy to win big. However, the actual African American women of Chicago, Detroit, and Harlem who used dream books in their work as spiritualists or mediums and those who sold occult goods were nothing like the caricature. Their realities contest the racist mockery that characterized the cover not only of this dream book but many others as well.

The books portrayed Black women not as consultants but in stereotype. This is another instance of Black women's navigation of their visibility within the policy gambling industry. But in this racist iteration of Black

women's labor, they became commoditized. W.E.B. Du Bois's description
of double consciousness helps us understand that the cover image of *Aunt
Sally's* signified mediums' confrontation with others' perception and por-
trayal of mediumship:

> [It is] a peculiar sensation, this double consciousness, this sense of always
> looking at one's self through the eyes of others, of measuring one's soul by
> the tape of a world that looks on in amused contempt and pity. One ever
> feels his two-ness, an American, a Negro; two souls, two thoughts, two
> unreconciled strivings; two warring ideals in one dark body, whose dogged
> strength alone keeps it from being torn asunder.[114]

This bifurcation emerges from the dream book cover—the caricatured
woman pictured in contrast to the reality of Black women. Divining women
were both the subject and object of capitalist desire, both perceiver of the
supernatural world and perceived as frauds by churches. This dichotomy
was full of tension; the African American medium was both present on the
cover and made absent because she wasn't needed for consultation—readers could interpret their dreams for themselves.[115]

Most dream books were printed by publishers owned by white businessmen. One notable exception to the white dominance of the dream book
publishing world was Herbert Gladstone Parris, an African American born
in 1893, who wrote his own books under the pseudonyms Prof. De Herbert, Dr. Pryor, and Prof. Uriah Konje. A manufacturer of "Japo-Oriental
products," and "spiritualist adviser" from Chicago, Dr. Pryor eventually
sold his business to the Lama Temple, owned by Max Kanovsky, a cos-
metics manufacturer, in the early 1950s.[116] This white company eventually bought out *Aunt Sally's* and *Three Witches*, books targeted to Black
readers.[117] By 1969 the company was headquartered at West Sixty-Second
Street in Bronzeville.[118]

Dream books were indexes—the entries were topics/images that appeared in one's dreams, and the "definitions" were the meanings of these
images or numbers assigned to those topics/images. "A dream," asserted the
Policy Player's Lucky Number Dream Book, "is a motion or fiction of the soul,
signifying good or evil to come, and it depended on the character or class
as to whether it may signify its true meaning or directly the contrary."[119]
This dream book pointed to class and character as keys to understand the
true meaning or (more ominously) the trickery that could result from poor

character. Therefore, to reveal a dream's true meaning—or else be threatened by the risk of an inaccurate reading—one had to consult a diviner.

Dream books linked dream images to divinatory meanings (e.g., if you dream of a cook, "you will receive a letter," or if you dream of a locomotive, "beware a strange man"), or they linked dream images to fancy gigs for betting. A field reporter of the Illinois Writers Project, a study of Chicago's policy gambling industry, who did his fieldwork along the South Side of Chicago, described a woman interpreting a dream:

> Player A dreams, the night before, that she sees her dead mother. In the dream book that's the "dead mother row," and is interpreted as a series of numbers. Player A will not rest until she has put a quarter or half dollar in the three drawings and in two or three of the popular books. She is likely to invest several dollars on the gig. But before she becomes discouraged and gives up, she will have another dream about her sweetheart (30-47-72), and the player jumps to this row.[120]

Descriptions of dreams bring to the waking world the rhythms and scenes of segregation. For example,

> WHITE POLICEMAN—if you dream of meeting up with a white policeman play numbers 28-35-67; COFFIN—to dream of a coffin signifies that you will soon be married and own a house of your own. Play numbers 9-49-50; TOMBS—to dream of being among the tombs denotes a speedy marriage. Play numbers 7-8-31; TUMMY—To dream of one's tummy as great and large predicts a fair and large estate. Play 10-11-22; GIN—To dream of gin denotes pleasure and disappointment in life. Play numbers 8-16-42; POLICY OFFICE—To dream of a policy office foretells riches. Play numbers 4-11-44. This is the favorite of all numbers.[121]

This list of dreams and their corresponding numbers provides access to the anxieties of African American life as well as the strategies gamblers used to cope with these anxieties. Some appeals were ominous, such as numbers that corresponded to dream images from real life: The "KKK," "white policeman," and "riot" all had corresponding number combinations.

Other dream books were explicit about racism. Spiritualist Herbert Gladstone "Professor Uriah Konje" Parris's *H. P. Dream Book* included a section titled "To the Black People of the World," which was an appeal to Black people: "It is quite evident that all of us cannot be highly intellectual, for if it were so, how would the world be served? . . . A nation's success is measured by its educational and industrial attainment. It is time for the Colored People of the world to hold their industrial and educational preeminence." In a portion of the book titled "All Oppressed People of the World," he gave his readers the following instructions:

> To become an able and successful person in any profession, two things are necessary, study and practice. The one who succeeds in life is the one who early on clearly knows his object and toward that object routinely directs his powers. Education has the magnificent quality of setting one apart from others. It can provide one with something that not only meets the needs of today, but rather the means to meet the demands of the day after tomorrow and the day after that. Education can have as its function the changing of social status or the preservation of the status quo. The final choice lies with each and every one of us. I am appealing to all to make the former choice.[122]

Parris's direct entreaty was an attempt to use his successful dream book medium to move gamblers to political action.[123] The African American gambling population, Harris argues, believed "supernatural traditions were integral to helping them deal with and overcome limited employment and economic hardship, and race, class, and gender discrimination."[124]

Dream books were the most consistently used numbers source for gamblers, and specific sets of numbers were so popular with patrons that some sets of numbers—or "gigs"—were given their own category.[125] In policy gigs had a popular recognized hierarchy. Numbers assigned to particular dreams—of adultery or death, for example—were known as "fancy gigs" and were always especially noted on drawing slips.[126] Rarely, however, did any two dream books assign the same numerical combination to the same image or topic. For example, magician "Black Herman," who included advice on policy in his book of simple tricks, listed 9-11-17 as the proper number combination for "women of color," while the gig 6-14-66 was assigned to the same phrase in *The Three Witches*, which *Ebony* touted as the 1950s' most popular numbers dictionary.[127] Despite this conflicting information, players and policy operators were not discouraged. The multiplicity of predictive possibilities made things *more* rather than *less* believable. Instead of "bad luck," patrons may have reconciled loss with the belief that they simply had consulted the wrong dream book. In that scenario, reality could still be predicted, confirming an order in the chaos of policy gambling, even if it was hard to find or discern. The multiplicity of dream books offered a comforting cosmology.

Evidence from the Illinois Writers Project identified the so-called policy station gig as the most popular combination in 1940. But by 1950, according to *Ebony*, the most frequently played fancy gigs were the dead numbers (9-19-29) and the money numbers (5-10-20).[128] These numbers were easily recognizable and were played daily. Thus, while *Three Witches* may have been the most trusted and therefore most popular dream book in 1950, it supplanted earlier books that had once claimed that famed spot. This trend also testifies to the need for dream books to adapt to the ever-shifting demands of the urban market. As Black America's experiences altered in response to segregation, so too did the nuances of dreams; dream books had to be able to be altered quickly, constantly being adjusted to the shifting terrain of segregation and hopes for relief from its grinding effects. Dream books, then, offered alternative interpretations of life, segregation, and patriarchy in Bronzeville.[129]

Spiritualist Commerce

Drawing further on the rich tradition of supernaturalism, some women sold material goods at highly visible church services or in the secular realm. In doing so they drew on African American women's long tradition as arbiters of divination and supernaturalism. As Harris explains, "Slaves believed that magic powders and spells would prevent physical abuse and being sold, and provide some with the courage and opportunity to run away or defy their owners. Supernatural traditions and the use of magic charms and amulets were 'integral to slaves' strategies of resistance' and helped to build an inner and autonomous Black world."[130] African Americans selling powders, potions, and talismans to improve their customers' odds were a vital part of the new urban landscape. Women sold products out of their homes, storefront churches, and local businesses like African American drugstores.[131] As entrepreneurs, many Black female mediums made a living from selling these homemade spiritual products.[132] Furthermore, Wolcott writes, by selling these goods, African American spiritualists developed new methods of gaining economic independence outside the purview of white employers.[133]

As Black spiritualists' success increased, white- and African American-owned companies that sold spiritual paraphernalia sought to get a share of the profit. Mediums were skeptical; when asked about the catalogs that

offered powders, talismans, and lucky oils for sale, Madame Lindsey, a spiritualist of Louisiana, replied, "I notice they say it's only sold as curios, so if
you risk your money, well, then you're just out [the price of the product] if it
don't work."[134] Some companies, most of them owned by whites, overcame
charges of inauthenticity by relying on stereotypes of authentically Black
spiritual traditions hailing from the South—particularly New Orleans—or
the "Orient." For example, mail-order suppliers extolled the South as the
birthplace of "genuine hoodoo specialists, . . . the only authentic vista from
which city dwellers could find the most potent Hoodoo items."[135] Aunt Sally's
image resurfaced in advertisements for incense. Images of women from the
"Orient" reading crystal balls emerged as well.

Patrons could mail-order items from catalogs put out by companies such
as the King Novelty Company based on Chicago's South Side.[136] These items
and many more were also available from King and dozens of other companies. Chicago's spiritual supplies industry began in the 1920s. By 1930
anything required by a spiritualist could be obtained from spiritual stores
or mail-order companies.[137] At that time, King's Curio Catalog touted novelty goods such as lucky rings and amulets. Early spiritualist suppliers in
Chicago, such as Ar-Jax and DeLaurence, continued the trend of Eastern
imagery, using a Hindu swami in their logos.[138] Of the many charms prescribed in these catalogs for capturing good luck in gambling, the most
famous, according to George J. McCall, in his study of hoodoo and the
numbers racket, was "John the Conqueror Root," with its associated oils
and incenses.[139] Other popular items included pairs of lodestones, miniature
bone hands (later replaced by plastic hands), and goldstone snake vertebrae.
Magical perfumes were recommended to control relationships while also
curing minor ailments. The latter would be of primary importance for African Americans experiencing the frustrations of segregated medical care.
These substances included magical oils with names like Lucky Dog, Essence
of Van Van, Three Jacks, and King. Powders were available as well to "dust
the courtroom."[140] Further proof of the blend of organized religion and the
commodification of divination were psalm prayer candles. When lit, these
candles revealed a "psalm number" as the wax melted away.[141]

In her study of Detroit's numbers rackets, Wolcott states, "If one opens
any African-American newspaper published during the interwar period,
one is confronted with numerous advertisements for dream books and
'lucky products' designed to help players pick numbers that are likely to 'hit'
on a particular day."[142] This was certainly true on the pages of the *Chicago*

Defender, which, despite the fact that it ran story after story criticizing policy, contained advertisements from many companies selling gambling aids. In 1919 R. D. Wester of Montgomery, Alabama, placed an advertisement in the *Chicago Defender* for "roots, herbs, lodestones, magic sand, the Book of Black Magic, Underground Treasure Book, the Wonderful Pow-Wow, secrets for growing hair, the Key of Solomon, magic finger ring, magic mirror, and herb medicine."[143] Advertisements for charms, amulets, powders, and candles, like advertisements for fortune-telling, appeared weekly in the *Chicago Defender*. These charms, or "adjuncts to the faith," were believed not only to secure great gigs but also to be efficacious in "rent[ing] houses, draw[ing[crowds, and eliminate[ing] the evil works of the devil."[144] Contrary to aiding Black women mediums' popularity and helping them gain customers, though, advertisements for curios contributed to their erasure.

Even as the *Chicago Defender* carried advertisements for substitutes for professional Black women mediums, the paper was not averse to shedding light on the financial instability of Bronzeville, on which gambling thrived. On Saturday, May 25, 1940, the newspaper ran the story "The Wheels Spin in Havana," an exposé on gambling in Cuba that depicted gambling as a vice:

> There is gambling and gambling—it's one of those things that make men brothers under the skin, and seems to flourish wherever life is insecure, as during times of depression and among people condemned to poverty, as well as among the heady upper class circles where there is almost as little psychological stability as among the masses.[145]

Running such a story also presented the *Chicago Defender*'s view of the lack of stability in Bronzeville. By making the point that gambling flourished best in those places where life was insecure, the journalist levied a critique at city infrastructure but also Black political leadership and the gambling industry. One of the mechanisms that African Americans deployed to overcome this instability and the mixed messages of the paper was consulting African American women and the products they sold—viable strategies meant to introduce stability into an unstable world.

Conclusion

Mail-order companies—Chicago's Valmor and Kings, for example—are not merely things of the past, nor are dream books, as evidenced by the many facsimiles one can purchase online. The intersection of policy and women's divination labor also continues to inspire. In 2016, for example, Laurence Fishburne and Larenz Tate produced the podcast "Bronzeville" dramatizing the excitement of Chicago's policy era and evoking the history of the thriving and self-sufficient neighborhood. The podcast stages the social striving of its main protagonist, Jimmy Tillman, an African American migrant fleeing from rural Arkansas, who finds employment as a policy runner for the very wealthy and successful Copeland brothers. The Copeland brothers are fictionalized versions of the Jones brothers, sons of Harriett Jones, the focus of chapter 3 of this book. The podcast is historically accurate; the fictional Copelands, like the Jones brothers, own several successful policy wheels and a department store in the heart of Bronzeville. In episode 3 of the series, the brothers reach out to Tillman, concerned that wins on their wheels have gone up 50 percent and that someone internal is hemorrhaging money. The brothers ask Tillman to look into the rise in wins.[146] He starts canvassing the area for the winners, asking them how they got their policy numbers. His landlady points him to Madame Marie's consultation service and dream book, stating that Madame Marie "has the real deal."[147] When Tillman walks through her beaded hanging doorway, Madame Marie greets him with a seductive "Welcome, seeker."[148] After a quick consultation, he plays her numbers and wins one hundred dollars; for this, Madame Marie charges only a nickel. Without hesitation, the Copelands dispatch him to retrieve Madame Marie. Arriving at her door unannounced, Tillman opens her door, uttering under his breath, "If she's the real deal, she already knows we're coming."[149] When Tillman and his partner open the door, they find her mutilated body on her apartment floor, murdered for peddling an extremely threatening dream book. Madame Marie never appears in another episode.

The podcast frames a fate for Madame Marie that speaks to the precariousness of Black women's divination labor and their work adjacent to policy gambling. Many persons relied on Black women mediums and their personal dream books not only for interpretation of dreams but also for the translation of personal experiences and public occurrences into numerical expressions.[150] Drake and Cayton stated that the dream book was "indispensable" to the policy player, valuable for its ability to translate dreams and significant occurrences into "gigs."[151] These lucky numbers and modes of obtaining them, whether through a medium or her divination objects, represent strategies that gamblers used to navigate Bronzeville's spiritual and secular landscape; evidence shows they chose to do so with gigs from Black women mediums. When played successfully, possession of a fancy gig meant a gambler had distinctiveness, personal meaning, exceptionality, and, perhaps on one's best day, untold riches. Dream books, powders, perfumes, and psalm candles available through African American women mediums, serve as powerful devices to discern the historical legacies of race and gender relations. Most importantly, mediumship and spiritual commerce show us that mediums used highly and dangerously visible strategies to appease gamblers' preference for their expertise. Every serious gambler consulted a medium—whether by individual consultation or through organized religion. Those who couldn't relied on the peddling of products in mail-order catalogs, with advertisements that used racialized characterization to sell "authentic" access to the divine. Their immense popularity put Black women mediums in harm's way, most notably in police crosshairs. The fact that their stories still resonate proves that Black female mediums' defiance of the law and their desire to offer numbers visibility show they left a historical legacy worth reconsidering.

5
What Arrest Records Reveal

Up until this point, my analysis of Black women's labor in the policy gambling industry has focused on the opportunities presented by informal economic labor. I've showcased the success stories of Elizabeth Slaughter, Eudora Johnson Binga, Harriett Jones, and several mediums to prove that policy's conspicuousness was difficult but not impossible to navigate. My analysis has shown that by leveraging their associations with policy gambling, some Black women found innovative ways to keep their respectability intact. But these women are the exceptions to policy's narrative not the rule. Far more numerous were the women who were constantly harassed by the Chicago police for their lower-level employment in the policy industry and their gambling habits. Also far more numerous are the stories of policy writers and gamblers arrested for policy work and play and then harassed for being "fallen" or "unrespectable" women. Their stories provide insight into the racist and sexist ways Chicago's white legal structures and Department of Police surveilled Black women policy workers and players. Therefore, the last two chapters of this book present a different type of visibility—a consuming surveillance that Black women policy workers and gamblers found extremely difficult to survive, yes, but that did not ultimately prevail. Indeed Black women were constrained, but their experiences can't be reduced to those constraints. Black women arrested for policy gambling join a tradition of Black women who, Keeanga Yahmatta Taylor argues, "'made a way out of no way,' . . . born from pure defiance and a refusal to do what you are told."[1]

Black women thrived despite severe challenges. Because Black women's homes and jobs, regardless of their ties to policy gambling or degrees of visibility, did not enjoy the legal protections that white women's homes did, Black women had to innovate. Arrest records for policy gambling in Cook County, Illinois, between 1925 and 1968 reveal that Black women's spaces of residence and employment were purposefully destabilized by a particularly aggressive police force. Archival data, arrest records, and the *Chicago Defender* verify that African Americans were the primary targets of police activity in Bronzeville.[2] Police arrests and surveillance disrupted African American women's authority over their homes, workplaces, marriages, and children. And unlike the ways in which Black women policy workers navigated their conspicuousness in policy gambling, their daily strategies of visibility had to contend with law enforcement's unrelenting sexist and racially motivated modes of surveillance.

Although policy gambling ran rampant in many urban centers, seldom were white offenders pursued with the same rigor as their Black counterparts.[3] Rather than seeking to stop policy gambling, police actions were primarily aimed at the social control of specific racial populations.[4] Social control of African American women's spaces required establishing and normalizing the association of Black feminine space with vice. Although white women's labor in the domestic sphere remained sacrosanct, Black women did not have the same luxury. The effects on Black women's lives of labor and leisure were dire. Without legal enforcement and protection of their domestic and working spheres, which often overlapped, the realities of Black womanhood were incongruous with the potential benefits of the separation between public and private spheres enjoyed by whites.[5] In the case of Bronzeville's policy women, public spheres, or "vice areas," operated simultaneously as both living and working spaces for African American women.[6] Their workplace and domestic sphere were always dangerously visible to police. Segregation, too, perpetuated the police's tendency to connect vice and urban Black women. This, in turn, justified police pursuit of Black women involved in policy gambling; whether operating wheels from home or enjoying time off the clock, these women were under constant police surveillance and the threat of home invasion.

That law enforcement used arrest as a means of social control rather than vice control was nothing new to the African American community.[7] Simon Balto's work demonstrates that the relationship of the Chicago Police Department (CPD) to the Black community was always one of devaluation.[8]

One must contextualize the findings of this chapter within broader historical conversations on the Jim Crow North, urban police brutality, and African American women's long histories with police violence and surveillance.[9] Police surveillance, the arrest of Black women workers, and the cultural sanction of such arrests led to the destabilization of Black feminine spaces. This destabilization had detrimental consequences for African American women policy workers, both at home and at work.

Methodology

The holdings at the Cook County Circuit Court Archives (Chicago, Illinois) lend rich archival insight into the plight of local African American women policy workers during the early to mid-twentieth century. The archives house the records of four hundred misdemeanor offenses from 1900 to 1968 for gambling-related crimes committed in Cook County. To better understand the resultant effects of arrests, I identified fifty-two cases in which African American women were stopped for gambling-related charges between 1925, the year of the first record, and 1968, the year of the last arrest record. When I first began to examine this sliver of archival data, I hoped to find evidence of success and defiance—a narrative of triumph over an aggressive police system. However, it gradually became clear that there was more evidence of police aggression. Black women and their families were continually threatened by an aggressive police force that failed to recognize their rights as citizens. The history of African American women's encounters with Chicago law enforcement is an uncomfortable one to tell, but it is at least intellectually honest and true to the labors of Black women policy workers.

To give voice to Black women policy workers' unique experiences, much of this chapter consists of vignettes of individual African American women arrested by the CPD for policy gambling infractions. These brief narratives provide a point of entry into the systemic surveillance of African American women by the police department and the resultant disruption of their home lives.

Demographic arrest slips completed by receiving officers serve as a basis for these vignettes. These sources offer a glimpse—albeit fraught with receiving officers' racism and therefore inadequate—into the distress these women endured while incarcerated. As is often the case in reconstructing the past from written sources, there is much left unsaid in these documents.

They are methodologically reductionist; although the arrest records shed light on how police viewed and described women, they fail to offer a record of women's own perspectives or their interior lives. Bearing this in mind, additional sources—namely, the *Chicago Defender* and archival records from the Kefauver Senate Committee to Investigate Organized Crime in Interstate Commerce—are used to lend further context to the stories of these women and focus attention on the plight of African American policy operators. I conclude the chapter by analyzing examples in which African American women resisted objectification and physical abuse and tried to turn their visibility and invisibility into sites of resistance. Building on the scholarship of Saidiya Hartman's *Wayward Lives*, I engage pivotal moments when Chicago's African American policy women exercised radical agency in the midst of seeming powerlessness. Women's arrest dockets demonstrate the extent to which the women configured resistance in the face of constant police scrutiny; they demanded to be seen as the *respectable women* they were, regardless of the legal and criminal consequences. They also demonstrated explicitly gendered efforts to challenge the notion of what is private, domestic, and invisible. But I turn first to a brief discussion of policy in Chicago's municipal codes.

Criminalizing Policy

Chicago's Municipal Code banned lotteries in 1866.[10] The city adopted specific penalties for policy gambling in 1911,[11] describing the official charge as a "conspiracy to injure the [public's] morals in the operation of policy gambling games."[12] The Illinois state legislature introduced an act to prevent playing policy on April 29, 1905.[13] For policy gamblers and leaders, the passing of Illinois State Bill 30: An Act for the Prevention of Policy Playing, also known as the Anti-Policy Law of 1905, meant that the game went underground. The General Assembly rationalized that the threat of imprisonment for up to a year or a fine of two hundred to one thousand dollars, or both, for a first offense would be enough to prevent policy playing (upon conviction for a second offense, the prison sentence was extended to more than two years; Illinois State Bill 30, section 412, chapter 38). The act was also intended to deter people from aiding those who played the game; those found in the presence of others playing policy received the same penalty as those who actively sold, distributed, or wagered lottery paraphernalia. Merely possessing policy paraphernalia—a slip, device, or article of any kind—was also viewed as promoting or playing the game (section 414, chapter 38) and was a further violation of the act.[14] Even janitors and caretakers could be punished if policy playing or sales were carried out on their properties with their knowledge.[15] Finally, landlords were warned not to rent to policy writers or shops. The *Defender* counseled readers:

> Attention HOME OWNERS: should someone call at your home requesting information about rental of your basement, that may be a vacant apartment check them closely before agreeing.—With things as hot as they are policy "station[s]" regularly seek new places to draw and may well desire yours for that purpose—If they rent the place and turn it into a policy wheel you are just as guilty as anyone else if the law moves in and raids the place.[16]

Chicago was not unique in its prohibitive lottery codes, but it was unique in its moralizing legal language about policy gambling. New York banned lotteries in 1895, yet the language it employed differed from that used in Chicago's laws. New York attacked gambling as a legal issue: "Section 324 of the New York State Penal Code of 1895 declared lotteries to be unlawful and a public nuisance. Under this law, an individual who 'contrives, proposes, draws a lottery' committed a felony."[17] After 1901, the New York State Assembly added new measures to the 1895 law that included "Section 344a—; 344b: Possessing policy slips and Section 344c: Removing persons occupying premise used for playing policy."[18] New York's initial criminalization law was more aggressive than that of Illinois, as New York classified participation in the lottery as a felony, but in 1926 the latter's laws on policy gambling were reclassified from a felony to a misdemeanor.[19] Through a lengthy process, Chicago's municipal codes, municipal courts, and the Illinois General Assembly rendered everyone who participated in the policy industry immoral. These legal institutions relied on the police force to remediate offending behavior to bring the individuals back in line with normative behavior. Chicago attacked gambling as a moral issue. As a result, any association with policy might tarnish one's respectability status; this meant African American women policy workers had to innovate when faced with the possibility, and perhaps reality, of arrest.

Through action from the mayor's office, enforcement of gambling laws came to be the responsibility of the Chicago Police Department. Mayoral candidates in Chicago sanctioned the push to eradicate policy gambling. Mayor Anton Cermak, with a term running from 1931 to 1933, was fundamental in both the policing of policy in Black Chicago and the criminalization of poverty.[20] Cermak ran for mayor as a tough-on-crime candidate and turned his police force aggressively against Black Chicago.[21] Cermak ordered the creation of a special vice and gambling unit that operated under his supervision. In 1931 over half of all those arrested in the city on gambling charges of some kind were Black—in a city where Black people made up less than 5 percent of the population.[22]

Edward Joseph Kelly, Cermak's successor who served from 1933 until 1947, and then Martin H. Kennelly, serving from 1947 to 1955, continued this trend. During Kelly's term in office, Police Commissioner James P. Allman arrested an average of 5,883 persons per year between 1941 and 1946 (including approximately 940 women a year) for gambling.[23] Under Mayor Kennelly and the new police commissioner, John C. Prendergast, this number rose to approximately 7,354 policy-related arrests per year between 1947 and 1955 (including about 992 women per year).[24] By the summer of 1947, Kennelly had ordered a new crackdown on policy, which produced reports claiming that 20,000 arrests had been made in the Fifth District (Bronzeville) since the beginning of that year. Neither the mayor nor Prendergast believed the reports, and after making a personal tour of Bronzeville, Prendergast told the *Defender*: "I know that policy still exists. I will give delinquent captains and their men time to clean it up. If they continue to overlook gambling of any sort they must suffer the consequences and regardless of support from politicians and Ward Committeemen. . . . Those who insist on bootlegging policy are playing with fire because the drive to clean the city of this type of gambling is really on."[25]

Prendergast's force responded to his threats enthusiastically. In 1951 alone, the CPD orchestrated 3,181 gambling raids, and the police arrested 7,937 persons.[26] Things were so bad that the *Defender* ran an article describing the melancholy policy player wandering aimlessly around Bronzeville looking for a station in order to make a play.[27] Starting in 1953, Chicago's annual police reports included racial demographic data for gambling arrests. This data indicates that African Americans totaled 80 percent of all arrests for gambling in 1953, 84 percent of all arrests in 1954, and 85 percent of all arrests in 1955.[28] Of those arrested, nearly a thousand were cataloged in Kennelly's personal files as lower-level policy employees: 151 as "Walking Bookmakers" and 847 as "Policy Runners."[29] The mayor maintained detailed, albeit scattered, notes on who was running policy games and where.

Kennelly relied on the Vice Control Division (VCD) of the Chicago Department of Police, an arm of the Organized Crime Division in existence since the early twentieth century. The VCD investigated prostitution, gambling, and license violations in bars and restaurants. Its gambling unit consisted of detectives and veteran police officers who wore civilian dress or plain clothes, drove unmarked cars, and conducted citywide gambling investigations.[30] Evidence persists that subsequent mayoral officials, through the end of Mayor Richard J. Daley's term in 1976, continued their scrutiny of African Americans playing and profiting from policy.[31] Balto's conclusion that "from the 1940s onward, the primary purpose of the police was to control supposedly unruly and dangerous racial minorities and to keep crime out of white neighborhoods" is particularly apt.[32]

Eleanor Smith: "Housewife," 1968

Official charges levied at offenders reflected the assumptions that Black women's status as independent laborers and respectable women was suspect. Most of the women arrested on policy gambling–related charges between 1925 and 1968 also worked in a variety of service industries. But white officers filling out arrest slips failed to recognize that labor.

For example, on February 2, 1968, Detective Robert Davis Jr., an officer of the gambling unit of Chicago's VCD, arrested Mrs. Eleanor Smith at her apartment building along with two other women. Police charged her with keeping a policy station and possession of policy and set her bail at one thousand dollars. A judge eventually found Smith guilty of possession and charged her a fine of ninety dollars.[33] The VCD team took Smith into custody and transferred her to a station that she entered willingly. The receiving officer processed her demographic information on a small pink arrest form that was required to be completed for every arrest.

Though intake registers are exhaustive—most contain the perpetrator's name, address, height, weight, skin color, date of birth, social security number, place of birth, length of residence in Chicago, occupation, and occupation status—the documents contain only sparse information about the nature of the crimes.[34] Though wanting for more substantive information, the records create a general demographic profile of Black women arrested for informal activity. On Smith's arrest sheet, the following information was recorded: married or single: "married"; race: "colored"; complexion "dark"; nativity: "Ohio"; occupation: "housewife"; and occupation status

or employment status: "none." Smith's recorded data that she had an occupation (housewife) but no occupation status poses multiple problems
and leaves questions unanswered. Operating a policy station was indeed an
occupation, but her occupation was listed as a housewife; therefore it is clear
on the arrest docket that that occupation did not fit institutional criteria
at the time. This ambiguity, along with the charge that she "kept a policy
station," is incongruent. Smith could not occupy the occupation of both
housewife and policy operator simultaneously and still be listed without an
occupational status. In direct conflict with this occupational designation,
African American women listed themselves as "policy operator," "policy
runner," and "policy clerk" as their source of employment in census data
from 1900 to 1960, which by virtue of being listed on the census should
convey something about these occupations as legitimate occupations. It is
clear that the police and women disagreed on this matter. The refusal of the
police to recognize Smith's work as operator of a policy station as legitimate
while also being a housewife may have resulted from the limitations of
white patriarchal understandings of legitimate domestic dependency and
labor. This exposes a visible racist and sexist casting that the CPD applied
to Black women's labor.

Of the fifty-two arrest records of women arrested for policy gambling
on file at the Cook County Archives, thirteen were listed as housewives,
two as maids, one woman engaged in housework outside the home, one
was a waitress, one a policy clerk, one a policy writer, two machine operators, one a tavern owner, and one a hairdresser.[35] All the women, except
the two who were recorded as participating in the policy industry, used
policy to supplement their income. Therefore, it's important to note that
one can't evaluate Black women's labor in policy gambling in isolation. A
composite understanding of their work must include an understanding of
the labor and work they engaged in in other industries.[36] However, actual
percentages of women who secured employment at policy establishments
are difficult to discern, since many took up informal labor intermittently,
weaving in and out of informal labor.[37] This intermittence, LaShawn Harris
notes, "reflected their broad beliefs that informal labor markets potentially
offered alternative paths toward monetary social benefits [and] new labor
identities."[38] Harris continues: "Informal labor afforded many Black women
the prospect of bypassing unskilled employment or combining legitimate
work with that of off-the-books labor. To make financial ends meet and
burdened by the harsh realities of poverty, house eviction, and hungry

children, urban women labored simultaneously in multiple occupations."[39] This simultaneous labor might also have been a survival strategy for poor and working-class Black women, who historian Joe Trotter explains were often a particular "target for 'uplift'" and preyed upon by enterprising philanthropic Black elites.[40]

Smith's ambiguous occupation status reflects Black women's precariousness as independent laborers in a competitive and racist labor market and uncertain social hierarchy. The occupational designation "housewife," assigned to thirteen of the women, was accompanied by inconsistent occupation statuses. Five of the thirteen women were listed as "housewife employed inside the home," three were listed as "housewife unemployed," and the remaining five were listed simply as "housewife" followed by neither an employed nor unemployed designation at all.[41] Women across every category of housewifery were charged with selling policy out of their homes as well as keeping a gambling house; fewer were charged with "possession of policy" or "promotion of policy writings." Supplementing domestic work with informal labor like policy work reflects its poor pay, their husbands' substandard wages in other industries, their desire to get out of domestic service altogether, and a desire to subvert the link between Black women's work as domestics and notions of Black women's domesticity.[42] Racism and perceived criminality influenced Black women's ability to obtain, administer, and endure domestic work, which, as the arrest records show, influenced their vulnerability in the face of law enforcement. This tension also reflected Black women's own responses to limited employment options and demonstrated their effort to exert autonomy within the domestic service field, their homes, and marriages. What Wolcott and Kali N. Gross have shown in the cases of Detroit and Philadelphia, respectively, may well have been at work in Chicago: although many desperately needed work, a large proportion of women refused to work in the domestic service industry in order to maintain their self-respect.[43] Instead, they sought employment elsewhere or supplemented it with illegal activity to afford both social status and a degree of personal autonomy.[44]

Mabel Robinson: "Married," 1959

When two officers arrested an astonishing forty-nine people after a gambling raid at an "after hours spot," a police matron helped process eight women. Among these was Mrs. Mabel Robinson, a successful, married, private business owner of a record shop and mother of three. Detective Frank Hackel and Lieutenant Edward Walsh became violent with Robinson, her niece, and the six other women. The matron watched as Hackel and Walsh hurled racial epithets and obscene remarks at the women and brutally manhandled them. Robinson later reported that Hackel "became enraged when she insisted on her right to make a telephone call (which he denied) and picked her up bodily by the neck and the seat of her dress and flung her across the cell room . . . throwing her down the stairs and then after handcuffing both her hands behind her back, of flinging her bodily into a squadrol [a vehicle used by police as both a squad car and an ambulance]."[45] Robinson did her best to defend herself: "When Hackel picked her up for a third time and flung her into the squadrol, she dug her nails into his face."[46]

Robinson's relationship to policy gambling is unclear. She may have been a policy worker or a legitimate business owner who mistakenly got caught up in a gambling raid. It is possible she was both, as it is well proven that men and women who ran legitimate businesses ran policy shops out of the back.[47] What is clear is the white officers' disrespect for the women; when one officer noticed an engagement ring on one of the women's fingers, "he propositioned her" and another officer also joined in on the abuse. The lockup keeper "snatched her coat one way and her pocket book another. . . . Called her a Black n[*****] whore."[48] The violence escalated further when the police lined the women up to take them to the downtown lockup. Robinson reported:

> When they got us into the station where the cell blocks are located one of the officers flung [a friend] down to the floor. My niece . . . 22, was shoved onto this woman and I was flung against the bars. Officers . . . entered the room where the cells are located and they were drinking Miller High Life beer. Cunningham and Sexton were making obscene remarks and suggestions to the women.[49]

Black women often endured abuse in the presence of racist white police-women and police matrons, and this was true regardless of their formal or informal employment status. Cities across the Northeast and Midwest began employing police matrons in their station houses in 1878. Chicago did so in 1880. They were employees but were not considered officers:[50] "The matron's duties varied considerably from city to city, but the core of her office was to shelter and protect women and children in police custody."[51]

As promoted in the literature of charities and corrections—in Chicago the Women's Christian Temperance Union approached Mayor Harrison about the post—a matron was always on duty when officers brought women to the station house. "She searched them for contraband, supervised their imprisonment, accompanied them to court, and, most important, offered assistance and encouragement to those who wished to reform."[52] Based on these duties, one can reasonably assume that white police matrons may have been the ones filling out demographic arrest sheets, passing out sandwiches, and supervising bathing facilities. The *Chicago Tribune* reported that police matrons' expertise lay in their femininity, their innate ability to protect a woman, because "it takes a woman to save a woman. That is one reason why there are matrons at the various police stations in Chicago."[53] However, as several lawsuits show, this was often not the case when women were brought to the stations, and white women's anti-Black racism is evident as is their support of sexual terrorism.[54] Police matrons and policewomen were present when Ms. Viola Hardin and Ms. Mildred Green were forced to strip nude in front of several people at police headquarters; the matrons and policewomen did nothing to shield the arrested women, nor did they do anything to protect them. Police matrons were touted as women who could shield other women from humiliating treatment.[55] However, no one in this situation expressed the importance of protecting Hardin and Green from women—namely, the women in uniform.[56] Claims that police matrons as "good women" could protect incarcerated "good women" meant little in the face of sexual terrorism and carceral violence against Black women. For Robinson, the matron's attempts failed to protect her from Hackel's and Walsh's sexual harassment. Yet, Robinson described the matron working with her at the Englewood station as kind and womanly: the matron "took Hackel to task . . . but he ignored her."[57] She also "told Hackel once before that he was not supposed to lay his hands on women prisoners."[58] When they went to the lockup, Mrs. Robinson "thanked the policewoman for attempting to intercede" and for order[ing] the handcuffs removed after they got downtown."[59] The brutality Robinson was subjected to resulted in the need for extensive medical care, including surgery, which moved her case back several years. She amassed a debt of $1,503.15.[60]

Hardin and Green filed damage suits against the mayor and police totaling four hundred thousand dollars. The women named Mayor Kennelly, Commissioner of Police Timothy J. O'Connor, Policewoman Ruther Biederman, and an undesignated Mary Doe in the action.[61] In 1961 Robinson resurfaced in the *Defender*, this time filing a one-hundred-thousand-dollar suit against Hackel. A hearing before the circuit court revealed that Hackel had conducted the raid without a search warrant. In the circuit court, Robinson was convicted of assaulting a police officer by scratching him on the face, but no disciplinary action was taken against Hackel, who remained on the force. Historian Kali N. Gross points out that partial justice and inefficiencies of the judicial system left women like Robinson very vulnerable.[62] Hackel and Walsh were left to continue their raids, targeting and brutalizing Black women.

On May 1, 1959, during another gambling raid, they broke into the home of Mrs. Margaret Pierce and arrested six people. Another tenant in the building, Mrs. Louise Marshall, said the pair kicked her door down and searched her apartment without a warrant.[63] But the six persons who were arrested in the raid were absolved of both gambling charges and being inmates of a disorderly house. Hackel admitted under oath that he broke into the home without a warrant, had no admissible evidence, and found nothing sustainable. But he suffered no consequences.[64] Such disregard for legal procedure and aggression illustrates the challenges African American women faced in their work. Both surveillance and intrusion plagued the private spaces they occupied over the course of nearly sixty years. Police interference, in which white women police matrons were complicit, amounted to a destabilization of Black women's spaces, making African American women's bodies, relationships, and homes/workspaces vulnerable. The CPD, following orders from the mayor's office, refused to see Black policy work as legitimate. Therefore, the police-orchestrated assaults on Black women's workplaces were motivated by racism and sexism. Hardin's and Green's heightened visibility before law enforcement, with officers literally demanding to see their bodies, prove the racist and sexist visible assault on Black women policy workers.

Mary Morrow: "Unlawfully and Willingly Did Gamble for Money," 1954

Arrest records from the Cook County Circuit Court Archives reveal how arrests disrupted women's social patterns: women were often arrested in pairs or groups, the timing of arrests fell when women were socializing with friends or meeting family obligations, and incarceration made it nearly impossible for women to meet family obligations such as child care. Whether socializing with friends in their apartments, enjoying a night out, or at work, African American women's work and leisure time was under constant surveillance by the police force. This heightened sense of being watched at all hours of the day and night led to women's suffering. For example, shortly after their Sunday noontime meal, Mary Morrow and her friend Alice Simmons sat down at Mary's dining room table to play cards. Mary had lived in Chicago for a short time after moving north from Tennessee six years earlier. She was married and worked as a machine operator for Lab-Line Instruments Inc., a division of Chicago Surgical and Electrical Company, which manufactured a wide variety of laboratory apparatus and instruments for research laboratories, on North DesPlaines Street.[65] Unbeknownst to the women, four officers had congregated outside Mary's apartment to ambush their card game. The officers charged into the dining room and handcuffed the two women. Both women reportedly "did gamble for money" and were charged with "unlawfully and willingly playing in a card game."[66]

Leisure time was a double-edged sword, and women who were found congregating together were especially conspicuous in the eyes of law enforcement. Cheryl Hicks confirms that in most Black urban centers, "women (and men) found that the cheap and pleasurable practice of visiting friends in their tenement rooms was a dangerous form of leisure. The simple act of enjoying the company of friends could mean an arrest."[67] This was the case as well for Addie Calvin and Elizabeth Johnson, who, along with six other women, were arrested during an early afternoon game of cards. They were charged with "gambling dice cards" and "possession of policy" and then taken to a women's lockup facility.[68] The simple act of enjoying a game of cards with friends landed them in jail for a night.

The notes on demographic sheets show that police swoops often took place late in the afternoon or early evening, when women were working at home, with children present, or socializing with friends. For example, Joanne Morgan, a nineteen-year-old housewife, was arrested for being "found in a house of ill fame or gaming house" on May 21, 1950 at 5 p.m. Her friend Katherina Harris was also arrested and sent to the women's lockup facility. They arrested her for the same offense. Neither Harris nor Morgan was found guilty.[69] The timing of arrests indicates that Chicago police paid particular attention to the socializing habits of African American women. The effect was to undermine the fabric of social community among these women.

The duration and state of women's detention after arrest made it difficult for them to meet family obligations. This was another way that police practices interfered with women's home responsibilities. After arrest and booking, women were taken to lockup at Eleventh and State. The facility had been built in 1928 to replace the old headquarters in the Loop and at that time was valued at an extravagant three million dollars. Yet it quickly became notorious for its filthy and brutal conditions. The *Tribune* did an eight-story series on Chicago's lockup squalor in 1947, highlighting the findings of a lockup study conducted by a penal reform organization known as the John Howard Association, financed by a group of prominent Chicagoans. The study found that "the city's 37 police dungeons are substandard and unfit for human habitation."[70] The report continued: "Lighting is the most inadequate in all the outlying stations. Twenty-four of the lockups have janitors, some of them two or more, the report says, but some lockup keepers said their janitors did nothing about cell cleaning. The only prisoner bathing facilities available are in the women's lockup at headquarters."[71]

Women hoped their time in jail took place on a weeknight, since the municipal court did not have sessions on Sundays or holidays. Being arrested on the weekend placed an additional burden on women, who had to wait in vermin-infested jails during that time.[72] Furthermore, they also had to worry about their children, who were left alone or in the care of relatives while they waited for bail or their court date. Even if a woman was granted a hearing during the week, she had to secure child care for the long hours spent in court. Victoria Perez recalled, "We women stayed in jail until midnight. We were taken to a downtown lock up on 11th and State because there was only a men's lockup on Racine and Monroe."[73] Jeanne Galatzer-Levy, a white activist working with the Chicago Women's Liberation Union, an abortion counseling service, remembers her time at Eleventh and State as uncomfortable:

> And then we were put in paddy wagons—which are really unpleasant—and driven to 11th and State, and the drive in the paddy wagon was a riot. It was all women and of course everybody else who was arrested was a hooker, because that's all they arrested women for then. And one woman was just giving hilarious stories, regaling us with stories of the street. It was really quite funny. And then we were in the women's lockup at 11th and State. We'd each made a phone call I guess. We knew that things were happening, and that they were going to pay the bail, and then there was the question

of whether they could get us out that night or whether we'd have to wait until the morning. It was very unpleasant. In the morning, they gave us bologna sandwiches, which I couldn't eat, and coffee. It was awful, but that was breakfast at Cook County Jail.[74]

Ironically, the same black coffee and bologna sandwiches that Galatzer-Levy detested had once been heralded as "the fanciest improvement" to the station.[75] When the building was new, the vittles had been "wheeled from cell to cell in the style of the best restaurants,"[76] but by 1961, according to one *Tribune* columnist, they were simply "shoved through the bars."[77] Furthermore, women sat under harsh electric lights all night and got little rest on the "beds" they were offered—hard and unforgiving wooden benches. Detention in such squalid conditions showed the carceral state's disregard for Black women's labor, families, and friendships. Police pursuit of policy gamblers interfered with African American women's community-building rituals, their friendships, their time for rejuvenation after a long and hard week, and domestic responsibilities such as the care for their children.

Anna Mae Robinson: "Contributing to the Delinquency of a Minor," 1955

Whether playing cards or running a policy station out of one's home, Black women were heavily scrutinized for the type of leisure and labor that took place in their domestic spaces. For example, as a frigid Saturday evening crept into Sunday morning, twenty-seven-year-old Annie Mae Robinson dealt her neighbors, Robert Milam and Emmitt Williams, another round of cards. It would be the last hand to be dealt that night. Yet, what ended the card game was not late-night fatigue but the law. Both Robinson and Williams were arrested on January 23, 1955, at 2:30 a.m. in Robinson's home during an investigation of gambling with cards. Robinson was charged with "contributing to the delinquency of a minor" because she "encouraged the juvenile" Robert Milam to gamble.[78]

It was not clear where Robert Milam's mother had been. Was she working or enjoying a night out? The answer was not cited and, in a sense, is irrelevant—whether African American women were working, socializing, or going out for an evening, their activities were equally liable to scrutiny and punishment. Judgment of Robinson and of Milam's mother for being absent rested on the idea that acts of individuality minimized Black women's ability or obligation to create wholesome domestic spaces.[79]

Adding to this judgment was the type of work required by Black women policy workers and how that work informed their domestic space. Policy workers had to be transitory, moving from apartment to apartment to avoid detection by an aggressive police force or to find a better pool of clients.[80] To make matters worse, rent was exorbitant; between 1901 and 1919, Black Chicagoans paid on average at least one hundred dollars more per month in rent than whites.[81]

Policy work was a costly affair in more ways than one. Managing a policy station in the same house where one was supporting multiple generations of family members risked embroiling one's entire home in a police raid or violent break-in. There was also a real danger of getting arrested or even murdered by having policy workers, gamblers, or cash in one's home, or running the risk of it being planted in one's home by nefarious police. For example, in 1967 Mrs. Verna Grimette was found murdered on her apartment floor. Police connected her murder to her policy-writing activities, which led her to keep large sums of money in her apartment in a safe.[82] Housing their policy business in their homes, women hoped, would afford the cover necessary for protecting both their source of revenue and their families, especially their children. But as Grimette's fate suggests, that combination would prove disastrous.

Rather than reflecting an inability to create domestic spaces, women's decisions to conduct policy gambling operations in their homes shows the undue burden of mothering in hostile spaces. For example, Mrs. Edith Roberts witnessed two men murder her son, who had been operating a policy station in her basement.[83] She and the rest of her family—several other residents and small children—lived in the floors above. Newspaper articles bore witness to Roberts's determination to reclaim her son in the face of death. She asserted that "she could identify the killers of her son 'even if I was buried'." She identified two men from a *Defender* photograph, and they appeared before the state attorney in connection with the slaying of her son. However, her son was dead and her family had been robbed of fourteen hundred dollars. Mrs. Roberts was left to grieve, pick up the pieces of the basement policy station, console her son's widow and children, and reestablish her own reputation as a virtuous mother despite her unrelenting hardships.

Lee Brown: "Policy Raid," 1968

Chicago police's use of informants to entrap policy workers and even non-policy players symbolized the reach and extension of police power and authority and how law officials and enforcers found different ways to monitor and control Black women, their bodies, and their homes. Officer James Alexander of the VCD gambling unit staked out policy clerk and housewife Lee Brown's place of employment for six months. Starting his days at 6:15 a.m., Alexander watched policy players enter, stay briefly to place their morning gigs, and then exit to go about their daily business. The scenario repeated itself between 4:15 and 5:45 p.m., when players arrived to place their evening numbers. On February 2, 1968, Alexander sent in an informant to purchase a ticket for the morning drawing. The man returned with a slip of paper stamped "Windy City." Officer Alexander explained in a search warrant, "From this information I've made six arrest[s] and had two convictions and four cases now pending. . . . This reliable person told me that a policy station was on the premise."[84]

Brown, a young African American migrant from Ohio, was taken in as part of Alexander's raid. After booking her and taking her possessions as evidence, officers put her in a police car and transferred her to the women's detention center, putting her in cell forty-six. On Brown's arrest sheet, where demographic information described her as having a medium build and a "medium" complexion free of scars; the receiving officer scrawled the words "blk purse" and "compcts," for powder application. The purse and beauty products are powerful representations of Brown's middle-class sensibilities.

Informants and tips on policy gambling that came in from the community reveal the complex relationship between law enforcement and policy gambling. Documents from the Kefauver Committee expose informants' desires to seek revenge on police officers taking a cut from policy gambling, or policy kings and queens who pushed others out of business, but not the concern for eradicating gambling itself. Policy was viewed as "ordinary" behavior by informants. Harris explores the "reconnaissance of the ordinary" in her study of informants used in New York Police Department investigations. She argues that surveillance prompted police, "without questioning the validity of anti-vice agents' investigative methods, to orchestrate raids and entrap assumed underground laborers and to monitor and criminalize New Yorkers' ordinary daily behavior."[85] In Chicago women like Lee Brown could find no rest in an ordinary card game with her neighbors on a late, cold, January evening.

Chicago police relied on informants to gather intelligence in Kennelly's haste to rid the South Side of vice. Officers relied on African American men to initiate contact with policy operators, gamblers, and vice establishments. Lottie Wolf, a policy clerk, was arrested after a raid when, as the officer reported, an informant entered "the apartment and he emerged about five minutes later. Subject came directly to me and gave me result tickets for the [R]oom and [B]oard and [W]indy [C]ity policy wheels. The informant told me that he got the result tickets from a Coca Cola box in the room where two females were accepting bets."[86] The raid resulted in the apprehension of the two women, policy lottery bet slips, policy lottery result tickets, and $22.76.[87] Officers acted quickly, often only on the word of paid police informants or based on letters or calls from concerned neighbors. Officials raided "home-based churches and had no problems interrupting church services to apprehend numbers bankers or players."[88]

Cayton and Drake describe policy gambling as "on the level,"[89] but policy also received harsh scrutiny from middle- and upper-class African Americans in civic organizations and churches. Complaint letters, telegrams, and postcards offer clues to the competitive and thriving nature of policy gambling in Chicago. For example, an anonymous tip dated December 18, 1950, from the Kefauver Committee described the illegal activities of a police captain working for three policy stations. The captain "directs the go and stop lights on all gambling and shady hotels, and the lights stay green if the consideration is coming in." The informant continued: "This man is also associated with Wasel Donaldson[,] a professional bondsman. . . . In three policy station[s] . . . pay off men for four policy wheels."[90] A similar note came in from a retired policy operator. He wrote, "Well to do—policy—will sing if pressed and will try to get out from under. Knows policy from beginning to end. . . . Signed, Colored. Policy. Tough. In by Choice."[91] A Reverend Ford called and left the name of a man running the Landlady and Landlord wheel at 4939 Michigan Avenue. Reverend Ford complained that "the hoods cut in on [his policy business] and their cut was 25% of the take."[92] Finally, a detailed letter with the names and addresses of twenty-five policy stations located throughout the Fifth District (Bronzeville) arrived on October 18, 1950. The author indicated that their motivation for reporting on these other stations was being "forced out of business because of their unfair racket," signing off with the words "former station owner forced out of business."[93] Complainants wanted in on the game; they did not necessarily want police to ramp up the raids.

Mayor Kennelly, however, drew different conclusions from the public's grievances. He used the information to criminalize African American behavior while declaring victory over citywide vice. He concluded in his testimony before the Senate committee:

> [KENNELLY:] There is a policy racket that is very prevalent there. We drove it off the streets, as one minister out there said, and drove it into the alleys.
> MR. HALLEY: Is it peculiar to any one location?
> [KENNELLY:] To the Negro districts.[94]

African American arrests for policy ordinance violation stood in for actual systemic reform for citywide criminal activity and economic injustice.

Arrests and fines were significant disruptions in African American women's family life. Federal investigator W. D. Amis, in his final report before the Kefauver Committee, stated that "fines average from $25 up, and are absorbed by the wheel operator. Judging from sums taken out of the policy operations by the men who control them, these fines amount to no more than a reasonable expense of doing business."[95] In his testimony before the Kefauver Committee, Theodore Roe indicated that his wheel, formerly the Joneses' wheel, bore the expense of fines, bail bonds, lawyers' fees, and so forth "when one of the pickup men or one of the writers is arrested." He added, "I got to pay it; nobody else to."[96]

Raids were strategic in that the VCD sought to obtain information and paraphernalia related to policy gambling. For example, Matilda Hobson, born in Jackson, Mississippi, in 1924 but a longtime resident of Chicago, was arrested as part of a raid in 1968. The officers' inventory slip of objects obtained on an invasive search of her person—the contents of her purse, pockets, and bra—indicated she had a quantity of policy writings, both slips and result tickets, from four policy wheels: Wagon-Wheel, Horse-Room-Board-Inn, Atlantic-Pacific Big-Creek-Wheel, and Windy-City-Subway-Big Town. Slips held no monetary value. However, they could tell officers which wheels she worked for or the wheels she frequented. Her bail was set at five hundred dollars.[97]

Another search warrant inventory from the archives for Leo Napa, arrested on policy gambling charges, listed all the necessary policy accoutrements. He was brought in with a lottery policy stand, a plastic bag

FIGURE 5. In 1949 women clerks, who were eventually arrested, sell numbers for the policy game to customers just before a police raid at 610 E. Fiftieth Street, Chicago, Illinois. (Chicago Tribune Historical Photos/TCA)

containing wooden balls used in numbers, a lottery cage containing numbered wooden balls, a pad containing policy relay, a quantity of policy writings, a quantity of policy result tickets, and a brown canvas bag, all of which were confiscated. His bail, too, was set at five hundred dollars.[98] Without the necessary policy paraphernalia, Napa's wheel was lifeless. Furthermore, any policy writers or runners connected with Napa's source of revenue were put in jeopardy as well. The VCD's raids disrupted the financial well-being of thousands of African Americans on the South Side.

Raiding was relentless. Police raids were so commonplace that they were part of the policy kings' and queens' business plans. Large raids were ubiquitous, with groups of women arrested in numbers as high as eight and eleven during Chicago's coldest winter months—February and March.[99] Theodore Roe commented that he had never known a time when police were not raiding but had seen only one person serve jail time.[100]

One proprietor, raided fifteen times in sixteen nights, reported that nearly thirty-one of his employees had been arrested but he was never

fined. The operator concluded, "No, they never did get much fines, because
the raids wasn't [sic] properly made and they raided without warrants and
a lot of times we had a pretty big fine in the courts, but we usually paid
those cases. Of course, they got others where there were warrants and we
got fines."[101] The case of Flora Mitchell, a repeat policy offender, illustrates
the Chicago Municipal Court's unwillingness to collect on multiple offenders. Mitchell was fined twice for policy violations: five dollars on June 20,
1945, and ten dollars on April 22, 1947. On February 18, 1949, she was convicted a third time and an application for probation was overruled; she was
sentenced to the county jail for five days. In her previous arrests she had
not been issued the two-hundred-dollar minimum fine prescribed by the
state statute. State attorney John S. Boyle commented on the case, calling
the sentence "a light touch on the cheek" in light of previous convictions.
Others in the same case were fined or placed on probation. The prosecutors
asked the judge to "give the public a break for a change."[102]

African American women weathered raiding throughout their entire
lives. Raiding statistics show a sustained commitment to disrupting domestic tranquility as women aged. The average age of women arrested between
1931 and 1954 was thirty years, the average age of women arrested in 1955
was forty years, and in 1968 it was sixty years. A 1968 raid at 3132 West
Maypole resulted in the apprehension of ten African American men and
one woman, the latter in her late fifties.[103] Theodore Roe noted that raiding
in 1949, which totaled two hundred fines, nearly put his wheel out of business because his cashiers, some of whom were women, would take money
during a raid and put it in their "pocket." Instead of giving it to the police,
the cashier would keep it and come home "in a new suit."[104] Roe's frustration
with his cashiers provides a glimpse into how Black women policy workers
spoke at a time when arrests and fines resulted in uncertainty.

Resistance

The cases of Leatrice Marrow and Sarah Goodwin demonstrate policy's
troubling matrix of visibility and women's ability to use it to figure forth
new structures of resistance. Marrow and Goodwin were the only women
arrested listed as "policy clerk" and "policy writer" on the arrest dockets
in the cases I studied.[105] The two women were both arrested in 1955 but
on separate occasions. The receiving officer listed Marrow's occupation as

"policy clerk" and indicated that she was "employed outside" of her home. Clerks were usually employed at policy stations and were usually the first person one saw when entering. Goodwin's occupation was listed as "policy writer," one who solicited bets throughout the neighborhood. Her place of employment was listed as "unknown." Both women were tried in a court presided over by Judge Fred W. Slater. Slater found Marrow "guilty of keeping a policy station" at 4032 Indiana Avenue, a few blocks away from her home. She was a little over twenty-five years old, a Chicago native, and married. The charge that she "kept" a policy station implies control over the station, but it also rendered her visible in the eyes of law enforcement, making her more vulnerable. Marrow was fined fifty dollars, but evidence obtained by the police was deemed inadmissible because it was illegally obtained.

The description of Goodwin as a policy writer, "place of employment unknown," exhibits policy's tensions of visibility in a different way. This description afforded her agency while making her vulnerable in the face of law enforcement. As a policy writer, she violated a city ordinance, but the indiscernibility of her place of employment before law enforcement ensured that her livelihood remained intact in ways that Marrow's did not. At the same time, white legal authorities refused to recognize the viability of Goodwin's informal labors as a policy writer, rendering her work inconsequential. Goodwin's policy writing was not seen as legitimate work, and one might surmise that this is the reason why the receiving officer listed her place of employment as "unknown." This could be read as a refusal to recognize feminine capitalist space. However, Goodwin possessed the potential to turn this lack of recognition into an advantage and a moment when new structures of resistance emerged. She could return to work after release from lockup because her place of employment was impossible to track, since the CPD did not recognize it as a place. Marrow, unfortunately, could not return to her place of employment—the station of which she was keeper—because the CPD had recognized it as a visible space. Goodwin could capitalize on her invisible status in the law, while Marrow could not do that so easily. Marrow might need to rely on more hidden mechanisms to reestablish her policy station.

Black women were never uniformly silent partners in the policy industry or in the face of its resultant violence, criticism, and injustice.[106] Policy was a vocation of movement, evasion, quick thinking, persuasion, and fast talking. Reading against the grain of the arrest records, we can access the moments when the women showed resistance against legal authorities who refused to recognize their rights and status as women. Edith Roberts's remarkable bravery in the aftermath of her son's murder, and her statement that she would know the face of his killers even if she were buried, is her testament to her status as a legitimate mother. Jessie Mae Robinson's lawsuit, her vivid testimony against officers Hackel and Walsh in the *Chicago Defender*, and her ability to survive their brutal attack were a testament to her bravery and her ownership of her maternal and feminine power. Finally, a purse on an arrest sheet was a testament to Lee Brown's ability to keep what she valued close by. Policy women were bold in the face of terrorizing structures that sought to extinguish them. The women had to be bold—their lives and their families depended on such bravery. Black women mobilized their resources, subverting the uncertain designation of their labors on arrest dockets, and their voices are reflected in court documents explored in the next chapter.

6

Legal Strategies for Policy Women

Both inside and outside the courtroom, particularly between 1925 and 1968, a troubling visibility continued to mark Black women policy workers and gamblers. When investigating conviction rates of Black policy women in the Chicago Municipal Court and their CPD arrest records, a striking phenomenon becomes evident—namely, the disparity between the high number of arrests and low number of convictions for policy-related crimes among African American women. As non-conviction rates in the Chicago Municipal Court prove, judges did not see policy labor or gambling among Black women as a liability. Chicago police, on the other hand, perceived policy as problematic, as suggested by the arrest-to-conviction ratio. Further investigation of Chicago Police Department files, including arrest records, search warrant inventories, and lockup reports, along with records of the Chicago Municipal Court, Illinois Appellate Court, and Illinois Supreme Court, reveal that the imbalance between frequent arrests and infrequent convictions for the same crimes created a perilous "quasi-criminal" status for Black women. This status, not quite discernible before the judiciary but more than legible before predatory law enforcement, had a range of adverse social consequences and reveals the status of Black women policy workers and women who gambled as collateral in Chicago's graft and payoff system.

As I illustrated in the previous chapter, Chicago police were aggressive in invading the supposedly private domestic sphere for the purpose of making arrests and disrupting policy gaming. This chapter takes that line of inquiry further into the Chicago municipal courts. What I find is that Chicago's courts were uninterested in actually obtaining convictions, preferring to drop the cases and take advantage of money that could be extracted via the bail system. Chicago's Municipal Court covered up this system by deploying a racialized logic of quasi-criminality in order to arrest but not convict Black women policy workers—a logic gobbled up by whites fleeing to the suburbs. What is most pressing when trying to fully understand the contours of Black women's policy labor and police surveillance is the extent to which Black women policy defendants were able to parlay the quasi-criminal status engendered by the dearth of criminal convictions into a competitive edge both inside the courtroom and after returning to the world of policy gambling. The courts' verdicts of non-conviction enabled some women to return to their communities and policy labor. But even when women received a favorable verdict, regulatory action—defined by over-policing and underprotection—of Black communities with thriving informal economies continued.[1] This chapter examines the imbalance between arrest and conviction in greater detail and the extent to which Black women policy workers benefited from the court's failure to convict them on policy-related charges. Like the women featured in the previous chapter, courtroom defendants attempted to challenge the court's notion of what was private, domestic, and viable labor, but over-policing prevailed.

Quasi-Criminality

Black women policy gambling defendants were tried in Chicago's Municipal, or "quasi-criminal," Court, which helps us understand the legal strategies applied by policy women, including queens, their employees, and gamblers, who were arrested and tried for policy gambling–related charges. "Quasi-criminal" was a term used by the Chicago Municipal Court to denote the category of prosecution that encompassed violations of local ordinances while also reflecting how police and prosecutors saw Black women policy workers. Prosecution generally covered proscribed behavior of minor "blameworthiness" and was handled in a civil context. However, Chicago's Municipal Court also prosecuted disorderly conduct, prostitution, gambling, fortunetelling, housing code violations, and traffic offenses, but it handled these violations under a single system of procedure.[2] Municipal courts were vital because they handled the vastly larger spectrum of lesser offenses and small claims cases that involved the "everyday rights and wrongs of the great majority of an urban community."[3] Municipal courts, "the ground floor of the American legal system, were where the action was."[4]

The Chicago Municipal Court, established in 1906, had jurisdiction over all criminal cases—but called them *quasi*-criminal actions—for which the appropriate punishment was a fine or imprisonment.[5] The court also heard all proceedings for the "prevention" of crime.[6] The municipal court could also issue search warrants to bring in stolen property and the person who possessed it. If a defendant failed to appear in court after being summoned, the court would issue a warrant for the person's arrest.[7] Despite being heard at a low-level court, municipal cases could be costly for the defendant. In these quasi-criminal cases, a jury trial and the presence of a bailiff, sheriff, and coroner incurred an additional cost to the defendant.[8]

Through its branches, the court upheld social mores of domesticity and morality, significantly extending the arm of the municipal court into defendants' homes. The court showed this extension in its domestic, morals, and vagrancy branches (often referred to as "domestic court" or "morals court").[9] Michael Willrich writes that "just as important as the extent of the court's reach was the way it reached."[10] Each branch employed a team of experts that included social workers, probation officers, and medical professionals.[11] The domestic branch developed legal statuses that dovetailed with the period's overarching social economic objectives, those being that the nuclear family comprised mothers/wives and fathers/husbands and that wage labor ensured independence and productive citizens, on the one hand, while protecting state resources from the impoverished, destitute, and dependent, on the other.[12] The court saw its purpose as uplifting the poor into suitable postures of proper wage laborers and making them members of patriarchal domestic units.[13] Through the domestic court, the city showed its preference for the white patriarchal family. Chief Justice Harry Olson launched the domestic relations branch of the court in August 1911 to "keep husband and wife together," to compel "delinquent deserters" to support their families, and to "provide watchful care over deserving and unfortunate women."[14] The court reflected an interest in keeping men, women, and children off state relief and proposed doing so by restoring negligent men to the position of independent patriarchs and independent women to that of dutiful and submissive wives.[15] As a result, the domestic relations branch failed to account for female heads of households, disavowing them of their independence and punishing those policy women who had new definitions for what counted as "domestic."[16]

The Chicago Municipal Court's morals and vagrancy branches reflected a desire on the part of the city to police the waves of African American migrant women who took up labor in policy gambling, prostitution, and other informal economic enterprises. The morals court was established in 1913 and handled all cases related to prostitution.[17] The vagrancy branch was established in 1918. It prosecuted defendants arrested for having no visible means of support and was the means by which police detained and regulated those they regarded as suspicious, deviant, or disturbing.[18] African American women in particular struggled with Chicago's labor market, thus they turned to the sex industry, policy gambling, and pickpocketing.[19] A morals court judge attempted to explain the disproportionate presence of Black defendants in his court. Dismissing the conclusion that "there is any greater percentage of immorality among Black women," Judge Wells Cook opined that "colored people living largely in one section of the city . . . are apt to congregate in places and in resorts where the police could more easily raid them, and are much more easily apprehended."[20] Cynthia Blair sees in these comments three intertwined factors contributing to the preponderance of Black women before the court on "morals" charges: racial segregation, the concentration of prostitution in the Black Belt, and increased police attention to the Black Belt sex trade.[21] Blair's observations are instructive for my examination of policy gambling, the municipal court's treatment of it, and police surveillance of gambling in Black communities.

The branches of Chicago's municipal court pushed African American women policy workers further to the margins of those familial structures it was willing to protect. The court's vision of the nuclear family as organized around the male provider was not one that resonated with every Black woman policy worker. This is one indication of the many ways the assumptions underpinning the quasi-criminal status of Black working women were shaped by sexist and racist attitudes about employment, social space, and the family.

The lack of African American women's representation on the municipal court bench and their overrepresentation as defendants caused much frustration in Black Chicago and sparked the interests of many activists. Ida B. Wells-Barnett made progress when she worked as a probation officer in the municipal court during the 1910s. She handled cases of Black men convicted of desertion and filed several complaints herself.[22] The *Chicago Defender* protested the lack of Black judges in the municipal court with its headline "Our Race Needs Judge," on March 31, 1917.[23] The *Defender* pressed the court on its favoritism: "There are many instances noted in the Morals court, and particularly acts of favoritism are shown in cases in which colored and white persons are concerned."[24] The newspaper called upon readers to openly criticize any public official, judges in particular, who demonstrated prejudice and partiality. The paper offered unhesitatingly to publish these complaints.

Mistreatment of Black Chicagoans also gained exposure in the extensive 1922 report by the Chicago Commission on Race Relations, *The Negro in Chicago: A Study of Race Relations and a Race Riot.* The report graphically detailed the discrimination African Americans faced throughout Chicago's entire criminal justice system. The authors began by pointing out that "testimony is practically unanimous that Negroes are much more liable to arrest than whites, since police officers share in the general public opinion that Negroes 'are more criminal than whites.'"[25] Police arrested African Americans more frequently, the report explained, saying, "There is little risk of trouble in arresting Negroes, while greater care must be exercised in arresting whites," because, according to police officers, whites were more violent when being arrested than African Americans. According to the commission's findings, African Americans, although comprising less than 4 percent of the city's population, accounted for 21 percent of all male and female felony arrestees in 1920 and 30 percent of all women arrestees in 1930. By 1930 a stunning 70 percent of prostitutes brought into the morals court were Black.[26]

Not only does this imbalance indicate the racism of the courts; it also exposes cooperation between the judicial and executive branches in handling Black offenders. The authors of the *Illinois Crime Survey* (1929) hinted at such a relationship between the defense attorneys, prosecution, and bailiffs. Some lawyers were known to divide the profits from their activities among officers who gave them business, especially if direct evidence was not easy to obtain and officers would not readily provide it. Examining crime from November 1927 to February 1928, the *Survey* concluded:

> The majority of the judges sitting are fitted neither by experience, education, nor, what is more important, sufficient professional standard to discharge

with credit the great responsibilities and powers which they possess under the law. The court is full of incompetence, of political influences, of lamentable laxness in meeting an unprecedented tide of crime.[27]

According to the *Illinois Crime Survey*, displays of mediocrity like this took place daily at municipal court branches all over Chicago and hint at the level of police payoffs and collusion between the prosecution and police department. Nicole Gonzalez Van Cleve confirms this when she observed during her time in Cook County courts that "the cultural practices and structural codependences between police and prosecutors create a dangerous dynamic."[28]

Although the number of African American women arrested was generally disproportionate, they were slightly less likely to be found guilty for nonviolent crimes than native-born white women (29 versus 34 percent in the 1910s and 39 versus 44 percent in the 1920s). For violent crimes, however, African American women were two to four times more likely than white women to be convicted; the type of crime—felony or misdemeanor—informed their prison sentencing. Although they were only 4.1 percent of the city's population in 1920, African American women comprised 36 percent of robbery arrestees; 61 percent of assault arrestees; and 31 percent of murder arrestees.[29] These high arrest rates translated into Black women's overrepresentation in the state's prison population with long sentences but underrepresentation in the state's misdemeanant population with shorter sentences. Laura Dodge argues that this imbalance confirms that racial stereotypes regarding the naturally hardened character, inherent immorality, and innate criminality of Black women factored into their higher proportion of the female prison population.[30]

The absolute number of Black women's commitments to female prisons in Illinois with longer sentences remained unchanged throughout the Depression.[31] Chicago police arrest statistics and Illinois imprisonment patterns confirm African Americans' vulnerability before law enforcement. Thus, the most formidable obstacle to Black women policy workers would continue to be an omnipresent Chicago Police Department and an unpredictable municipal court.

Politics and Payoffs

Simon Balto confirms that the likelihood of conviction for African Americans was always higher than for whites but that the overall rate of conviction was low because of the court's historic reputation for corruption, stressing that "Black people were more likely than whites to be convicted of crimes of which they were accused, but [that] Chicago's court system during the twenties was so disjointed and overburdened that overall rates of conviction were low, much to the chagrin of tough-on-crime proponents."[32] This relationship was cemented at policy's infancy, continued through the 1920s, as Balto points out, and, importantly for this chapter, shaped the way arrests and convictions played out in the civic arena from the second election of William Hale Thompson in 1927, to Anton Cermak's election in 1931 and assassination in 1933, to Edward Kelly's tenure lasting from 1933 to 1947, through to the end of Martin H. Kennelly's term in 1955.

Chicago's tough-on-crime politicians, police commissioners, and justices have always had a relationship to policy gambling defined by the omnipresence of payoffs and graft. Commentary from Shane White and his colleagues on Harlem's unique legal system with respect to numbers is apropos when engaging that of Chicago: "Payoffs and graft were undoubtedly a part of everyday life in the numbers game, and it is necessary to bear this in mind when the legal record is examined."[33] Payoffs and graft informed the relationships between Chicago's policy kings and queens and the mayor, police commissioner, and the court. What emerges from these arrangements is that low-level policy workers were often treated like collateral when delivering city hall Black voters and policy kings and queens the protection they needed to keep their wheels running. Protection included a reduction in the number and frequency of raids, cases never making it to court, or, if they did, a non-conviction. Non-conviction, many believed, was the strategy used by both the court and the police to extract revenue from Chicago's poor. Some argued it exposed collusion between the judicial and executive branches, revealing the impossibility of greater supervision of both. These accusations against the municipal court were plentiful and came from all directions. Time and again, it was African American women policy workers who were caught in the crosshairs of this twofold engine of exploitation through police and judicial payoffs.

Nathan Thompson asserts that "policy became the biggest political football in town. Ruthless political battles of the parties were fought over the Black vote, resulting indirectly in one Chicago mayor's murder."[34] Thompson also goes to great lengths in his informal history of Chicago's policy kings to prove that policy flourished because municipal authorities (mayors, judges, prosecutors, court clerks, and members of the police department) depended on policy kings to deliver a sizeable Black vote. When policy kings did not want to involve themselves in electoral politics, they secured operations by way of arrangements they made directly with police—"the cash cow every cop in town probably wanted in on."[35] Claude Murphy, an infamous policy worker, outlined details about the payoff system in his court testimony, stating that he had

> collected up to $30,000 a month in one Police district alone. Simultaneously, collected $12,000 a month from wheel operators citywide for a group of powerful police officers. Further, that a "politician" split the $30,000 with 40% going to himself, 10% to one cop in the district and the remaining 50% being cut between the lieutenants, sergeants, and vice cops of that district.[36]

It was a costly affair for policy station owners. Thompson claims that on one occasion station owners spent nearly half a million dollars in six months for fines, court costs, bail bondsmen fees, lawyer fees, and money given to police officers for protection against raids.[37] When kings delivered the vote or large sums of cash, they found that policy flourished free from interference. However, when they failed to deliver, authorities created problems for people at every level of the policy gambling industry. These patterns are evident throughout the tenure of several Chicago mayors, but Mayor Martin Kennelly merits closer examination when scrutinizing the rates of arrests versus non-convictions for gambling-related crimes.

Mayor Kennelly accelerated his assault on vice in the Black Belt as part of his effort to seek reelection in the 1940s and because of continual pressure from the Italian mob. Thompson reports that by the "summer of 1947, Chicago had a new mayor, Martin Kennelly, who as Chicago tradition held, ordered a new crackdown on Policy."[38] Kennelly formed a special squad led by Detective Tim Allman and tasked with keeping track of policy gambling. Kennelly relied on this squad and an aggressive police force ready to bring in a steady stream of defendants. The data indicates that African Americans totaled 80 percent of all arrests for gambling in 1953, 84 percent of all arrests in 1954, and 85 percent of all arrests in 1955.[39] But few of these arrests led to conviction (see table 1).

During Kennelly's term, newspapers not only identified schemes that put defendants in harm's way but also accused city officials of lining their pockets with court fines from Chicago's vulnerable populations. One such

Table 1. Comparison of arrest data to conviction data, 1941–1955, Chicagoans, white and Black, arrested for policy gambling–related infractions.

Year	Number Arrested	Number Guilty	% of Total Arrest
1941	4,771	485	10%
1942	6,571	1,697	25%
1943	6,861	1,857	27%
1944	7,814	629	8%
1945	5,061	607	12%
1946	4,220	630	15%
1947	5,283	784	15%
1948	9,889	724	7%
1949	8,649	665	8%
1950	5,253	562	11%
1951	7,602	573	7%
1952	7,653	597	8%
1953	7,327	1,199	16%
1954	7,159	938	13%
1955	7,373	989	13%

Source: Edward J. Kelly, Mayor, *Chicago Police Department Annual Reports, 1941–1955* (City of Chicago).

scheme involved bail, and when the defendant could not pay the amount of bail on their own, many sought help from bail bonds. A bail bond is a type of surety bond provided by a company or bail agent that secures the release of a defendant from jail. Corruption abounded around bail bonds. For example, the Chicago Crime Commission exposed a municipal judge named Joseph B. Hermes in an elaborate bail bond fraud scheme that stole from unknowing defendants.[40] Kefauver files provide a detailed description of bail bond fraud "where in illiterate defendants [were] duped out of cash bail bonds and money paid ostensibly as a fine."[41] The *Chicago Daily News* gathered extensive files documenting a startling thirty-year-long bail bond "alliance of the gambling interests" and municipal court officials, a problem that had not been corrected as of 1950.[42] The journalists alleged that judges committed fraud by entering: (1) a phony ex parte motion to vacate, (2) a phony suspension of fine and costs, or (3) several continuances followed by granting a new trial that either found the defendant not guilty or lowered the original fine and costs.[43] Defendants may not have known of the motion to vacate or the subsequent lowering of the fines but willingly handed over their bail bond receipt in lieu of cash in satisfaction of the judgment. After a counterfeit suspension or motion to vacate was entered, the judge or clerks of the court sold the bond receipts at a discounted rate. Judges and clerks were counting on a steady stream of defendants supplied by police.

Catherine Reiser, a reader of the *Tribune* in 1950, voiced her skepticism of city officials' oversight of the municipal court. She reminded Kefauver officials that the Crime Commission official Virgil W. Peterson and his boss, Austin L. Wyman, were "not unfamiliar with the shabby devices used by some practitioners in obstructing justice, and he knows from first-hand experience that 'justice freely, and without denial, promptly and without delay' is a hollow mockery as observed in the Circuit Court."[44] In the eyes of many, the mounting evidence of corruption among the domestic, moral, and vagrancy branches of the municipal court proved the court's reliance on police for the inexhaustible supply of defendants. This corruption made it incredibly difficult for policy laborers and gamblers to navigate arrest and trial. The courts' practice of dropping these cases while still extracting money absorbed and appropriated most women's legal strategies of resistance.

Strategies of Evidence Suppression

Leatrice Marrow and Sarah Goodwin found themselves caught in this axis in 1955, Kennelly's last year in office. The women's defense lawyers argued that arresting officers had illegally obtained policy slips from the women during their arrests in 1955. Their cases were brought before a municipal court judge and ended after they entered, via their defense attorneys, a "motion to suppress the evidence."[45] This phrase appears on the back of nearly every policy arrest docket in the Cook County Circuit Court Archives. The motion meant that the police had illegally obtained evidence to be used against the defendants in court. Filing the motion to suppress improperly seized evidence would not dismiss an entire case, usually, but it would make materials like policy slips inadmissible in court—a crucial piece of evidence in these cases. The defendant issued this motion to make the policy slips or whatever evidence had been presented by the police inadmissible in the courtroom because it was unlawfully seized during the arrest.[46] In these cases the defense argued that the Fourth Amendment had been violated.[47]

The Fourth Amendment of the U.S. Constitution states:

> The right of the people to be secure in their persons, houses, papers, and effects, against unreasonable searches and seizures, shall not be violated, and no Warrants shall issue, but upon probable cause, supported by Oath

or affirmation, and particularly describing the place to be searched, and the persons or things to be seized.[48]

The Illinois Criminal Code makes this provision: "An arrest may be made by an officer or by a private person without warrant, for a criminal offense committed or attempted in his presence, and by an officer, when a criminal offense has in fact been committed, and he has reasonable ground for believing that the person to be arrested has committed it."[49] Therefore, an officer may act on the suspicion that a crime has been committed without the written documentation of a warrant.

A distressful contradiction between the amendment and the Illinois Criminal Code may have paved the way for officers to enter Goodwin's home. The officers may not have had a warrant, but perhaps they did not need one according to the Illinois Criminal Code. In the Marrow and Goodwin cases, Judge Slater "sustained the motions, and the defendants were discharged."[50] But after Judge Slater did this, there was no follow-up on the actions of the officers that would hold the Chicago police accountable for violating Marrow's and Goodwin's Fourth Amendment rights. Instead, the women's cases demonstrate that the courts upheld Kennelly's aggravation policing strategy. However, the courts did not convict the women for ordinance violation; courts would not punish them for policy gambling. They wanted fines but did not convict them. The legal system sustained the ongoing arrests of Black women in Bronzeville.

There were mechanisms in place to protect women from this never-ending cycle of arrest, and the invasion of their private spaces without warrants was disruptive to women's businesses and privacy. The exclusionary rule of the U.S. Constitution exists to benefit people subjected to search and seizure. It states that if law enforcement invades a home without meeting certain exceptions or without possession of a warrant or sufficient grounds for suspicion, any evidence obtained cannot be used against the defendant; it affords the defendant some invisibility before the law. Without this rule there would be no incentive to adhere to the Fourth Amendment, which protects citizens from unreasonable search and seizure. This is the more mysterious and less tangible check and balance of the police force.

Several cases in which the courts denied defendants' motions to suppress evidence provide a glimpse into Fourth Amendment jurisprudence. Numerous defendants pursued appeals in Illinois's higher courts, and their cases illustrate when and where Black women tried to appeal their convictions.[51]

The court decisions also highlight moments when the law relied on search and seizure to make women more vulnerable. These decisions also help us consider whether and to what extent the policy workers' challenges actually got pressed, how much resistance they found themselves able to make, and how such challenges were absorbed by the state at the judicial level.

For example, Rexford Clark presented a written petition to suppress policy slips and sheets as evidence in 1956 when he was arrested for a parking violation.[52] Clark argued that his property was unlawfully taken by Chicago police officers Roland, Mitchell, and Mullin when he was unlawfully taken into custody on the pretext that he had violated a city parking ordinance. Around noon on October 10, the three officers observed Clark parking his car in front of his residence at 4508 Forrestville Avenue. Clark got out and was about to cross the street when Mullin asked him if he always parked his car like that. Clark responded, "What's wrong with it?" Mullin accused him of parking too close to the curb. Mullin testified that he saw a package sticking out of Clark's right rear pocket that was only partially obscured by a handkerchief. When he asked Clark what he had in the package, Clark replied, "Policy slips." Mullin took the policy slips as Roland and Mitchell searched the car, found some policy sheets, and formally charged the defendant with violating gambling statutes. The police admitted they had no warrant for Clark's arrest.[53]

Traffic stops, for example, were particularly vulnerable moments for policy gamblers. Black men and women were unexpectedly prosecuted for policy gambling ordinances after being pulled over for routine parking violations, turn-signal malfunctions, or simply walking down the street. This is what happened, for example, to Fletcher and Edna Galloway, who lobbied to get their 1965 Chevrolet back in an appeal after Fletcher's arrest. Police Officer Daniel Nagle testified that on January 13, 1967, he arrested Fletcher Galloway for not having a turn signal and traveling too fast for the conditions. Allegedly, when Nagle had asked the defendant what he did for a living, Fletcher replied that he was a policy runner. Nagle testified that he found policy slips on the seat of the car and arrested the defendant. The policy slips were admitted in evidence—brought into the court's vision—despite the objection of the defendant. The Galloways admitted that they were the owners of the vehicle in question and were policy runners but maintained that the automobile was not used in the commission of gambling. The Galloways never got their car back from auction.[54]

There were very few victories in the appeals process for individuals who moved to suppress evidence and were denied. But Barbara Heard and Gertrude Moore were able to force a higher court's desire to adhere to due process despite its unwavering support of police overreach. On June 28, 1968, Officer William Mitchell of the gambling division of the Chicago Police Department entered the first-floor apartment located at 4729 South Prairie with a search warrant. He testified that after identifying himself and announcing the purpose of his call, he proceeded into the dining room, where he observed Barbara Heard and Gertrude Moore seated at a table on which there were policy slips, tickets, and $21.65 in cash. On this basis, the Cook County Circuit Court found Heard and Moore guilty of gambling, since they had knowingly possessed policy slips and tickets.[55]

On July 11, 1968, a criminal complaint was filed in the Circuit Court of Cook County charging Heard and Moore with the offense of gambling. The court denied Heard and Moore's motion to suppress both the search warrant and the evidence seized, and, after waiving a jury trial, they were tried by the court and found guilty. Each was later sentenced to serve ninety days in a correction house. The Illinois Supreme Court took up their appeal because of the charge that their constitutional rights were violated due to the nature in which the prosecution initiated the proceedings and the lack of specificity of the charge. The women argued that the offense for which they were tried and sentenced, policy gambling, required prosecution by indictment rather than by complaint.[56] The complaint charged that each defendant committed the offense of gambling inasmuch as "she set up or promoted a Policy Game or (Sold) or (Offered to Sell) or (transferred) a ticket or (share) for a lottery or (sold) or (offered to sell) or (transferred) or (knowingly possessed) a policy ticket or other similar device: To Wit: Policy results tickets, Policy bet writings and other related gambling policy paraphernalia."[57] The state supreme court found that "the promoting of a policy game is not the same act as transferring a policy ticket, for example. The use of the disjunctive under these circumstances causes uncertainty and conjecture as to which of the alternatives the accused is charged with committing. The result was that the complaint was void because it did not set forth the nature and elements of the charge with the certainty [required]."[58] The women's savvy defense attorneys destroyed the prosecution. By exposing the ineptitude and lack of due process in the handling of their original case, Heard and Moore gained traction in the Illinois Supreme Court, which reversed the circuit court's decision. Reversal, however, was not contingent upon a violation of the defendants' Fourth Amendment rights due to the motion to quash the search warrant and suppress the evidence seized—the supreme court kept police leeway on search and seizure firmly intact. Again, this case proves that the court upheld the police's continual assault on Black women policy workers, and police surveillance would continue with the court's help.

Being a "Known" Policy Runner

The aforementioned court cases illustrate the problem of being a known policy runner—being too visible in the eyes of an eager police force. A reputation of notoriety put African American women in serious jeopardy, but to be a successful policy writer required a certain degree of fame and a rejection of traditional notions of what was considered women's private sphere. The job was also an outward rejection of the court's notions of what was domestic, private, and acceptable labor for women. Being a known policy worker was a catalyst for suspicion by the police, and significantly decreased one's odds in the appeals process. For example, Estele Johnson, a woman arrested for policy gambling, who issued a motion to suppress evidence in 1968, discovered that search warrants did not have to be factual and, in fact, were immaterial if the search could be otherwise justified by officers.[59] Johnson's case illustrates that if one were seen near a known policy station or engaging individuals deemed "known" by police, as in being too visible or too familiar to police because of one's policy labor, one could be convicted of policy gambling, and motions to suppress were rendered useless.

A police officer's ability to mark someone as "known," on the other hand, was a mark of success. It provided evidence of a police officer's years on the force; it established the credibility and seniority of the officer—both highly desirable masculine qualities. It also emboldened police during the era of Kennelly's raids on policy gamblers. In Johnson's case, Herman Waller, a Chicago police officer with four years of experience, estimated he had made approximately three hundred policy arrests—he knew a policy situation when he saw one. Waller secured a search warrant for surveillance of a second-floor apartment of a two-story frame building at 1702 North Bissell because he had been informed that a policy operation was going on inside. During the surveillance, Waller observed persons who were allegedly engaged in policy entering the first-floor apartment, not the second-floor one, yet his warrant permitted him access to only the latter. Waller testified that he recognized some of these people as "known policy runners" whom he had arrested many times before, and after some thirty-five minutes spent watching the front of the building, he moved to the rear of the premises to look into a window of the first-floor apartment, which was partially covered by curtains. Through a crack in the window curtain, Waller could see the heads of the people inside, and through the closed window, he could hear an adding machine being operated and a female voice inquiring, "Are all your books in? Who has any short books? Where is all the money?" After about ten minutes of watching and listening, Waller grew impatient, went to the front door of the apartment, knocked, and announced who he was. When the person who answered the door told him to "get lost," Waller forced his way inside. He charged into the kitchen at the rear of the apartment, where he found Estele Johnson and Francis Spires sitting at a table with an adding machine, policy writings, and policy result slips. Another defendant, Charles Wright, yelled "Police!" and threw a bag containing $179.35 behind a washing machine. Wright and the other defendants pursued an appeal based on the fact that the trial court had refused to suppress the evidence because Waller's search warrant authorized a search of only the second-floor apartment in the two-story building. The Illinois Supreme Court upheld the municipal court's denial of the motion to suppress.[60] While in the Heard and Moore case, the courts ruled in favor of the defendants, the case of Estele Johnson reminds us that being a known policy worker was dangerous. Courts denied Black women and men working in the policy industry the protections of the Fourth Amendment, and they also did not offer them the invisibility afforded by petitions to suppress evidence, which kept evidence about their policy work out of the courtroom.

What Did Women Gain?

Little is known about what happened to Heard and Moore after their supreme court trial in 1968. Did they return to their policy station? Did they have to find a new apartment? Were they able to reassemble their customer base and ticket exchange, rendezvous with pickup men, and reestablish their trustworthiness with policy wheel operators? How long were they out of touch with men such as Theodore Roe and Edward Jones or women like Irene Coleman who might offer them protection or bail? What would be the fallout from their long-term absence from the world of wheels and books? Answers to these questions would provide us with a glimpse into what women gained, if anything, from their victories in court, but we do not know. Answers would also reveal the unstable status of women in the policy industry and how significant the disruptions of law enforcement were on their lives. What we can track is the degree to which sexism created new disparities and problems for women returning to policy work upon being released from jail. The difficulties of making bail, establishing new domiciles, and disparities in payroll reveal the complex world of the underground economy for women.[61] These factors illustrate women policy workers' uncomfortable proximity to men who were not always their allies in the business of policy gambling. Recovering from arrests, jail time, and court cases illustrates policy's tensions. Bail and surety, payroll and the provenance of policy gambling complaints show us that run-ins with Chicago's legal system exacerbated policy's discriminatory practices and hierarchical systems of bias. And as ever, upon release from prison, Black women policy workers and gamblers remained leery of police surveillance.

Due to the visibility their labors required, policy writers were more vulnerable to arrest by police compared to others in the policy industry. They, therefore, more often faced expensive bond fines that their meager salaries, which relied on commissions, could not cover. Theodore Roe, when questioned by Kefauver authorities, denied paying for protection from the police, but he confirmed drawing from his accounts for expenses such as bonds and fines for his runners. Clifford Davis, former treasurer for the Jones brothers and a partner with Roe in the Idaho-Maine wheel, employed between sixty and seventy people. But he did not pay his writers—they operated on a commission of 25 percent before they turned in the books and cash to a cashier.[62] Their relationship to the policy station was of a different nature. Roe stated that it was not hard to find a job as a cashier or writer but that writers had to ingratiate themselves to the door-to-door population.[63]

Cashiers and clerks, however, enjoyed more security than writers; they were less visible to the police on the streets. Cashiers and clerks drew weekly salaries from twenty-five dollars to one hundred dollars. The payroll list from Davis and Roe's wheel from June 30, 1950, informs us that the income of women varied considerably and that some were earning more than men.[64] But when they needed bail, they turned to policy operators, usually men, like Theodore Roe or Walter J. Kelly. For example, Kelly bailed out Gertrude Patterson and Leona Spratling, ages thirty-four and twenty-seven, respectively, when they were arrested for policy violations, offering up his property worth seven thousand dollars. Kelly listed his occupation as "real estate" and his net worth at twenty thousand dollars. Both Patterson and Spratling pled not guilty, waived a jury trial, and were found not guilty later that summer.[65]

Because men like Kelly and Roe dominated underground vice, they had access to a broader range of socioeconomic and political opportunities, networks, and occupations and could rebound from run-ins with the law more quickly than most. Harris comments that in both numbers and policy "on account of race and gender exclusion and male patriarchy, some women were kept at the bottom of the gambling hierarchy."[66] She notes that the "urban informal economy catered to men's desires and interests, creating a homosocial world that sanctioned and rewarded men's aggressive and competitive behaviors and legitimatized their substantial control over various quasi-legal and illegal labor rackets."[67] Consequently, informal laborers had to cope with forms of sexism that "kept the vast majority of female numbers games laborers out of positions of power and in low- and midlevel positions as runners, collectors, and clerks."[68] For example, if Gertrude Patterson were apprehended at her home, she would have had to find a new apartment in which to set up her policy business. Roe informed authorities in his testimony before the Kefauver Committee that his network provided employees with apartments. Lower-level policy workers were dependent on Roe for help when law enforcement raided and ransacked their homes. He nonchalantly explained that the expense of moving was incurred by the company, and an individual cashier or checker might "pay the bill, but he would get a receipt." The interviewer pressed Roe on his last point, inquiring, "Isn't that sort of a difficult thing for the individual concerned to keep moving to get a new apartment some place periodically?" Roe answered, "He can always get places for those writers. There are so many people out there that want to collect that money every day."[69] Roe's lack of sympathy in this exchange indicates that lower-level policy workers had an unstable status in the policy game, especially as they lived in spaces rife with hostile law enforcement. But as previous chapters have shown, many women also excelled because of this unstable status. Certainly women working as runners, writers, clerks, and cashiers, who encountered police on a daily basis, exhibited undue tenacity before law enforcement and legal systems that were stacked against them. The success of lower-level policy women in the face of policy's masculine tilt and the sexist carceral strategies of the municipal court reveal women's agency from queens to writers.

Conclusion

The Chicago Police Department and the city's municipal court, as well as the Illinois Appellate Court and Supreme Court, however, refused to support policy women's solidarity. Instead, the municipal court relied on a peculiar strategy of police surveillance and non-conviction to adjudicate policy gambling ordinance violations and the surveillance of Black women policy workers and gamblers throughout the twentieth century. Defendants fought back as best they could using sanctioned legal conduits by petitioning to suppress illegally obtained evidence, issuing claims that officers had invaded their homes without a search warrant and had violated their Fourth Amendment rights, or through the appeals process. But the state's unwavering support of the strategy to criminalize Black women's labor in the informal economy, shake up Black communities that depended on Black women's informal labor, and refuse to offer formal reformatory measures or economic assistance for struggling Black communities persisted. Before the law on the streets and inside the courtroom, Black women remained vulnerable.

The quasi-criminal status of Black women in Chicago cannot be understood outside the broader context of African American women's relationship with the law during this period. Black women's legal status was measured as "quasi-criminal" while society's racist structures measured them as "wholly Black." Quasi-criminal, quasi-labor, and quasi-domestic were the key theoretical components through which the Chicago Municipal Court and Illinois Supreme Court assessed the status of all Black women. Black women had an uneasy classification inside and, most distressingly (as the previous chapter showed through its investigation of arrest records and police brutality), outside the courtroom. Nicole Van Cleve, in her book *Crook County*, provides guidance on the court's approach, explaining that "distinctions about morality and criminality, on the one hand, and morality and racism, on the other, meddle within the context of our criminal courts; there, one's moral status is conferred by both legal categories and racial categories. As such, the 'immorality' of defendants is both a criminal distinction and a racial one."[70] This logic worked itself out in adverse ways for Black women policy workers and gamblers caught in the legal realm. Van Cleve draws this conclusion further by stating that "with the authority of the law, a host of racialized abuses are not only allowable in public spaces but are seen as deserved and justified."[71] The executive branch arrested African Americans by the thousands for policy-related charges, but the judiciary branch dropped most cases.

This poses an interesting quandary. Certainly, non-conviction presented opportunities for Black women to return to work and families, but it reveals the extent to which the court affirmed arrests and predatory policing. Black women responded to these dilemmas and their quasi-criminal status with innovation, but the masculine world of policy gambling offered little in return. Black women found themselves dependent on Black men running the game, as Roe's testimony before the Kefauver Senate Committee illustrates, reflecting the troubled vectors of patriarchy, racism, and capitalism.

Conclusion

For Black women whose husbands had made millions off policy but who now found their partners in prison; for women who longed to further their educations or their children's lot in Chicago's rigidly segregated world; for women who dreamed of owning their own businesses; for children who loved to tell a tall tale for a few cents on the dollar; and for women who could scarcely make it as domestic laborers, maids, or laundresses, policy was the answer. Black women's success in policy, whether as policy queens, policy writers, clerks, cashiers, or mediums, illuminates just how multilayered their movements though the Black urban market were. Policy added a hint of hope to the grinding poverty of everyday life for residents of the South Side of Chicago as its African American neighborhood turned from a small enclave to the bustling Black Metropolis during the mid-twentieth century—but not without constant state scrutiny.

Queens Irene Coleman, Leslie Williams, Ann Roane, and Florine Reynolds Irving Stephens, and lower-level employees such as Celeste White, whose drop station funneled about twelve thousand dollars a day into the Windy-City-Subway-Big Town policy wheel's coffers, bring to light a sophistication in entrepreneurship when surveillance from the Chicago Police Department was omnipresent and violent. Coleman and Williams, instead of competing against each other, were co-owners of the Belmont and Old Reliable policy wheels, which they inherited from Coleman's father.[1] Ann

Roane partnered with men in both the policy industry and legitimate businesses. Roane and Matt Bivins partnered in the Alabama-Georgia, Jackpot, and Whirlaway wheels.[2] She and Ed Jones Jr. opened the Hawthorn Milk Store, a milk delivery business.[3] As an equal partner in both formal and informal economies, Roane worked in the tradition of policy queen Elizabeth Slaughter. Roane and Slaughter showed how Black women could straddle the informal and formal economic binaries with great success.

Perhaps most exciting was the success and revolutionary business tactics of Florine Reynolds Irving Stephens, who navigated a public divorce from the once famed "King of Policy," James D. Irving.[4] She negotiated a divorce settlement that included a $250 weekly allowance, a sizeable cash settlement, and, perhaps most importantly, the possession of one of her husband's policy wheels that was reported to bring in $25,000 a week. She purchased several other wheels, expanding her operations to over sixty policy runners, clerks, and writers, many of whom were women. By 1961 the *Chicago Tribune* described Stephens as "the operator of the largest policy wheels on the Southside . . . [whose Spaulding-Silver-Dunlap wheel, which is only one of her wheels] nets $14,000 a day in income for her, totaling up to more than five million dollars annually. . . . The wheel operates seven days a week, 52 weeks a year." The same reporter related that they found women, policy clerks, counting large stacks of money upon entering a policy station in Stephens's district.[5]

The gains of Bronzeville's policy queens are nothing short of incredible. But as previously mentioned, the accomplishments of queens were the exception, not the rule. Most women involved in policy gambling worked as policy writers, clerks, cashiers, or labored as mediums. Their position in the hierarchy of policy gambling was far more precarious than queens, as the stories of the arrest and surveillance records in chapter 5 prove. Lower-level policy writers navigated policy's demanding environment of visibility and invisibility in exciting ways. Policy demanded writers', clerks', and cashiers' visibility inside the industry. Writers had to be mobile throughout their workplace, and notoriety served them well. Clerks and cashiers were the visible front lines for writers and customers coming in and out of policy stations; they often worked the front counter at policy stations. Mediums had to be well known and made names for themselves in the Black press; they tried to mitigate scrutiny by joining organized religion. Black women working at the lower levels of policy and its tertiary industries challenged the visibility of policy gambling while also challenging the invisibility the legal system imposed on them, and for some this proved advantageous through the state's takeover of most informal lotteries in the early 1970s.

The beginning of policy's demise in Bronzeville started when Chicago's most famous policy queen, Harriett Jones, fled Chicago and moved to Mexico City. Theodore Roe took over managing Jones's wheels until his murder in 1952. Then "white-organized crime successfully subordinated or eliminated Black-controlled gambling operations throughout the 1930s and 1940s."[6] At first, white organizations employed African Americans to solicit bets from policy's Black client base, but as "white involvement in the upper levels of the policy business increased, so too did the playing of the daily numbers among poor and working-class whites."[7] Eventually, historian Matthew Vaz states, white policy operators went from "extorting what was a Black practice to operating a game with a substantial white customer base and a significant number of white workers at all levels."[8] Policy gambling was never the same.

The State of Illinois took steps to transform policy into the Illinois State Lottery starting in 1974; Illinois was the last of several states to initiate lotteries between 1967 and 1974, seeing them as easy ways to raise revenues without raising taxes.[9] According to Vaz, Black political leaders in New York and Illinois "opposed the state taking over numbers gambling, and they pressed instead for community control over a legalized game, with legislators in both New York and Illinois proposing laws to bring daily gambling in Black communities under local control."[10] Lewis A. H. Caldwell, then a representative of Illinois's Twenty-Fourth District, drove the push for local control of legalized gambling. Caldwell opened the hearings of Illinois's Policy-Numbers Game Study Committee with this appeal: "As a professional social worker for sixteen years, dating from 1933, I learned that policy was a major factor in the economic and social life of Black communities in the city. . . . The time has come that policy should be legalized."[11] Caldwell, along with Harold Washington, Chicago's first Black mayor, and activist Brenetta Howell Barrett, sought to legalize policy gambling to offer African American men and women employed by the game legitimate occupations. Barrett, a Black Chicagoan who had served as director of the Governor's Office of Human Resources, argued that "legalization of Policy will legitimize an industry which employs substantial numbers of Blacks, providing them on-the-job training in responsible positions which would otherwise not be so easily accessible to them in either the public or private sector."[12] Vaz tells us that Barrett was convinced that "legalization would go a long way towards removing the ever-resented intrusion of crime syndicate control from outside of the Black community usually in concert with and abetted by some public officials who wink at the existence of a thriving numbers game."[13] Vaz notes that Barrett "referred to the appropriation of the game by white gangsters as 'plagiarism,' and, she argued, 'policy should be legalized and restored, under regulation by the State, to the administrative hands of the Black community.'"[14] Barrett and Caldwell fought tirelessly for a community-controlled policy game that would give African American policy workers legitimate jobs. Ultimately, however, state lottery supporters quickly pushed through a lottery-controlled numbers game and the new game went into operation in 1979.[15] This failure to secure legitimacy for thousands of men and women policy workers revealed the government's perception of policy workers as criminals who cheated the tax and welfare systems.[16] Therefore, the lottery scripted policy workers as "undeserving"— not the gamblers from whom the state soon profited when it peddled lottery tickets to them every day.[17]

New state lotteries altered the dynamics of Black women's labor in the informal economy.[18] But instead of retirement, joblessness, or obscurity, men and women who labored in policy gambling were innovative and found ways to run the numbers. Historian Davarian Baldwin remembers in the early 1980s when a number of people congregated at his mother's friend's house to watch the Illinois State Lottery on television. What he soon realized was "that the house was a policy station, but instead of having an independent wheel, she use[d] the same numbers as the state lottery to generate an illicit economy . . . WOW!"[19] Baldwin's anecdote illustrates new fluctuations in policy gambling's dialectic of visibility and invisibility made necessary by the state lottery. As a result, queens, their employees, and gamblers perfected new ways to strategically evade detection by authorities.

Fannie Davis, who ran her own numbers operation out of her Detroit home, never lost confidence that her business could survive despite white takeover. Fannie's daughter Bridgett, then an undergraduate at Spelman College, captured Detroit numbers operators' feelings the first week Michigan Lottery tickets went on sale to the public: "Everyone in the business was confident that the Numbers would continue running right alongside the legal lottery, and that plenty of Black folks would stay loyal to them. Mama felt certain her own customers would stay loyal to *her*."[20] Fannie stayed in business and her daughter reported that the day-to-day operations of the numbers continued in full force despite competition from the state and a ramp-up of police raids. Bridgett said numbers had a distinct advantage over the weekly lottery: in numbers Fannie's clientele could pick their own combinations and wager several times a week, but in the weekly lottery, gamblers couldn't pick their own sets of numbers and placed bets only once.[21] In 1977, again seeing the profitability of numbers, Michigan's state authorities began to offer a daily lottery game; now players could select their own three-digit number, with drawings every day, six days a week.[22] Fannie had to innovate—she had to make herself visible to her clientele in ways she had not previously. She offered customers several options: play the daily lottery with her, play the traditional numbers as always, or play a combination of both.[23] Eventually, Fannie did away with traditional numbers altogether and exclusively used the lottery's daily winners in a fashion similar to that of Baldwin's aunt. And Fannie also made her business "more alluring by becoming more competitive: she started offering a higher payout than the estate, paying 600–1 winnings compared to the Daily's 500–1."[24] Her innovation paid off, Bridgett reported, as this approach—her navigation of the daily's attempt to make her invisible—"saved Mama's business and our livelihood. I returned to Spelman for the spring semester and promptly moved off campus."[25]

That there were overlapping gaming practices, such as those described by Baldwin and Davis, confirms the thesis set forth in this book that policy work required Black women's visibility and invisibility and that they navigated this matrix deftly. But the fact that Black-controlled and Black-operated policy gambling continues should come as no surprise; when faced with policy gambling's visibility and invisibility, African American women had been navigating these poles for decades. It is true that the state took over policy gambling, and as a result, innovations in the informal economy moved further and further from the record. Black women's maneuvers are now increasingly more difficult for historians to track but nonetheless urgent to uncover.

Examining Black women's visibility and invisibility in policy work can take us in many important new directions. Policy was passage out of poverty and patriarchy for Black women of the upper class or those aspiring to ascend the social ladder. Policy made Eudora Johnson Binga into a beloved philanthropist, but her husband's mismanagement of her fortune spelled her demise. Queen Ann Roane discovered, after she divorced her husband and moved to Chicago to set up her own policy wheels, that the game rendered women vulnerable before law enforcement. Their lives show how policy facilitated the seemingly protective trappings of respectability and access to the upper crust of Black Chicago society while it highlights just how tenuous their grasp on upper-class life was. African American women of Black Chicago's working classes also turned to policy gambling as a source of mobility, profit, and security. Policy work provided Black women with steady work inside the home, where they could watch over their children and establish a domestic sanctuary. Runners, writers, and clerks, however, found Chicago law enforcement relentless and the court system difficult to navigate, as was the return to the patriarchal world of policy gambling after arrest, trials, or incarceration. *Dream Books and Gamblers* opens up the previously mysterious world of dream books, séances, and mediumship as the urban domain of Black women while it renders the sanctioned economic world anew by establishing the many connections between Chicago's shadowy underworld and Black women's everyday lives.

African American women's capitalist influence through the informal economy must receive recognition if the story of Black working women in Chicago is to be fully understood. People all over the city of Chicago knew about and played policy, but its existence was rarely recorded for posterity. By bringing the women's stories of policy gambling to the forefront, I hope that Black women's policy work does not suffer the same fate.

Notes

Introduction

1. "Gives Check to Provident Hospital," *Chicago Defender*, February 8, 1947, 11.

2. "Testimony of Theodore Roe," December 18, 1950, Kefauver Senate Committee to Investigate Organized Crime in Interstate Commerce, box 183, "Hearings: Public," folder Part 5 Illinois, 1137, National Archives, Washington, DC.

3. The scholarly literature on "respectability" is dynamic and interdisciplinary. For further engagement with this literature, see Evelyn Brooks Higginbotham's important work on respectability politics and the Black church, *Righteous Discontent: The Women's Movement in the Black Baptist Church, 1880–1912* (Cambridge, MA: Harvard University Press, 1993); E. Frances White, *Dark Continent of Our Bodies: Black Feminism and the Politics of Respectability* (Philadelphia: Temple University Press, 2001); Patricia Schechter, *Ida B. Wells-Barnett and American Reform 1880–1930* (Chapel Hill: University of North Carolina Press, 2001); Victoria W. Wolcott, *Remaking Respectability: African American Women in Interwar Detroit* (Chapel Hill: University of North Carolina Press, 2001); and Brittney C. Cooper, *Beyond Respectability: The Intellectual Thought of Race Women* (Urbana: University of Illinois Press, 2017). And for a study that pushes back against the sinister politics of respectability in urban Black women and girls' lives, read Saidiya Hartman's *Wayward Lives, Beautiful Experiments: Intimate Histories of Riotous Black Girls, Troublesome Women, and Queer Radicals* (New York: Norton, 2019).

4. Paisley Jane Harris, "Gatekeeping and Remaking: The Politics of Respectability in African American Women's History and Black Feminism," *Journal of Women's History* 15, no. 1 (2003): 212.

5. Wolcott, *Remaking Respectability*, 8.

6. Bridgett M. Davis, *The World According to Fannie Davis* (New York: Little, Brown, 2019), 56.

7. Ibid.

8. Studies of illegal lotteries and African American women include LaShawn Harris, *Sex Workers, Psychics, and Numbers Runners: Black Women in New York City's Underground Economy* (Urbana: University of Illinois Press, 2017); Ann Fabian, *Card Sharps and Bucket Shops: Gambling in Nineteenth-Century America* (London: Routledge Press, 2013); Robin Bachin, *Building the South Side: Urban Space and Civic Culture in Chicago, 1890–1919* (Chicago: University of Chicago Press, 2004); Sharon Harley, "Working for Nothing but for a Living: Black Women in the Underground Economy," in *Sister Circle: Black Women and Work,* ed. Sharon Harley and the Black Women and Work Collective (New Brunswick, NJ: Rutgers University Press, 2002); Wolcott, *Remaking Respectability*; Victoria W. Wolcott, "The Culture of the Informal Economy: Numbers Runners in Inter-War Black Detroit," *Radical History Review* (Fall 1997): 46–75; and Shane White, Stephen Gordon, Stephen Robertson, and Graham White, *Playing the Numbers: Gambling in Harlem between the Wars* (Cambridge, MA: Harvard University Press, 2010).

9. Isabel Wilkerson, *The Warmth of Other Suns: The Epic Story of America's Great Migration* (New York: Vintage Books, 2011), 9.

10. Darlene Clark Hine, *Hine Sight: Black Women and the Re-construction of American History* (Bloomington: Indiana University Press, 1997), 94; U.S. Bureau of the Census, *Fifteenth Census of the United States, 1930* (Washington, DC: National Archives and Records Administration, 1930), T626, 2,667 rolls; U.S. Bureau of the Census, *Sixteenth Census of the United States, 1940* (Washington, DC: National Archives and Records Administration, 1940), T627, 4,643 rolls.

11. Joe William Trotter Jr., *Workers on Arrival: Black Labor in the Making of America* (Berkeley: University of California Press, 2019), 77.

12. Ibid., 83.

13. Hine, *Hine Sight*, 89 and 102.

14. Ibid., 103.

15. Trotter, *Workers on Arrival*, 85.

16. Isabel Wilkerson, "Fresh Air Interview: Journalist Isabel Wilkerson," *National Public Radio*, September 13, 2010.

17. Monroe Nathan Work, "Negro Real Estate Holders of Chicago" (PhD diss., University of Chicago, 1903), 6.

18. Allen Spear, *Black Chicago: The Making of a Negro Ghetto* (Chicago: University of Chicago Press, 1967), 11.

19. Beryl Satter, *Family Properties: How the Struggle over Race and Real Estate Transformed Chicago and Urban America* (New York: Picador Press, 2009), 39. Recent studies of Black migration and community formation pushing this analysis include Brian McCammack, *Landscapes of Hope: Nature and the Great Migration in Chicago* (Cambridge, MA: Harvard University Press, 2019); and Jeffrey Helgeson, *Crucibles of Black Empowerment: Chicago's Neighborhood Politics from the New Deal to Harold Washington* (Chicago: University of Chicago Press, 2014).

20. Christopher Robert Reed, *Black Chicago's First Century*, vol. 1: *1833–1900* (Columbia: University of Missouri Press, 2005), 437.

21. Satter, *Family Properties*, 36.

22. Ibid.

23. Wilkerson, *Warmth of Other Suns*, 8.

24. S. White et al., *Playing the Numbers*, 20.

25. See Higginbotham, *Righteous Discontent*.

26. Ibid., 55.

27. Nathan Thompson, *Kings: The True Story of Chicago's Policy Kings and Numbers Rackets, An Informal History* (Chicago: Bronzeville Press, 2006), 13.

28. L. Harris, *Sex Workers*, 54.

29. Ibid., 55.

30. Richard Wright, *Black Boy (American Hunger)* (New York: Harper Perennial Deluxe Edition, 2008), 267.

31. S. White et al., *Playing the Numbers*, 101.

32. Ibid., 143.

33. Ibid.

34. W.E.B. Du Bois, *The Philadelphia Negro* (Philadelphia: University of Pennsylvania Press, 1899), 311.

35. St. Clair Drake and Horace Cayton, *Black Metropolis: A Study of Negro Life in a Northern City* (New York: Harcourt, Brace and World, 1945, repr., Chicago: University of Chicago Press, 1993), 470. Citations refer to the 1993 edition.

36. Black Chicagoans found work in many parallel illicit industries like sex work. For excellent engagement on this topic and how it impacted working-class Black communities, see Cynthia M. Blair, *I've Got to Make My Livin': Black Women's Sex Work in Turn-of-the-Century Chicago* (Chicago: University of Chicago Press, 2010).

37. Robert Weems, *Black Business in the Black Metropolis: The Chicago Metropolitan Assurance Company, 1925–1985* (Bloomington: Indiana University Press, 1998); Robert Weems and Jason P. Chambers, eds., *Building the Black Metropolis: African American Entrepreneurship in Chicago* (Urbana: University of Illinois Press, 2017); Robert Weems, *Desegregating the Dollar: African American Consumerism in the Twentieth Century* (New York: New York University Press, 1998).

38. Matthew Vaz, "'We Intend to Run It': Racial Politics, Illegal Gambling, and the Rise of Government Lotteries in the United States, 1960–1985," *Journal of American History* 101, no. 1 (2014): 71–96.

39. See Davarian Baldwin, *Chicago's New Negroes: Modernity, the Great Migration, and Black Urban Life* (Chapel Hill: University of North Carolina Press, 2008).

40. For a discussion of the origins of the informal economy, see Louis Ferman and P. Ferman, "The Structural Underpinnings of the Irregular Economy," *Poverty and Human Resources Abstracts* 8 (1978): 3–17; Victor E. Tokman, "The Informal Sector in Latin America: From Underground to Legality," in *Beyond Regulation: The Informal Economy in Latin America*, ed. Victor E. Tokman (Boulder, CO: Lynne Rienner Publishers, 1992), 3–4; Philip Harding and Richard Jenkins, *The Myth of*

the Hidden Economy: Towards a New Understanding of Informal Economic Activity (Maidenhead, Berkshire, UK: Open University Press, 1989). For a nuanced approach to recent scholarship on the underground economy, see L. Harris, *Sex Workers*, 210n28. For a provocative counterargument on labeling Black Chicago's policy gambling industry as "underground," see Simon Balto, *Occupied Territory: Policing Black Chicago from Red Summer to Black Power* (Chapel Hill: University of North Carolina Press, 2019), 69.

41. Sudhir Alladi Venkatesh, *Off the Books: The Underground Economy of the Urban Poor* (Cambridge, MA: Harvard University Press, 2006), 10.

42. Wolcott, "Culture of the Informal Economy," 72.

43. Blair, *I've Got to Make My Livin'*, 23. Harris positions her inquiry into the informal and formal labor habits of Black women in Harlem along similar lines: "New York's burgeoning underground economy served as a catalyst in working-class Black women's creation of employment opportunities, occupational identities, and survival strategies that provided financial stability and a sense of labor autonomy and mobility. A number of material and intangible benefits drew women of African descent to New York's informal mob market. With its flexible and fluid structure, the informal labor sector offered employment and economic opportunities that complemented Black women's desire to secure occupational mobility." L. Harris, *Sex Workers*, 2.

44. Balto, *Occupied Territory*; Hazel V. Carby, "Policing the Black Woman's Body in an Urban Context," *Critical Inquiry* 18, no. 4 (1992): 741; Blair, *I've Got to Make My Livin'*; Kali N. Gross, *Colored Amazons: Crime, Violence, and Black Women in the City of Brotherly Love, 1880–1910* (Durham, NC: Duke University Press, 2006); Cheryl D. Hicks, *Talk with You Like a Woman* (Chapel Hill: University of North Carolina Press, 2010); Sarah Haley, *No Mercy Here: Gender, Punishment, and the Making of Jim Crow Modernity* (Chapel Hill: University of North Carolina Press, 2016).

45. Wolcott, *Remaking Respectability*; L. Harris, *Sex Workers*.

46. Here I rely on Hazel Carby's masterful example of this line of inquiry: "It Jus Be's Dat Way Sometime: The Sexual Politics of Women's Blues," *Radical America* 20, no. 4 (1986): 9–24.

47. "Characters, Gambling," April 7, 1937, Ernest W. Burgess Papers, box 23, folder 13, Special Collections, University of Chicago Library.

48. Harris's *Sex Workers* leads the way in scholarly analysis of numbers and policy's other world. See also LaShawn Harris, "Madame Queen of Policy: Madame Stephanie St. Clair and African American Women's Participation in Harlem's Informal Economy," *Black Women, Gender, and Families* 2, no. 2 (2011): 75–76; Victoria W. Wolcott, "Mediums, Messages, and Lucky Numbers: African-American Female Spiritualists and Numbers Runners in Inter-War Detroit," in *The Geography of Identity*, ed. Patricia Yeager, 273–306 (Ann Arbor: University of Michigan Press, 1996). Wallace Best offers an unparalleled description of policy gambling and spirituality in Bronzeville in his book *Passionately Human, No Less Divine: Religion*

and *Black Culture in Chicago, 1915–1952* (Princeton, NJ: Princeton University Press, 2013). Jamie L. Pietruska helps theorize American's turn to predicting the future in the late nineteenth century in *Looking Forward: Prediction and Uncertainty in Modern America* (Chicago: University of Chicago Press, 2017).

49. L. Harris, "Madame Queen of Policy," 75–76.

50. See Higginbotham, *Righteous Discontent*.

51. Treva B. Lindsey, *Colored No More* (Urbana: University of Illinois Press, 2017), 10.

Chapter 1. *"The Best Job I Ever Had"*

1. S. White et al., *Playing the Numbers*, 20.

2. Ibid.

3. "Playing Policy All over City," *Chicago Daily Tribune*, February 24, 1901, 1.

4. Ibid.

5. "War to a Finish against Policy," *Chicago Daily Tribune*, May 1, 1903, 13.

6. "Forces Arising to Crush Policy," *Chicago Daily Tribune*, May 3, 1903, 10.

7. Matthew Vaz, *Running the Numbers* (Chicago: University of Chicago Press, 2020), 2.

8. S. White et al., *Playing the Numbers*, 34.

9. Ibid.

10. Will Cooley, "Jim Crow Organized Crime: Black Chicago's Underground Economy in the Twentieth Century," in *Building the Black Metropolis: African American Entrepreneurship in Chicago*, ed. Robert E. Weems Jr. and Jason P. Chambers (Chicago: University of Illinois Press, 2017), 152.

11. S. White et al., *Playing the Numbers*, 55.

12. Cooley, "Jim Crow Organized Crime," 152. The "Black Belt" refers to the geographical region where African Americans were allowed to settle, a narrow strip of land adjacent to Lake Michigan.

13. Ibid.

14. Simon Balto, *Occupied Territory*, 132.

15. Thompson, *Kings*, 26.

16. Vaz, "'We Intend to Run It,'" 76.

17. Cooley, "Jim Crow Organized Crime," 153.

18. Vaz, "'We Intend to Run It,'" 74.

19. Drake and Cayton, *Black Metropolis*, 29.

20. Ibid.

21. Gustav G. Carlson, "Number Gambling: A Study of a Culture Complex" (MA thesis, University of Michigan, 1940), 49.

22. Ibid., 51.

23. Ibid., 52.

24. Lewis A. H. Caldwell, "The Policy Game in Chicago" (PhD diss., Northwestern University, 1940), 54.

25. Carlson, "Number Gambling," 51.

26. See Blair, *I've Got to Make My Livin'*; Gross, *Colored Amazons*.

27. "Policy Raid Nets Printer, Three Presses," *Chicago Defender*, December 5, 1953, 21; see also Carlson, "Number Gambling," 51.

28. Caldwell, "Policy Game," 57.

29. Carlson, "Number Gambling," 53.

30. Caldwell, "Policy Game," 57.

31. Ibid.

32. Ibid., 29.

33. "Policy Raid Prisoners Clutter Chicago Courts," *Chicago Defender*, May 3, 1941, 12.

34. Caldwell, "Policy Game," 49.

35. Robert Roy, "Behind the Scenes," *Chicago Defender*, October 31, 1960, A17.

36. "Detectives Hit Southside Policy Collection Station," *Chicago Defender*, December 21, 1967, 3.

37. Caldwell, "Policy Game," 32.

38. "Mrs. G. W. Neighbors," Social Stratification, 1938, St. Clair Drake Papers, box 56, folder 6, Schomburg Center for Research in Black Culture, New York Public Library, New York (hereafter "Drake Papers").

39. Carlson, "Number Gambling," 51–53.

40. Ibid., 50.

41. For an excellent firsthand account of policy gambling in Detroit, see B. Davis, *World According to Fannie Davis*.

42. Carlson, "Number Gambling," 53.

43. Ibid.

44. Blair, *I've Got to Make My Living*, 23.

45. U.S. Bureau of the Census, *Fifteenth Census of the United States, 1930* (Washington, DC: National Archives and Records Administration, 1930), T626, 2,667 rolls; U.S. Bureau of the Census, *Sixteenth Census of the United States*, 1940 (Washington, DC: National Archives and Records Administration, 1940), T627, 4,643 rolls.

46. Caldwell, "Policy Game," 29.

47. Baldwin, *Chicago's New Negroes*; Marcia Chatelain, *South Side Girls: Growing Up in the Great Migration* (Durham, NC: Duke University Press, 2015); Reed, *Black Chicago's First Century*; Christopher Robert Reed, *The Rise of Chicago's Black Metropolis, 1920–1929* (Urbana: University of Illinois Press, 2014); Drake and Cayton, *Black Metropolis*; James Grossman, *Land of Hope: Chicago, Black Southerners, and the Great Migration* (Chicago: University of Chicago Press, 1989).

48. Carlson, "Number Gambling," 50.

49. "Mrs. G. W. Neighbors," Social Stratification, 1938, Drake Papers, box 56, folder 6.

50. "Cops Raid Four Gambling Joints," *Chicago Defender*, January 5, 1967, 4; "Policy Writer Nabbed," *Chicago Defender*, July 17, 1926, A7.

51. Caldwell, "Policy Game," 18.

52. Elizabeth Schlabach and Jose Ignacio, "Map of Policy Station and Worker Distribution in Chicago, 1930–1939." Authors' own unpublished source.

53. Carlson, "Number Gambling," 49.

54. Caldwell, "Policy Game," 27.

55. Carlson, "Number Gambling," 49.

56. B. Davis, *World According to Fannie Davis*, 86.

57. "Policy and Numbers," *Ebony*, 1950, 27.

58. "The Garnet Girls Bridge Club," Interview, 1938, Drake Papers, box 38, folder 10.

59. "Mid-West Horse Show Is Parade of Fashion," *Chicago Defender*, October 5, 1940, 3.

60. "Society," *Jet*, November 8, 1951, 41; "Designers Discover New Markets," *Jet*, April 3, 1952, 47.

61. "Society," *Jet*, November 8, 1951, 41.

62. "$11,140 and a Divorce Ends Roanes' Fight," *Chicago Defender*, December 2, 1939, 8.

63. "Roxborough, Manager of Joe Louis," *Chicago Defender*, May 4, 1940, 1.

64. Russ J. Cowans, "Roxborough, Officials Face Racket Trial," *Chicago Defender*, September 27, 1941, 1; Russ J. Cowans, "Wheel Boss Tells of Fix in Policy Racket," *Chicago Defender*, October 18, 1941, 1.

65. Al Monroe, "Swingin' the News," *Chicago Defender*, November 15, 1941, 21.

66. Ibid.

67. Thompson, *Kings*, 233.

68. "Snag Policy Wheel in Raid at Funeral Home," *Chicago Defender*, December 7, 1964, 10.

69. "Witness Flunks Out at Policy Hearing," *Chicago Defender*, June 20, 1942, 2.

70. Grossman, *Land of Hope*, 3, 48, and 79.

71. "Woman Jails Local Cleaner in Libel Suit," *Chicago Defender*, August 12, 1939, 19.

72. "Policies on Numbers Vary with Numbers of Policies," *Chicago Defender*, February 8, 1941, 3.

73. Ibid.

74. "Lady Racketeers," *Ebony*, 1952, 46.

75. For more on urban policing of Black womanhood, see Blair, *I've Got to Make My Livin'*; Hicks, *Talk with You Like a Woman*; Chatelain, *South Side Girls*.

76. Adam Green, *Selling the Race: Culture, Community, and Black Chicago, 1940–1955* (Chicago: University of Chicago Press, 2007), 9.

77. "Interview with Mrs. Mitchell," Olivet, 1938, Drake Papers, box 57, folder 16.

78. "Mrs. G. W. Neighbors," Olivet, 1938, Drake Papers, box 57, folder 16.

79. Ibid.

80. "Interview with Mrs. Pearl Managree," Member of the Church of the Good Shepherd, May 14, 1937, Drake Papers, box 57, folder 16.

81. Ibid.

82. "Around and About in Chicago," *Chicago Defender*, August 14, 1915, 5; "Indiana News," *Chicago Defender*, August 3, 1939, A6; "Women's Civic League Sponsors Style Revue," *Chicago Defender*, December 7, 1935, 7.

Chapter 2. Chicago's First Policy Queens

1. Reed, *Black Chicago's First Century*.

2. Ibid.

3. Work, "Negro Real Estate Holders of Chicago," 13.

4. Spear, *Black Chicago*, 14.

5. Blair, *I've Got to Make My Livin'*, 87.

6. Reed, *Black Chicago's First Century*, 239.

7. Drake and Cayton, *Black Metropolis*, 45.

8. "Forces Arising to Crush Policy," *Chicago Daily Tribune*, May 3, 1903, 1.

9. "Playing Policy All over City," *Chicago Daily Tribune*, February 24, 1901, 1; "Policy Games Infest Chicago," *Chicago Daily Tribune*, August 23, 1901, 3.

10. "Forces Arising to Crush Policy," *Chicago Daily Tribune*, May 3, 1903, 1.

11. "Girl Praised; Color Pitied," *Chicago Daily Tribune*, July 23, 1907, 7.

12. Ibid.

13. "Final Account, January 2, 1912," in Inventory in the Matter of the Estate of John V. Johnson, deceased, Probate Court of Cook County, Estate file of John V. Johnson, Archives of the Clerk of the Circuit Court of Cook County, Daley Center, Chicago, quoted in Don Hayner, *Binga: The Rise and Fall of Chicago's First Black Banker* (Evanston, IL: Northwestern University Press, 2020), 79.

14. "Attacks His Mother's Will," *Chicago Defender*, February 4, 1908, J3; "Find No 'Mushmouth' Will," *Chicago Defender*, September 15, 1907, A3. The February 1908 headline denotes the seriousness of the situation as it reads "Attacks His Mother's Will." Elijah sought to expose the "fraudulent" means his sisters used to obtain the buildings and properties Johnson left to his mother (although he left no will). Johnson's estate was valued at $54,400 ($50,000 in real estate and $4,400 in personal property). This amounts to $1.3 million in 2016.

15. Elijah Johnson was the father of Fenton Johnson, a famous poet of the mid-twentieth century Chicago Black Renaissance.

16. *Slaughter v. Johnson*, 181 Illinois Appellate Court 693, 694 (1st District, 1913).

17. Hayner, *Binga*, 79.

18. Ibid.

19. See Richard A. Courage and Christopher Robert Reed, eds., *The Roots of the Chicago Black Renaissance: New Negro Writers, Artists, and Intellectuals 1893–1930* (Urbana: University of Illinois Press, 2020), Grossman, *Land of Hope*; Baldwin, *Chicago's New Negroes*; Chatelain, *South Side Girls*; Reed, *Black Chicago's First Century*; Reed, *Rise of Chicago's Black Metropolis*; Cayton and Drake, *Black Metropolis*; Wolcott, *Remaking Respectability*; L. Harris, *Sex Workers, Psychics, and Numbers Runners*.

20. Reed, *Black Chicago's First Century*, 231.

21. Christopher Robert Reed, "The Rise of Black Chicago's Culturati," in Courage and Reed, *Roots of the Chicago Black Renaissance*, 34n5.

22. Sallie L. Powell, "Elizabeth B. Slaughter," in *The Kentucky African American Encyclopedia*, ed. Gerald L. Smith, Karen Cotton McDaniel, and John A. Hardin (Lexington: University of Kentucky Press, 2015), 458.

23. Ibid., 923.

24. Ibid., 926.

25. "Womanhood's True Type," *Colored American*, June 3, 1899, 5.

26. Ibid.

27. Ibid.

28. Ibid.

29. "The Green-Lilly Millinery Co.," *Chicago Defender*, May 17, 1913, 2.

30. "Chips," *Broad Ax*, November 26, 1904.

31. Ibid.

32. G. F. Richings, *Evidences of Progress among Colored People*, 11th ed. (Philadelphia: Ferguson, 1902), 506.

33. Ibid., 507.

34. Ibid., 508.

35. Tiffany Gill, *Beauty Shop Politics: African American Women's Activism in the Beauty Industry* (Urbana: University of Illinois Press, 2010), 2.

36. Tanisha Ford, *Liberated Threads: Black Women, Style, and the Global Politics of Soul* (Chapel Hill: University of North Carolina Press, 2015). See also Gill, *Beauty Shop Politics*.

37. "Company 'B' Is the Crack Company of the Eighth Regiment," *Broad Ax*, July 22, 1905.

38. "Chips," *Broad Ax*, July, 15, 1905.

39. Powell, "Elizabeth B. Slaughter," 458.

40. Ibid.

41. "Chips," *Broad Ax*, February 20, 1904.

42. "Chips," *Broad Ax*, June 8, 1907.

43. "Nervous Breakdown," "Chips," *Broad Ax*, May 23, 1908.

44. "Miss Elizabeth B. Slaughter . . . Brought Suit in the Circuit Court of Cook County against Miss Eudora Johnson," *Broad Ax*, September 12, 1908.

45. *Slaughter v. Johnson*, 695.

46. Ibid.

47. Deborah Gray White, *Ar'n't I a Woman? Female Slaves in the Plantation South* (New York: W. W. Norton, 1999).

48. "Seen Leaving for Philadelphia," "Chips," *Broad Ax*, 1908.

49. Morris, like Slaughter, was a Kentucky native who had moved around before making Chicago his permanent residence. Some sources cite him hailing from Cincinnati or Louisville before settling in Chicago. Morris made his historical mark as the fifth African American admitted to the Illinois bar in 1879 and by serving

in the Illinois State Legislature from 1890 to 1892. See Frank Lincoln Mather, ed., *Who's Who of the Colored Race: A General Biographical Dictionary of Men and Women of African Descent*, vol. 1 (Chicago: State Historical Society of Wisconsin, 1915), 199; "Forces Arising to Crush Policy," *Chicago Daily Tribune*, May 3, 1903, 1.

50. "Guest of Morris," "Chips," *Broad Ax*, October 7, 1911; "Elizabeth B. Slaughter Guests from Lexington, Kentucky," "Chips," *Broad Ax*, August 26, 1911.

51. "The Green-Lilly Millinery Company," *Broad Ax*, April 8, April 11, and April 15, 1911.

52. "The Successful Close of the State Street Fair and Carnival," *Broad Ax*, August 31, 1912.

53. *Slaughter v. Johnson*, 699.

54. Ibid.

55. Ibid., 698.

56. Ibid.

57. Ibid.

58. *Stenographic Verbatim Report*, April 1, 1936, 6, quoted in Hayner, *Binga*, 192.

59. Powell, "Elizabeth B. Slaughter," 458.

60. "The Slaughter-Douglas Nuptial," *Broad Ax*, December 30, 1916.

61. Hayner, *Binga*, 83.

62. "The Slaughter-Douglas Nuptial," *Broad Ax*, December 30, 1916.

63. Ibid.

64. Ibid.

65. Ibid.

66. Powell, "Elizabeth B. Slaughter," 458.

67. Margaret Garb, *Freedom's Ballot: African American Political Struggles in Chicago from Abolition to the Great Migration* (Chicago: University of Chicago Press, 2014), 115.

68. Inez V. Cantey, "Jesse Binga," *Crisis* 34 (December 1927), 329.

69. Carl R. Osthaus, "The Rise and Fall of Jesse Binga, Black Financier," *Journal of Negro History* 58, no. 1 (1973): 42.

70. Christopher Robert Reed, "Early Black Chicago Entrepreneurial and Business Activities from the Frontier Era to the Great Migration: The Nexus of Circumstance and Initiative," in Weems and Chambers, *Building the Black Metropolis*, 38.

71. *Broad Ax*, October 23, 1921, quoted in Osthaus, "Rise and Fall of Jesse Binga," 49.

72. Reed, "Early Black Chicago Entrepreneurial and Business Activities."

73. "Mr. Jesse Binga's Box Party," *Broad Ax*, January 1, 1910.

74. Ibid.

75. "Chips," *Broad Ax*, October 14, 1911.

76. The Choral Study Club was founded in 1878 by Mrs. Francis A. Powell, leading soprano in the Olivet Baptist Church choir. See St. Clair Drake, *Churches and*

Voluntary Associations in the Chicago Negro Community (Chicago: Works Progress Administration, District 3, 1940), 65.

77. "The Choral Study Club of Chicago in its 34th Concert," *Broad Ax*, December 2, 1911.

78. A. L. Foster, "Twenty Years of Inter-Racial Goodwill through Social Service," in *Chicago Urban Leagues: Two Decades of Service, 1916–1936* (Chicago: Urban League, 1936), 346, M. H. Bickman Papers, Special Collections, University of Illinois at Chicago.

79. Gerri Major and Doris E. Saunders, *Gerri Major's Black Society* (Chicago: Johnson Publishing, 1976), 305, quoted in Hayner, *Binga*, 81.

80. Hayner, *Binga*, 82.

81. Garb, *Freedom's Ballot*, 115.

82. "The Johnson Binga Wedding," *Broad Ax*, February 17, 1912.

83. The couple's marriage announcements ran on February 17 and 24, 1912, in *Broad Ax* and on February 17, 1912, in the *Chicago Defender*, where the newspaper lauded the Johnsons as one of Chicago's "oldest families."

84. Ibid.

85. "The Johnson-Binga Wedding the Most Elaborate and Fashionable," *Broad Ax*, February 24, 1912.

86. Major and Saunders, 304, quoted in Hayner, *Binga*, 85.

87. Hayner, *Binga*, 86.

88. Osthaus, "Rise and Fall of Jesse Binga," 46.

89. Reed, "Early Black Chicago Entrepreneurial and Business Activities," 37.

90. Osthaus, "Rise and Fall of Jesse Binga," 47. For more recent scholarship on Black Catholics in Chicago, see Matthew Cressler, *Authentically Black and Truly Catholic: The Rise of Black Catholicism in the Great Migration* (New York: New York University Press, 2017).

91. Osthaus, "Rise and Fall of Jesse Binga," 47.

92. Ibid.

93. This is just one example of how policy gambling funded the artistic and literary output of the Chicago Black Renaissance. For further exploration, see Elizabeth Schroeder Schlabach, *Along the Streets of Bronzeville: Black Chicago's Literary Landscapes* (Urbana: University of Illinois Press, 2013), specifically chapter 3 on policy gambling and the Chicago Black Renaissance, along with the growing canon of literature on the Chicago Black Renaissance by Darlene Clark Hine, Christopher Robert Reed, Anne M. Knupher, and Robert Bone and Richard Courage.

94. Osthaus, "Rise and Fall of Jesse Binga," 47.

95. "Christmas Party," *Chicago Defender*, January 3, 1920, quoted in Ostahus, "Rise and Fall of Jesse Binga," 47.

96. Ibid.

97. "With the Clubs," *Chicago Defender*, January 10, 1925, A3.

98. "The Garnet Girls Bridge Club, 1938," The Garnet Girls Bridge Club, Drake Papers, box 38, folder 10.

99. "Interview (77-3/9/38)," The Garnet Girls Bridge Club, 1938, Drake Papers, box 38, folder 10.

100. Ibid.

101. Wanda A. Hendricks, *Gender, Race, and Politics in the Midwest: Black Club Women in Illinois* (Bloomington: Indiana University Press, 1998); Anne Meis Knupher, *Toward a Tenderer Humanity and a Nobler Womanhood: African-American Women's Clubs in Turn-of-the-Century Chicago* (New York: New York University Press, 1996), 79.

102. Drake, *Churches and Voluntary Associations*, 146.

103. Mary Jo Deegan, "Williams & Black Feminist Pragmatism," in Courage and Reed, *Roots of the Chicago Black Renaissance*, 66.

104. Frederic H. H. Robb, ed., *1927 Intercollegian Wonder Book, or, The Negro in Chicago, 1779–1927* (Chicago: Washington Intercollegiate Club of Chicago, 1927), 53.

105. Osthaus, "Rise and Fall of Jesse Binga," 49. According to the Chicago Commission on Race Relations, Binga's home and offices were targeted several times in 1919. On November 12, 1919, an automobile "rolled by his [Binga's] realty office and a bomb was tossed from it," leaving his office in ruins. Weeks later a bomb "tore up the front porch of Binga's home." The police explained "that the explosion had been caused by 'racial feeling,' white men having said that 'Binga rented too many flats to Negroes in high-class residence districts.'" See Chicago Commission on Race Relations, *The Negro in Chicago* (Chicago: University of Chicago Press, 1922), 125.

106. Robert Howard, "The Rise and Fall of Jesse Binga: A Black Chicago Financial Wizard," in Weems and Chambers, *Building the Black Metropolis*, 66.

107. Dempsey Travis, *An Autobiography of Black Chicago* (Chicago: Bolden, 1981), 50.

108. Petition dated July 30, 1931, in "In the Matter of Jesse Binga, Bankrupt," 1, quoted in Hayner, *Binga*, 192.

109. Albert Harris, *The Negro as Capitalist* (Philadelphia: American Academy of Political and Social Sciences, 1936), 160, quoted in Osthaus, "Rise and Fall of Jesse Binga," 56.

110. *Stenographic Verbatim Report*, April 1, 1936, 6, quoted in Hayner, *Binga*, 192.

111. Howard, "Rise and Fall of Jesse Binga," 73.

112. Ibid.

113. Ibid.

114. "Binga Downfall Ends Spectacular Career," *Chicago Defender*, June 10, 1933, 10.

115. Ibid.

116. Osthaus, "Rise and Fall of Jesse Binga," 60.

117. Howard, "Rise and Fall of Jesse Binga," 75.

118. Ibid.

119. Travis, *Autobiography of Black Chicago*, 50–51.

120. Ibid.

121. Ibid.

122. "Mrs. Eliza Chilton Johnson," Church Federation Interviews, 1938, Drake Papers, box 57, folder 11.

123. See Baldwin, *Chicago's New Negroes*; Schlabach, *Along the Streets of Bronzeville*; N. Thompson, *Kings*; Wolcott, *Remaking Respectability*.

Chapter 3. Chicago's Most Famous Policy Queen

1. Rhonda Y. Williams, *The Politics of Public Housing: Black Women's Struggles against Urban Inequality* (New York: Oxford University Press, 2004), 40.

2. Year: 1880; Census Place: Beat 4, Washington, Mississippi; Roll: 668; Family History Film: 1254668; Page: 199B; Enumeration District: 094; Image: 0256, via ancestry.com. Accessed May 13, 2019.

3. Wilkerson, *Warmth of Other Suns*, 240.

4. *Census of the United States*, 1860, Tennessee State Marriages, National Archives and Records Administration, Washington, DC, 1860. M653, 1,438 rolls; digital image, via www.ancestry.com. Accessed May 13, 2019.

5. Willis E. Mollison, *The Leading Afro-Americans of Vicksburg: Their Enterprises, Churches, Schools, Lodges, and Societies* (Vicksburg, MS: Biographia Publishing, 1908), 10.

6. Jones was born on February 21, 1872, in Hinds County, Mississippi. His father, Rev. George P. Jones, was pastor at King Solomon M.B. Church. According to Patrick H. Thompson, Reverend G. P. Jones's "eminent qualities and distinguished abilities not only endear him to every Negro of Vicksburg, but our entire state." After his wife, Louvenia (or Laverna), passed when Edward P. was six years old, Rev. G. P. Jones's goal in life was to educate his son. See Patrick H. Thompson, *The History of Negro Baptists in Mississippi* (Jackson, MS: R. W. Baily Printing Co., 1898), 615–16. See also Mather, *Who's Who of the Colored Race*, 160; Mollison, *Leading Afro-Americans of Vicksburg*, 9.

7. P. Thompson, *History of Negro Baptists*, 616.

8. Garb, *Freedom's Ballot*, 57.

9. Milton Hinton and David G. Berger, *Playing the Changes: Milt Hinton's Life in Stories and Photographs* (Nashville, TN: Vanderbilt University Press, 2008), 3.

10. Mollison, *Leading Afro-Americans of Vicksburg*, 10.

11. "Preacher Acts Like Wildman at Meeting," *Chicago Defender*, October 3, 1914, 3.

12. Hinton and Berger, *Playing the Changes*, 9.

13. Ibid., 8.

14. Ibid., 9.

15. Wilkerson, *Warmth of Other Suns*, 8.

16. Ibid., 7.

17. Timuel D. Black Jr., "Interview with Representative Corneal Davis," in *Bridges of Memory: Chicago's First Wave of Black Migration* (Evanston, IL: Northwestern University Press, 2003), 53.

18. Hinton and Berger, *Playing the Changes*, 9.

19. Ibid.

20. Ibid., 10.

21. Ibid., 11.

22. "Baptists Meet at Kansas City," *Indianapolis Recorder*, September 23, 1916, 1.

23. "Baptists Decide on Course," *Chicago Defender*, February 26, 1916, 1.

24. "Guard Pastor in Pulpit," *Chicago Defender*, January 20, 1923, 1.

25. Ibid.

26. Ibid.

27. "Rev. E. P. Jones, Baptist Leader, Dies Suddenly," *Chicago Defender*, November 29, 1924, 1.

28. Nathan B. Thompson, *Kings: The True Story of Chicago's Policy Kings and Numbers Racketeers, An Informal History* (Chicago: Bronzeville Press, 2006), 42.

29. "Rev. E. P. Jones, Baptist Leader, Dies Suddenly," *Chicago Defender*, November 29, 1924, 1.

30. W. D. Amis, "Numbers and Policy Racket: Jones Brothers," Kefauver Senate Committee to Investigate Organized Crime in Interstate Commerce, Memorandum, folder "Policy Gambling–General," National Archives, Washington, DC.

31. U.S. Bureau of the Census, Fourteenth Census of the United States, 1920; Census Place: Evanston Ward 5, Cook, Illinois; Roll: T625_358; Page: 2A-2B; Enumeration District: 80; Image: 265 & 266; digital image, via ancestry.com. Accessed July 8, 2017; "Edward Jones Beats Auto Sellers in Higher Court," *Chicago Defender*, May 26, 1923, 1.

32. U.S. Bureau of the Census, *Fifteenth Census of the United States*, 1930, National Archives and Records Administration, Washington, DC.

33. N. Thompson, *Policy Kings*, 43.

34. "Testimony of Edward P. Jones," December 19, 1950, Kefauver Senate Committee to Investigate Organized Crime in Interstate Commerce, box 183, "Hearings: Public," folder part 5 Illinois, 1165, National Archives, Washington, DC. Rudolph Halley was the chief counsel for the committee.

35. "The Jones Brothers Financial Statements," December 31, 1942, Kefauver Senate Committee to Investigate Organized Crime in Interstate Commerce, box 183, Name Files, folder "Jones, George, P. and Edward P., Mexico City, Mexico," National Archives, Washington, DC.

36. Maureen Kallick et al., "A Survey of American Gambling Attitudes and Behavior," appendix 2, in Commission on the Review of the National Policy toward Gambling, *Gambling in America* (Washington, DC: Government Printing Office, 1976), 121.

37. Dempsey Travis, *An Autobiography of Black Chicago* (Chicago: Bolden, 1981), 48.

38. Ibid.

39. "Business in Bronzeville," *Time*, April 18, 1938, 70, quoted in Weems and Chambers, *Building the Black Metropolis*, 18.

40. Weems and Chambers, *Building the Black Metropolis*, 18.

41. "Business in Bronzeville," *Time*, April 18, 1938, 72, quoted in Weems and Chambers, *Building the Black Metropolis*, 18.

42. Weems and Chambers, *Building the Black Metropolis*, 16.

43. Ibid., 17.

44. Otis Dudley Duncan and Beverly Duncan, *The Negro Population of Chicago: A Study of Residential Succession* (Chicago: University of Chicago Press, 1957), 96, quoted in Lionel Kimble, *A New Deal for Bronzeville: Housing, Employment, and Civil Rights in Black Chicago, 1935–1955* (Carbondale: Southern Illinois University Press, 2015), 15.

45. Illinois General Assembly Oral History Program, "Corneal A. Davis Memoir, Volume I" (Springfield, IL: Legislative Studies Center of Sangamon State University, 1984), 60–61.

46. Williams, *Politics of Public Housing*, 27.

47. "Interview with Mrs. Henry Mae Mitchell," by E. R. Saunders, May 25, 1938, Drake Papers, box 57, folder 16.

48. Keeanga-Yamahtta Taylor, *From #BlackLivesMatter to Black Liberation* (New York: Basic Books, 2017), 6, 24.

49. A. L. Foster, "Twenty Years of Interracial Goodwill through Social Services," quoted in Kimble, *New Deal for Bronzeville*, 34.

50. Timuel D. Black Jr., "Interview with Thomas Ellis and Edith Ellis," in *Bridges of Memory: Chicago's First Generation of Black Migration—An Oral History* (Evanston, IL: Northwestern University Press, 2004), 26–27.

51. Eugene K. Jones, "The Negro Working Population and National Recovery: A Special Memorandum Submitted to Franklin Delano Roosevelt, President of the United States by the National Urban League for Social Service among Negroes, January 4, 1937," 5–6, National Urban League Papers, box 5, folder 1, National Archives, Washington, DC. On the disproportionate economic effect of African American workers during the Great Depression, see Richard B. Sherman, *The Negro and the City* (New York: Prentice Hall, 1970), 45–49; William Sundstrom, "Last Hired, First Fired? Unemployment and Urban Black Workers during the Great Depression," *Journal of Economic History* 52, no. 1 (1992): 415–29; Jacqueline Jones, *Labor of Love, Labor of Sorrow: Black Women, Work, and the Family from Slavery to the Present* (New York: Basic Books, 2009), 164–67.

52. Arvarh E. Strickland, *History of the Chicago Urban League* (Columbia: University of Missouri Press, 1966), 104.

53. Trotter, *Workers on Arrival*, 91.

54. Ibid., 92.

55. "Report on Interview with Mrs. Odessa Evans, Housewife," Social Stratification, Wilhelmina Warfield, February 17, 1938, Drake Papers, box 56, folder 6.

56. Trotter, *Workers on Arrival*, 92.

57. Christopher Robert Reed, *The Depression Comes to the South Side: Protest and Politics in the Black Metropolis, 1930–1933* (Bloomington: Indiana University Press, 2005), 16–17.

58. "Little Lucy" Collier, "Interview with Wallace D. Best, December 2, 1996," in Best, *Passionately Human, No Less Divine*, 164–65.

59. Reed, *Depression Comes to the South Side*, 17.

60. "Bulletin: Relief Illegal Occupation," December 18, 1933, quoted in Caldwell, "Policy Game in Chicago," 90; Caldwell, "Personal Interview with Mrs. Paige," July 8, 1937, quoted in Caldwell, "Policy Game in Chicago," 91.

61. Caldwell, "Policy Game in Chicago," 91.

62. Ibid., 90.

63. T. Black, "Interview with L. A. H. Caldwell," in *Bridges of Memory: Chicago's First Generation*, 260.

64. "So Is the Mayor," *Chicago Defender*, August 22, 1931, 2.

65. N. Thompson, *Kings*, 56.

66. "So Is the Mayor," *Chicago Defender*, August 22, 1931, 2.

67. Ibid.

68. Weems and Chambers, *Building the Black Metropolis*, 17.

69. Ibid. Like the Associated Numbers Bankers in Detroit, Chicago kings and queens attempted to mobilize against white encroachment. For more on bankers associations and syndicates, see Baldwin, *Chicago's New Negroes*; N. Thompson, *Kings*; Chris M. Smith, *Syndicate Women: Gender and Networks in Chicago Organized Crime* (Oakland: University of California Press, 2019).

70. N. Thompson, *Kings*, 45.

71. "Jones Bros. Get $435,111 Back Taxes," *Chicago Defender*, January 31, 1942, 1.

72. Ibid.

73. Chuck Davis, "Jail 'Richest' Policy Kings," *Chicago Defender*, December 30, 1950, 1.

74. "Testimony of Theodore Roe," December 18, 1950, Kefauver Senate Committee to Investigate Organized Crime in Interstate Commerce, box 183, "Hearings: Public," folder part 5 Illinois, 1137, National Archives, Washington, DC; Estes Kefauver, *The Kefauver Committee Report on Organized Crime* (New York: Didier, 1951), 9; Chuck Davis, "Jail 'Richest' Policy Kings," *Chicago Defender*, December 30, 1950, 1.

75. Kefauver, *Kefauver Committee Report*, 10.

76. Chuck Davis, "Jail 'Richest' Policy Kings," *Chicago Defender*, December 30, 1950, 1.

77. Gerald Horne informs readers that Edward and George were among the richest men in Mexico, a fact that Claude Barnett saw as an enticement for more African Americans to settle there. Horne does not point out that Harriett must

have been among the richest African American women who resided there. See Gerald Horne, *The Rise and Fall of the Associated Negro Press: Claude Barnett's Pan-African News and the Jim Crow Paradox* (Urbana: University of Illinois Press, 2017), 154.

78. "The Ed Jones Story: Rise and Fall of a Policy King, Part III," *Chicago Defender*, January 7, 1965, 1.

79. "Policy King Flee[s] Gangland Guns," *Chicago Defender*, October 19, 1946, 2.

80. "Jones Bros. Stores Near Completion," *Chicago Defender*, May 1, 1937, 3.

81. James J. Gentry, "Bill Robinson Opens Jones Bros' Store," *Chicago Defender*, July 31, 1937, 10.

82. Vera B. Slaughter, "Highlights of Opening of Ben Franklin Store," *Chicago Defender*, July 31, 1937, 3.

83. Ibid.

84. Ibid.

85. Robert S. Abbott, "An Editorial: The Three Musketeers," *Chicago Defender*, July 31, 1937, 4.

86. "New Business Project Near Completion," *Chicago Defender*, February 13, 1937, 10.

87. Darlene Clark Hine, "Rape and the Inner Lives of Black Women in the Middle West," *Signs: Common Grounds and Crossroads: Race, Ethnicity, and Class in Women's Lives* 14, no. 4 (1989): 917.

88. "Founding the Club," The Garnet Girls Bridge Club, 1938, Drake Papers, box 38, folder 10.

89. "Social Participation," The Garnet Girls Bridge Club, 1938, Drake Papers, box 38, folder 10.

90. "Interview (77-3/9/38)," The Garnet Girls Bridge Club, 1938, Drake Papers, box 38, folder 10.

91. "The Garnet Girls Bridge Club," 1938, Drake Papers, box 38, folder 10.

92. James C. Davis, *Commerce in Color: Race, Consumer Culture, and American Literature, 1893–1933* (Ann Arbor: University of Michigan Press, 2007), 39.

93. Drake and Cayton, *Black Metropolis*, 547.

94. Davis, *Commerce in Color*, 40.

95. Ibid., 41.

96. Drake and Cayton, *Black Metropolis*, 548.

97. "Class Position," The Garnet Girls Bridge Club, 1938, Drake Papers, box 38, folder 10.

98. "Extra-Club Interests," The Garnet Girls Bridge Club, 1938, Drake Papers, box 38, folder 10.

99. Ibid.

100. "Doing Something Worthwhile," The Garnet Girls Bridge Club, 1938, Drake Papers, box 38, folder 10.

101. "Interview (77-2/23/38)," The Garnet Girls Bridge Club, 1938, Drake Papers, box 38, folder 10.

102. "Spectacular Style Show Packs Glamorous Wallop," *Chicago Defender*, January 29, 1938, 13.

103. "Fashion's Interesting Creations," *Chicago Defender*, April 26, 1941, 18.

104. "Second Lawn Fete Proves Successful," *Chicago Defender*, August 12, 1933, 6.

105. "Gives Check to Provident Hospital," *Chicago Defender*, February 8, 1947, 11.

106. "Edward Peter Jones, Jr. Death Certificate," Illinois Department of Public Health, Division of Vital Records, Springfield, Illinois.

107. "Illinois, Cook County Birth Certificates, 1878–1922." Index. FamilySearch, Salt Lake City, Utah, 2009; Cook County Birth Certificates, 1878–1922, Illinois Department of Public Health, Division of Vital Records, Springfield, Illinois.

108. "Edward Jones, Ex 'Policy King,' Is Buried," *Jet*, December 17, 1964, 26–27.

109. "Countess Honored at Reception by Editor and Mrs. Abbott," *Chicago Defender*, October 26, 1935, 6.

110. "Policy King Dies in Car Crash," *Chicago Defender*, July 29, 1944, 2.

111. "George Jones and Wife to Visit Orient," *Chicago Defender*, November 28, 1936, 2.

112. "Testimony of Edward P. Jones," December 19, 1950, Kefauver Senate Committee to Investigate Organized Crime in Interstate Commerce, box 183, "Hearings: Public," folder part 5 Illinois, 1174, National Archives, Washington, DC.

113. Passenger and Crew Lists of Vessels Arriving at New York, New York, 1897–1957, Year: 1939; Arrival: New York, New York; Microfilm Serial: T715, 1897–1957; Microfilm Roll: Roll 6273; Line: 21; Page Number: 15. National Archives Microfilm Publication, digital image, via ancestry.com. Accessed July 10, 2017.

114. "The Ed Jones Story: Rise and Fall of a Policy King: Part III," *Chicago Defender*, January 7, 1965, 1.

115. "Edward Jones, Ex 'Policy King,' Is Buried," *Jet*, December 17, 1964, 26–27.

116. "Edward J. Jones, 66, Former Policy Wheel Kingpin, Dies," *Chicago Defender*, November 30, 1964, 3.

117. W. D. Amis, "Theodore Roe—Idaho-Maine Club, Jones Brothers—Policy Operators," October 25, 1950, Kefauver Senate Committee to Investigate Organized Crime in Interstate Commerce, Memorandum, folder "Policy Gambling-General," National Archives, Washington, DC.

118. T. Black, "Interview with Commander Milton Deas, Jr.," in *Bridges of Memory: Chicago's First Generation*, 417.

119. W. D. Amis, "Theodore Roe—Idaho-Maine Club, Jones Brothers—Policy Operators," October 25, 1950, Kefauver Senate Committee to Investigate Organized Crime in Interstate Commerce, Memorandum, folder "Policy Gambling-General," National Archives, Washington, DC.

120. "Policy King Flees Gangland's Guns," *Chicago Defender*, October 19, 1946, 2.

121. Ibid. The play on the Maine-Idaho-Ohio wheel, the largest wheel operating in Chicago at the time of the committee's report, grossed about $6,000,000 per

year; the net income in 1949 was close to $700,000, and in 1948 it came to over $997,000. For 1949 the gross was about $1 million and the gross for 1948 was $1.3 million. See Kefauver, *Kefauver Committee Report*, 38–39.

122. W. D. Amis, "Theodore Roe—Idaho-Maine Club, Jones Brothers—Policy Operators," October 25, 1950, Kefauver Senate Committee to Investigate Organized Crime in Interstate Commerce, Memorandum, folder "Policy Gambling–General," National Archives, Washington, DC; Al Monroe, "Swinging in the News," *Chicago Defender*, March 27, 1948, 8; "Testimony of Edward Jones," December 19, 1950, Kefauver Senate Committee to Investigate Organized Crime in Interstate Commerce, box 183, "Hearings: Public," folder part 5 Illinois, 1174, National Archives, Washington, DC.

123. "Wives of Negro Millionaires," *Jet*, January 17, 1952, 61.

124. Ibid.

125. N. Thompson, *Kings*, 346.

126. Al Monroe, "So They Say," *Chicago Defender*, January 23, 1962, 16.

127. T. Black, "Interview with LeRoy Martin," in *Bridges of Memory: Chicago's First Generation*, 465.

128. "Jones Brothers' Mother Dies in Mexico City," *Jet*, December 23, 1971, 7.

Chapter 4. Dream Books, Fortune-Tellers, and Mediumship

1. S. White et al., *Playing the Numbers*, 20.

2. Ibid., 12.

3. Drake and Cayton, *Black Metropolis*, 474.

4. Ibid.

5. Following the lead of historian LaShawn Harris, I use the terms "medium" and "mediumship" to describe Black women who worked as mediums, supernaturalists, spiritualists, clairvoyants, or fortune-tellers. See LaShawn Harris, "Dream Books, Crystal Balls, and 'Lucky Numbers': African American Female Mediums in Harlem, 1900–1930s," *Afro-Americans in New York Life and History* 35 (2011): 101n11.

6. B. Davis, *World According to Fannie Davis*, 136.

7. N. Thompson, *Kings*, 102, 260.

8. Ibid., 106.

9. Ibid., 155.

10. Ibid.

11. Ibid., 233.

12. Ibid., 293.

13. Ibid., 43.

14. Ibid., 200.

15. Pietruska, *Looking Forward*, 200.

16. Jeremy Patrick, *Faith or Fraud: Fortune-Telling, Spirituality, and the Law* (Vancouver: University of British Columbia Press, 2020), 99.

17. Ibid., 89.

18. Pietruska, *Looking Forward*, 201.

19. Jno. R. McCabe, City Clerk, *All Amendments to the Revised Municipal Code of Chicago of 1905 (passed March 20, 1905): And All New General Ordinances and Ordinances Creating Prohibition and Local Option Districts Passed . . . from March 20, 1905 to January 1, 1909. Supplement number III*, Catalog Hathi Trust, Hathitrust.org.

20. Ibid., 282.

21. The present-day code specifically bans "astrology, card reading, palm reading or fortune-telling in any form," and licenses cannot be obtained for these as a "home occupation." Chicago Municipal Code, 4-6-270 "Home Occupations," Chicago Decoded, https://chicagocode.org/4-6-270. Accessed December 12, 2017.

22. *Chicago v. Payne*, 160 Ill App 641 (1911), quoted in Patrick, *Faith or Fraud*, 93.

23. Patrick, *Faith or Fraud*, 92, 94.

24. See Patrick, *Faith or Fraud*; Pietruska, *Looking Forward*; Christine Corocos, "Seeing It Coming since 1945," *Thomas Jefferson Law Review* 37, no. 1 (2014): 53–63.

25. *Chicago v. Payne*, 160 Ill App 641 (1911), quoted in Patrick, *Faith or Fraud*, 93.

26. *Chicago v. Westergren*, 173 Ill App 562 (1912), quoted in Patrick, *Faith or Fraud*, 95.

27. Patrick, *Faith or Fraud*, 100.

28. Ibid.

29. Corocos, "Seeing It Coming," 42.

30. Patrick, *Faith or Fraud*, 92.

31. Ibid.

32. Ibid., 91.

33. Pietruska, *Looking Forward*, 202.

34. Ibid., 202–203.

35. L. Harris, "Dream Books," 75. Harris recommends John W. Blassingame, *The Slave Community: Plantation Life in the Antebellum South* (New York: Oxford University, 1972), 109–110; B. A. Botkin, *Lay My Burden Down: A Folk History of Slavery* (Chicago: University of Chicago Press, 1945); Savannah Unit Georgia Writers' Project, Works Projects Administration, *Drums and Shadows: Survival Studies among the Georgia Coastal Negroes* (Athens: University of Georgia Press, 1940).

36. Yvonne P. Chireau, *Black Magic: Religion and the African American Conjuring Tradition* (Berkeley: University of California Press, 2003), 139.

37. Best, *Passionately Human*, 2.

38. Ibid., 3.

39. U.S. Bureau of the Census, *Thirteenth Census of the United States*, 1910; U.S. Bureau of the Census, *Fourteenth Census of the United States*, 1920; U.S. Bureau of the Census, *Fifteenth Census of the United States*, 1930; U.S. Bureau of the Census, *Sixteenth Census of the United States*, 1940, all in National Archives and Records Administration, Washington, DC.

40. Pietruska, *Looking Forward*, 204.

41. Drake and Cayton, *Black Metropolis*, 476, 477.

42. Ibid., 139–40.

43. "Aunt Sally's Spiritual Dream Book," Luckymojo.com. http://www.lucky mojo.com/auntsallys.html. Accessed September 30, 2014.

44. Drake and Cayton, *Black Metropolis*, 476.

45. Ibid.

46. Ibid.

47. Pietruska, *Looking Forward*, 205.

48. Drake and Cayton, *Black Metropolis*, 477.

49. Ibid.

50. Advertisement, *Chicago Defender*, December 10, 1910, 5, quoted in Carolyn Marrow Long, *Spiritual Merchants: Religion, Magic, and Commerce* (Nashville: University of Tennessee Press, 2001), 130.

51. *Chicago Defender*, March 22, 1919, 3, quoted in Long, *Spiritual Merchants*, 130.

52. *Chicago Defender*, June 8, 1935, 3, quoted in Long, *Spiritual Merchants*, 131.

53. Ibid.

54. Drake and Cayton, *Black Metropolis*, 476, 477.

55. Chireau, *Black Magic*, 141.

56. Ibid., 141–42.

57. Ibid., 142.

58. Tammy Stone-Gordon, "'Fifty-Cent Sybils': Occult Workers and the Symbolic Marketplace in the Urban U.S., 1850–1930" (PhD diss., Michigan State University, 1998), 124, 141.

59. Chireau, *Black Magic*, 142.

60. L. Harris, "Dream Books," 86.

61. George M. McCall, "Symbiosis: The Case of Hoodoo and the Numbers Racket," in *Mother Wit from the Laughing Barrel: Readings in the Interpretation of Afro-American Folklore*, ed. Alan Dundes (Jackson: University Press of Mississippi, 1990), 421–22.

62. "Madame Harper," *Chicago Defender*, April 9, 1910, 4.

63. S. White et al., *Playing the Numbers*, 96.

64. Pietruska, *Looking Forward*, 206.

65. Henry C. Bolton, "Fortune-Telling in America To-Day: A Study in Advertisements," *Journal of American Folklore* 8, no. 31 (1895): 300, quoted in Pietruska, *Looking Forward*, 207.

66. Pietruska, *Looking Forward*, 214.

67. Drake, *Churches and Voluntary Associations*, 149.

68. Ibid.

69. Ibid., 165.

70. Ibid.

71. Best, *Passionately Human*, 2.

72. Ibid.

73. Ibid.

74. Drake, *Churches and Voluntary Associations*, 174.

75. U.S. Bureau of the Census, *Thirteenth Census of the United States*, 1910; U.S. Bureau of the Census, *Fourteenth Census of the United States*, 1920; U.S. Bureau of the Census, *Fifteenth Census of the United States*, 1930; U.S. Bureau of the Census, *Sixteenth Census of the United States*, 1940, all in National Archives and Records Administration, Washington, DC.

76. Higginbotham, *Righteous Discontent*, 9.

77. Drake and Cayton, *Black Metropolis*, 476.

78. Drake, *Churches and Voluntary Associations*, 109.

79. Drake and Cayton, *Black Metropolis*, 476.

80. Ibid. The authors qualify this when they conclude that this individual was an "atypical Spiritualist preacher."

81. L. Harris, "Dream Books," 85.

82. Ibid., 86.

83. Ibid.

84. Chireau, *Black Magic*, 143.

85. Drake and Cayton, *Black Metropolis*, 476.

86. Ibid.

87. Anthony Shafton, *Dream Singers: The African American Way with Dreams* (New York: Wiley and Sons, 2002), 68.

88. Carlson, "Number Gambling," 107.

89. Ibid.

90. Wolcott, "Mediums, Messages," 274.

91. Ibid.

92. Henry A. Bullock, "The Urbanization of the Negro Church in Detroit" (Second Semester Report to the Earhart Foundation for Community Leadership, May 30, 1935), *Extracts from the Experiences of Various Spiritual Leaders*, Appendix C-II, 49–50. Unidentified informant.

93. Wolcott, "Mediums, Messages," 287–88.

94. Best, *Passionately Human*, 150.

95. Ibid., 41.

96. B. Davis, *World According to Fannie Davis*, 137.

97. Best, *Passionately Human*, 41.

98. B. Davis, *World According to Fannie Davis*, 137.

99. Wolcott, "Mediums, Messages," 290.

100. L. Harris, "Dream Books," 76.

101. "Policy and Numbers," *Ebony*, 1950.

102. Caldwell, "Policy Game in Chicago," 50.

103. A middle-age woman who has been writing policy for years said this to an interviewer on the sources of gigs. Quoted in Drake and Cayton, *Black Metropolis*, 475–76.

104. Shafton, *Dream Singers*, 68, 69.

105. Ibid.

106. Ibid.

107. Drake and Cayton, *Black Metropolis*, 475.

108. J. Saunders Redding, "Playing the Numbers," *North American Review* 238, no. 6 (1934): 542, quoted in Shafton, *Dream Singers*, 73.

109. Anthony Shafton, interviews with prisoner no. 18 and anonymous dreamer no. 114, in *Dream Singers*, 73, 74.

110. Ibid., 74.

111. Chireau, *Black Magic*, 143.

112. Fabian, *Card Sharps and Bucket Shops*, 144.

113. J. H. Harvey, *Wehman's Complete Dancing Master and Call Book Containing a Full and Complete Description of All the Modern Dances, Together with the Figures of the German* (New York: H. J. Wehman, Publisher, monographic, 1889), 121, https://www.loc.gov/item/musdi.091/.

114. W.E.B. Du Bois, *The Souls of Black Folk* (New York: Dover Publications, 1903), 2–3.

115. Charles Johnson, *Middle Passage* (New York: Scribner, 1990), 98.

116. Carolyn Marrow Long, *Spiritual Merchants: Religion, Magic, and Commerce* (Nashville: University of Tennessee Press, 2001), 207.

117. Shafton, *Dream Singers*, 235, 236.

118. Long, *Spiritual Merchants*, 208.

119. Ibid.

120. Andrew G. Paschal, "Business–Policy: Negroes Number Game," n.d., Illinois Writers Project: Negro in Illinois Papers, box 35, folder 15, Vivian G. Harsh Research Collection, Chicago, Illinois.

121. Herman Clayton, "Local Policy Barons," October 1, 1940, Illinois Writers Project: Negro in Illinois Papers, box 35, folder 17, Vivian G. Harsh Research Collection, Chicago, Illinois.

122. Uriah Konje [Herbert Gladstone Parris], *H. P. Dream Book* (n.p., 1926), luckymojo.com. Accessed May 14, 2017.

123. Alonzo Kittrels, "'The Dream Book' Fed Dreams of Riches," *Philadelphia Tribune*, https://www.phillytrib.com/lifestyles/the-dream-book-fed-dreams-of -riches/article_359af0ac-8dac-53aa-9b87-7231b638925b.html. Accessed December 18, 2017.

124. L. Harris, "Madame Queen of Policy," 72.

125. "Policy and Numbers," *Ebony*, 1950.

126. Ibid.

127. Ibid.

128. Ibid.

129. Shafton, *Dream Singers*, 235–39.

130. L. Harris, "Dream Books," 75.

131. Wolcott, "Culture of the Informal Economy," 58.

132. L. Harris, "Dream Books," 87–88.

133. Wolcott, "Culture of the Informal Economy," 58.

134. Long, *Spiritual Merchants*, 100.

135. Chireau, *Black Magic*, 142.

136. Popular publishers in Chicago, New York, and Baltimore also printed dream books as cheap pamphlets. These too served as guides to interpreting and understanding dreams and symbols and were used to pick winning policy numbers. Some sold for thirty-five cents a copy and could be purchased at various women's candle shops, newsstands, or stationery stores.

137. Long, *Spiritual Merchants*, 99–100.

138. Ibid., 117.

139. McCall, "Symbiosis," 421.

140. Long, *Spiritual Merchants*, 106.

141. McCall, "Symbiosis," 422.

142. Wolcott, "Culture of the Informal Economy," 56–58.

143. Long, *Spiritual Merchants*, 130.

144. Drake and Cayton, *Black Metropolis*, 477.

145. Joaquin Pelayo, "The Wheels Spin in Havana," *Chicago Defender*, September 15, 1940, 13.

146. Laurence Fishburne and Larenz Tate, "Episode 3," *Bronzeville* (podcast), February 21, 2017, http://bronzevilleseries.com/episode-103/.

147. Ibid.

148. Ibid.

149. Ibid.

150. Drake and Cayton, *Black Metropolis*, 475.

151. Ibid.

Chapter 5. What Arrest Records Reveal

1. Keeanga Yahmatta Taylor, "Saidiya Hartman's 'Beautiful Experiments'," *LA Review of Books*, May 5, 2019, https://lareviewofbooks.org/article/saidiya-hartmans-beautiful-experiments/. Accessed March 4, 2021.

2. Walter Reckless, *Vice in Chicago* (Chicago: University of Chicago Press, 1933), 15, 16. Based on his study of early, now lost, arrest records, Reckless wrote, "Police were seven times more active in vice districts in 1928 than they had been in 1908."

3. Irma Watkins-Owens, *Blood Relations: Caribbean Immigrants and the Black Working Class* (New York: Free Press, 1996), 146.

4. Carby, "Policing the Black Woman's Body," 741. See also Blair, *I've Got to Make My Livin'*.

5. Brittney C. Cooper, *Beyond Respectability: The Intellectual Thought of Race Women* (Urbana: University of Illinois Press, 2017), 13.

6. Carby explains in greater detail that "Black urban life was viewed as being intimately associated with vice because Black migrants to cities were forced to live in or adjacent to areas previously established as red-light districts in which prostitution and gambling had been contained." See Carby, "Policing the Black Woman's Body," 751–52.

7. "Vice" was a term employed when Chicago's first vice commission met in 1911 to study prostitution in the Black Belt. See Chicago Vice Commission, *The Social*

Evil in Chicago: A Study of the Existing Conditions with Recommendations (Chicago: Vice Commission of Chicago, 1911).

8. Balto, *Occupied Territory*, 24.

9. See Hicks, *Talk with You Like a Woman*; Shannon King, *Whose Harlem Is This Anyway? Community Politics and Grassroots Activism during the New Negro Era* (New York: New York University Press, 2015); Gross, *Colored Amazons*; Balto, *Occupied Territory*; Blair, *I've Got to Make My Livin'*.

10. Joseph E. Gary, *Laws and Ordinances Governing the City of Chicago, January 1, 1866, With an Appendix, Containing the Former Legislation Relating to the City and Notes of Decisions of the Supreme Court of Illinois Relating to Corporations* (Chicago: Bulletin Printing Company, 1866), 334.

11. Edward J. Brundage, *The Chicago Code of 1911* (Chicago: Callaghan and Company, 1911), 383–84.

12. "Witness Flunks Out at Policy Hearing," *Chicago Defender*, June 20, 1942, 2.

13. Samuel H. Treat, Walter B. Scates, and Robert S. Blackwell, *The Statutes of Illinois Embracing All of the General Laws of the State Complete to 1865, with Marginal Notes, Showing the Contents of Each Section, and a Reference to the Decisions of the Supreme Court upon the Construction of Each Statute* (Chicago: E. B. Myers and Chandler, 1866), 756.

14. *Laws of the State of Illinois Enacted by the Forty-Fourth General Assembly* (Springfield: Illinois State Journal Company, State Printers, 1905), 192–93.

15. W. D. Amis, "Policy Business: The Benvenutis," n.d., Kefauver Senate Committee to Investigate Organized Crime in Interstate Commerce, box 48, folder "8-4: Policy–Numbers," National Archives, Washington, DC.

16. Rob Roy, "Behind the Scenes," *Chicago Defender*, July 10, 1961, 16.

17. *The Penal Code of the State of New York: In Force December 1, 1882* (New York: Banks and Brothers, 1895), 91; quoted in L. Harris, *Sex Workers, Psychics and Numbers Runners*, 76n2.

18. *The Penal Code of the State of New York: In Force December 1, 1882* (New York: Banks and Brothers, 1895), 91; quoted in L. Harris, "Playing the Numbers," 70n2.

19. See S. White et al., *Playing the Numbers*, 111, 127.

20. Balto, *Occupied Territory*, 69.

21. Ibid., 58.

22. Roger Biles, *Big City Boss in Depression and War: Mayor Edward J. Kelly of Chicago* (DeKalb: Northern Illinois State University Press, 1984), 89–90; *Chicago Police Department Annual Report 1931*, quoted in Balto, *Occupied Territory*, 70.

23. Edward J. Kelly, Mayor, and James P. Allman, Commissioner of Police, *Chicago Police Department Annual Reports, 1941–1946* (Chicago: City of Chicago, 1941–1946).

24. Martin H. Kennelly, Mayor, and John C. Prendergast, and Timothy J. O'Connor, Commissioners of Police, *Chicago Police Department Annual Reports 1947–1955* (Chicago: City of Chicago, 1947–1955).

25. "Order Cleanup of Gambling," *Chicago Defender*, July 5, 1947, 7.

26. "Summary of Arrests Made in 1951," Kennelly Collection, box 56, folder 1134J, Special Collections, University of Illinois, Chicago.

27. "Gambling Lid Hits Southside," *Chicago Defender*, March 29, 1947, 2.

28. Kennelly et al., *Chicago Police Department Annual Reports, 1947–1955.*

29. Ibid.

30. The gambling unit disbanded in 2009. See Chuck Goudie, "The End of the Line," *ABC-7 Eyewitness News*, https://abc7chicago.com/.

31. Mayor Richard M. Daly and Commissioners of Police, *Chicago Police Department Annual Reports, 1960–1968* (Chicago: City of Chicago, 1960–1968).

32. Balto, *Occupied Territory*, 94.

33. "Eleanor Smith," Arrest Record 812273, 1968, Cook County Circuit Court Archives, Chicago, Illinois.

34. Gross, *Colored Amazons*, 5.

35. Arrest Records Misdemeanor Files, 1925–1968, Cook County Circuit Court Archives, Chicago, Illinois.

36. Black women's working-class labor history and Chicago's labor history are worth noting when trying to understand women's policy labor in context with other informal labor and labor organizing. See the work of Marica Walker-Williams, *Reverend Addie Wyatt: Faith and the Fight for Labor, Gender, and Racial Equality* (Champaign: University of Illinois Press, 2016); Robin D. G. Kelley, *Race Rebels: Culture, Politics, and the Black Working Class* (New York: Free Press, 1994); Tera Hunter, *To 'Joy My Freedom': Southern Black Women's Lives and Labors after the Civil War* (Cambridge, MA: Harvard University Press, 1998); Talitha LeFlouria, *Chained in Silence: Black Women and Convict Labor in the New South* (Chapel Hill: UNC Press, 2015); and Trotter, *Workers on Arrival.*

37. L. Harris, "Playing the Numbers," 28.

38. Ibid., 34.

39. Ibid.

40. Trotter, *Workers on Arrival*, 69.

41. Arrest Records, Misdemeanor Files, 1925–1968, Cook County Circuit Court Archives, Chicago, Illinois.

42. Wolcott, *Remaking Respectability*, 27.

43. Wolcott, *Remaking Respectability*; and Gross, *Colored Amazons.*

44. Gross, *Colored Amazons*, 49.

45. Adolph Slaughter, "Mother Balks in Brutality Case," *Chicago Defender*, April 11, 1959, 3.

46. Ibid.

47. See Baldwin, *Chicago's New Negroes*; Fabian, *Card Sharps and Bucket Shops*; Drake and Cayton, *Black Metropolis.*

48. Adolph Slaughter, "Cop on Carpet for Race Slur," *Chicago Defender*, April 4, 1959, 3.

49. Ibid.

50. The first female police officers were appointed in 1913. Grace Wilson was the city's first African American woman appointed to the force, in 1918. See "History," Chicago Police Department, https://home.chicagopolice.org/about/history/.

51. Sharon E. Wood, *The Freedom of the Streets: Work, Citizenship, and Sexuality in a Gilded Age City* (Chapel Hill: University of North Carolina Press, 2005), 104.

52. Ibid.

53. "Police Matrons: Their Power for Good," *Chicago Tribune*, June 30, 1895, 42.

54. Gross, *Colored Amazons*, 21.

55. Wood, *Freedom of the Streets*, 121.

56. Gross, *Colored Amazons*, 21.

57. Slaughter, "Mother Balks in Brutality Case."

58. Ibid.

59. Ibid.

60. "Beaten Woman Sues Cop for $100,000," *Chicago Defender*, March 14, 1961, 3.

61. "Forced to Strip Nude, Women Sue Police," *Chicago Defender*, March 15, 1952, 4.

62. Gross, *Colored Amazons*, explains the patterns of partial justice in Philadelphia and how such patterns left Black women vulnerable.

63. "Six Found Not Guilty of Charges by Police," *Chicago Defender*, May 18, 1959, A7.

64. Balto, *Occupied Territory*, 45, comments that CPD work routinely devolved into retribution and violent extraction, both of which became embedded in the culture. The Illinois State Supreme Court heard nine separate cases involving Chicago-based police brutality between 1920 and 1930.

65. Lab-Line Instruments Inc., *Analytical Chemistry* 26, no. 4 (1954): 7A.

66. "Mary Marrow," Arrest Record 1999356, 1954, Cook County Circuit Court Archives, Chicago, Illinois.

67. Cheryl D. Hicks, "Confined to Womanhood: Women, Prisons, and Race in New York State, 1890–1935" (PhD diss., Princeton University, 1999), 41.

68. "Addie B. Calvin and Elizabeth Johnson," Arrest Record, 1968, Cook County Circuit Court Archives, Chicago, Illinois.

69. "Katherina Harris and Joanne Morgan," Arrest Records 149852 and 149853, 1950, Cook County Circuit Court Archives, Chicago, Illinois.

70. Harold Smith, "Chicago Jails Filthy, Full of Rats, Vermin," *Chicago Tribune*, March 9, 1947, 10.

71. Ibid.

72. Ibid.

73. Victoria Perez, "Defending My People and My Culture," in *Chicanas of 18th Street: Narratives of a Movement from Latino Chicago*, ed. Leonard G. Ramirez (Urbana: University of Illinois Press, 2011), 120.

74. Chicago Women's Liberation Movement, *Jane: Documents from Chicago's Clandestine Abortion Service, 1968–1973* (Baltimore: Firestarter Press, 2004), 31–32.

75. James C. Gavin, "Musty, Dusty Police Cells on Way Out: Map Lockup Reforms at Headquarters," *Chicago Tribune*, May 22, 1961, 33.

76. Ibid.

77. Ibid.

78. "Annie Mae Robinson," Arrest Record, 1955, Cook County Circuit Court Archives, Chicago, Illinois.

79. L. Harris, "Playing the Numbers," 43.

80. "Summary of Arrests Made in 1951," Kennelly Collection, box 56, folder 1134J, Special Collections, University of Illinois, Chicago.

81. Christopher Robert Reed, *The Chicago NAACP and the Rise of Black Professional Leadership, 1910–1966* (Bloomington: Indiana University Press, 1997), 200.

82. "List of Unsolved Murders Grows as Two Stabbing Victims Are Found," *Chicago Defender*, September 23, 1967, 2.

83. "Calls Two Robbery Suspects Killers," *Chicago Defender*, October 7, 1958, 21.

84. "Lee Brown," Arrest Record 812280, 1968, Cook County Circuit Court Archives, Chicago, Illinois.

85. L. Harris, "Playing the Numbers," 126.

86. "Lottie Wolf," Arrest Record, 1968, Cook County Circuit Court Archives, Chicago, Illinois.

87. Ibid.

88. L. Harris, *Sex Workers, Psychics, and Numbers Runners*, 114.

89. Drake and Cayton, *Black Metropolis*, 487.

90. "Letter to Mr. Robinson," December 16, 1950, Kefauver Senate Committee to Investigate Organized Crime in Interstate Commerce, box 132 "Investigative File Geographical Files, Ill.," folder "Policy Racket General," National Archives, Washington, DC.

91. "Police Captains," October 11, 1950, Kefauver Senate Committee to Investigate Organized Crime in Interstate Commerce, box 51 "Crime General," folder "Chicago Crime Commission," National Archives, Washington, D.C.

92. "Message for Mr. Robinson," December 18, 1950, Kefauver Senate Committee to Investigate Organized Crime in Interstate Commerce, box 132 "Investigative File Geographical Files, Ill.," folder "Policy Racket General," National Archives Building, Washington, DC.

93. "Letter to Senator Kefauver," October 18, 1950, Kefauver Senate Committee to Investigate Organized Crime in Interstate Commerce, box 132 "Investigative File Geographical Files, Ill.," folder "Policy Racket General," National Archives, Washington, DC.

94. "Mayor Martin Kennelly," October 5, 1950, Kefauver Senate Committee to Investigate Organized Crime in Interstate Commerce, "Public Testimony pages 131, 132," box 183 Hearings: Public, folder Part. 5 Illinois, National Archives, Washington, DC.

95. "Theodore Roe, Interview," October 25, 1950, Kefauver Senate Committee to Investigate Organized Crime in Interstate Commerce, box 113 "Investigative files names Rho-Ros," folder Roe, Theodore, National Archives, Washington, DC.

96. "Theodore Roe, Public Testimony pages 1151–1152," December 19, 1950, Kefauver Senate Committee to Investigate Organized Crime in Interstate Commerce,

box 183 Hearings: Public, folder Part. 5 Illinois, National Archives, Washington, DC.

97. "Matilda Hobson," Arrest Record, 1968, Cook County Circuit Court Archives, Chicago, Illinois.

98. "Leo Napa," Arrest Record, 1968, Cook County Circuit Court Archives, Chicago, Illinois.

99. Arrest Records, Misdemeanor Files, 1925–1968, Cook County Circuit Court Archives, Chicago, Illinois.

100. "Theodore Roe, Public Testimony pages 1151–1152," December 19, 1950, Kefauver Senate Committee to Regulate Interstate Commerce, box 183 Hearings: Public, folder Part. 5 Illinois, National Archives Building, Washington, DC.

101. "Theodore Roe, Interview," October 25, 1950, Kefauver Senate Committee to Investigate Organized Crime in Interstate Commerce, box 113 "Investigative files names Rho-Ros," folder Roe, Theodore, National Archives, Washington, DC.

102. W. D. Amis, "Policy Business: The Benvenutis," n.d., Kefauver Senate Committee to Investigate Organized Crime in Interstate Commerce, box 48, folder 8-4: Policy—Numbers, National Archives, Washington, DC.

103. "Pearl Cohen," Arrest Record, 1968, Cook County Circuit Court Archives, Chicago, Illinois.

104. "Theodore Roe, Interview," October 25, 1950, Kefauver Senate Committee to Investigate Organized Crime in Interstate Commerce, box 113 "Investigative files names Rho-Ros," folder "Roe, Theodore," National Archives, Washington, DC.

105. "Leatrice Marrow," Arrest Record 30145, 1955, Cook County Circuit Court Archives, Chicago, Illinois; "Sarah Goodwin," Arrest Record 55MC35764, 1955, Cook County Circuit Court Archives, Chicago, Illinois.

106. John Hope Franklin and Evelyn Brooks Higginbotham, *From Slavery to Freedom: A History of African Americans*, 9th ed. (New York: McGraw Hill, 2011), 379.

Chapter 6. Legal Strategies for Policy Women

1. Anne Gray Fischer, "Centering Women in *Occupied Territory*," *Black Perspectives*, April 7, 2020, https://www.aaihs.org/centering-women-in-occupied-territory/.

2. Gordon V. Levine and Ceil Misles-Reinglass, "Procedural Disarray in Illinois Ordinance Prosecution," *DePaul Law Review* 24, no. 2 (1975), 588–89.

3. Charles W. Eliot, Louis D. Brandeis, Moorfield Storey, Adolph J. Rodenbeck, and Roscoe Pound, *Preliminary Report on Efficiency of the Administration of Justice* (Boston: Caustis-Claflin Co., Printers, 1914), 29, quoted in Michael Willrich, *City of Courts: Socializing Justice in Progressive Era Chicago* (New York: Cambridge University Press, 2003), xxxv.

4. Willrich, *City of Courts*, xxxiv.

5. Ibid., xxxii; Harry Edward Smoot, *Manual of Juvenile Laws, Juvenile Protective Agency of Chicago* (Chicago: Hale-Crossley Printing, 1916), 100–102.

6. Willrich, *City of Courts*, xxxii.

7. Smoot, *Manual of Juvenile Laws*, 100–102.

8. James Langland, *The Chicago Daily News Almanac and Year Book for 1910* (Chicago: Chicago Daily News, 1909), 476.

9. Ibid., 133.

10. Willrich, *City of Courts*, xxxiii.

11. Ibid., xxxiv.

12. Joel Elan Black, "Idlers, Outliers, and Dependents: The Free Labor Order in Industrial Chicago, 1870–1930" (PhD diss., University of Florida, 2010), 63.

13. Ibid.

14. City of Chicago, Municipal Court, *Fifth Annual Report of the Municipal Court of Chicago: For the Year December 5, 1910, to December 3, 1911, Inclusive* (Chicago, n.d.), 68–72.

15. Ibid.

16. Ibid.

17. Ibid.

18. Mark H. Haller, "Historical Roots of Police Behavior: Chicago, 1890–1925," *Law and Society Review* 10, no. 2 (1976): 322.

19. Blair, *I've Got to Make My Livin'*, 220.

20. Ibid., 228.

21. Ibid.

22. Willrich, *City of Courts*, 156. For cases involving Wells-Barnett, see *People v. Willie Scott*, case 105630, March 20, 1914, Municipal Court of Chicago Criminal Records, Cook County Circuit Court Archives, Chicago, Illinois; and *People v. William H. Rhoden*, case 105634, March 25, 1914, Municipal Court of Chicago Criminal Records, Cook County Circuit Court Archives, Chicago, Illinois.

23. "Our Race Needs Judge," *Chicago Defender*, March 31, 1917, 10.

24. "Defender's Legal Helps," *Chicago Defender*, September 8, 1917, 12.

25. Chicago Commission on Race Relations, *Negro in Chicago*, 345, quoted in L. Mara Dodge, *"Whores and Thieves of the Worst Kind": A Study of Women, Crime, and Prisons, 1835–2000* (Dekalb: Northern Illinois University Press, 2002), 72.

26. "Adultery and Fornication String I," 50 cases: November 5, 1914, case 119001, to December 28, 1914, case 119073, Municipal Court of Chicago Criminal Records, Cook County Circuit Court Archives, Chicago, Illinois, quoted in Willrich, *City of Courts*, 190.

27. Illinois Association for Criminal Justice, *The Illinois Crime Survey* (Chicago: Blakely Printing, 1929), 393.

28. Nicole Gonzalez Van Cleve, *Crook County: Racism and Injustice in America's Largest Criminal Court* (Stanford, CA: Stanford University Press, 2017), 150.

29. Dodge, *"Whores and Thieves of the Worst Kind,"* 73.

30. Ibid., 291n11.

31. Ibid., 117.

32. Balto, *Occupied Territory*, 45.

33. S. White et al., *Playing the Numbers*, 133.

34. N. Thompson, *Kings*, 14.

35. Ibid., 59.

36. Ibid., 327.

37. Ibid., 273.

38. Ibid., 260.

39. Martin H. Kennelly, Mayor, and John C. Prendergast and Timothy J. O'Connor, Commissioners of Police, *Chicago Police Department Annual Reports, 1947–1955* (Chicago: City of Chicago, 1953, 1954, 1955).

40. "Memo to Mr. Klein," August 26, 1950, Kefauver Senate Committee to Investigate Organized Crime in Interstate Commerce, box 132 Investigative File Geographical Files, Ill., folder Chicago and Vicinity, Gambling General, National Archives, Washington, DC.

41. Ibid.

42. Ibid.

43. Ibid.

44. "Catherine Reiser to Editor, Voice of the People," September 11, 1950, Crime Commissions (Chicago Crime Commission), box 132 Investigative File Geographical Files, Ill., folder "Crime General, 14-3, folder "Chicago Crime Commission," National Archives, Washington, DC.

45. "Leatrice Marrow," Arrest Record 30145, 1955, and "Sarah Goodwin," Arrest Record 55MC35764, 1955, Cook County Circuit Court Archives, Chicago, Illinois.

46. James E. Spiotto, "Search and Seizure: An Empirical Study of the Exclusionary Rule and Its Alternatives," *Journal of Legal Studies* 2 (1973): 243–78.

47. I am indebted to Professor Erin Sheley, Professor of Law, University of Calgary, for her help on the legal interpretation of this data.

48. Fourth Amendment, U.S. Constitution, https://www.law.cornell.edu/wex/fourth_amendment.

49. Section 4 of division 6 of the Illinois Criminal Code (Ill. Rev. Stat. 1951, chap. 38, par. 657), Illinois General Assembly, https://ilga.gov.

50. "Leatrice Marrow" and "Sarah Goodwin," Cook County Circuit Court Archives, Chicago, Illlinois.

51. The Illinois Appellate Court had jurisdiction of all matters of appeal or writs of error from the superior, circuit, and county courts, and from the Municipal Court of Chicago, except in criminal cases and those affecting a franchise or freehold or the validity of a statute. Decisions were final except that an appeal could be granted on a certificate of importance, or a review could be allowed from the supreme court. See Langland, *Chicago Daily News Almanac*, 462.

52. *The People of the State of Illinois v. Rexford Clark*, 9 Ill.2d 400, 137 N.E.2d 820 (Ill. App. Ct. 1956).

53. Ibid. Under these circumstances, the appellate court ruled that the municipal court properly denied the defendant's petition to suppress the evidence and return the property.

54. *People of the State of Illinois ex rel. John J. Stamos, State's Attorney of Cook County, Plaintiff-Appellee, v. 1965 Chevrolet Chevy II*, 99 Ill. App.2d 201, 202 (Ill. App. Ct. 1968).

55. *The People of the State of Illinois v. Barbara Heard et al.* 47 Ill. 2d 501(Ill. 1970).

56. Ibid.

57. Ibid.

58. Ibid.

59. *The People of the State of Illinois v. Charles Wright et al.* 41 Ill.2d 170, 171 (Ill. 1968).

60. Ibid.

61. L. Harris, *Sex Workers, Psychics, and Numbers Runners*, 44.

62. W. D. Amis, "Theodore Roe—Idaho-Maine Club—Jones Brothers—Policy Wheel Operators," October 25, 1950, Kefauver Senate Committee to Investigate Organized Crime in Interstate Commerce, box 132 Investigative File Geographical Files, Ill., folder Policy Racket General, National Archives, Washington, DC.

63. "Theodore Roe to G. S. Robinson," Transcript of Interview, October 25, 1950, Kefauver Senate Committee to Investigate Organized Crime in Interstate Commerce, box 132 Investigative File Geographical Files, Ill., folder Policy Racket General, National Archives, Washington, DC.

64. "Payroll, Theodore Roe to Charles Davis," June 30, 1950, Kefauver Senate Committee to Investigate Organized Crime in Interstate Commerce, box 132 Investigative File Geographical Files, Ill., folder Policy Racket General, National Archives, Washington, D.C.

65. "Gertrude Patterson," Arrest Record, 1931, Cook County Circuit Court Archives, Chicago Illinois; "Leona Spratling," Arrest Record, 1931, Cook County Circuit Court Archives, Chicago, Illinois.

66. L. Harris, *Sex Workers, Psychics, and Numbers Runners*, 44.

67. Kathy Peiss, *Cheap Amusements: Working Women and Leisure in Turn-of-the-Century New York* (Philadelphia: Temple University Press, 2001), 20–21.

68. L. Harris, *Sex Workers, Psychics, and Numbers Runners*, 44.

69. "Theodore Roe, Testimony," December 19, 1950, Kefauver Senate Committee to Investigate Organized Crime in Interstate Commerce, box 132 Investigative File Geographical Files, Ill., folder Policy Racket General, National Archives, Washington, DC.

70. Van Cleve, *Crook County*, 6.

71. Ibid.

Conclusion

1. N. Thompson, *Kings*, 104; Schlabach, *Along the Streets*, 59.

2. N. Thompson, *Kings*, 233; Schlabach, *Along the Streets*, 59.

3. N. Thompson, *Kings*, 233.

4. George Bliss, "$763,233 Policy Cash Is Merely 'Peanuts'," *Chicago Daily Tribune*, February 23, 1964, 7.

5. Ibid.

6. Vaz, "'We Intend to Run It,'" 76.

7. Ibid.

8. Ibid.

9. Ibid.

10. Ibid., 73.

11. Caldwell quoted in Barrett, *The Policy-Numbers Game Study Committee* (Springfield, 1975), State of Illinois, transcript of floor debate, "House of Representatives, Seventy-Eighth General Assembly, Fiftieth Legislative Day, May 8, 1973."

12. Brenetta Howell Barrett, *The Policy Numbers Game Study Committee* (Springfield, June 1975), quoted in Matthew Vaz, "The Jackpot Mentality: The Growth of Government Lotteries and the Suppression of Illegal Numbers Gambling in Rio de Janeiro and New York City" (PhD diss., Columbia University, 2011), 152.

13. Ibid.

14. Ibid.

15. Vaz, "'We Intend to Run It,'" 90.

16. Ibid., 96.

17. See Herbert Gans, *The War against the Poor: The Underclass and Antipoverty Policy* (New York: Basic Books, 1995); Michael B. Katz, *The Undeserving Poor: America's Enduring Confrontation with Poverty* (Oxford, UK: Oxford University Press, 2013).

18. Vaz, "'We Intend to Run It,'" 72.

19. Davarian Baldwin, "Comment," "The Triangle African American History Colloquium," unpublished manuscript (Durham, NC: Duke University, 2008).

20. B. Davis, *World According to Fannie Davis*, 173.

21. Ibid., 177.

22. Ibid., 208.

23. Ibid., 231.

24. Ibid.

25. Ibid., 232.

Select Bibliography

Newspapers and Magazines

Broad Ax
Chicago Daily Tribune
Chicago Defender
Colored American
Crisis
Ebony
Jet
New York Age

Archival Collections

Cook County Circuit Court Archives, Chicago, Illinois
Arrest Records
Municipal Court of Chicago Criminal Records
Probate Records
Illinois Department of Public Health. Division of Vital Records, Springfield, Illinois
Illinois Writers Project: Negro in Illinois Papers, Vivian G. Harsh Research Collection, Chicago, Illinois
National Archives and Records Administration, Washington, DC
Thirteenth, Fourteenth, Fifteenth, Sixteenth Census of the United States, 1910, 1920, 1930, 1940
1860 U.S. Census, Tennessee State Marriages, 1780–2002

Kefauver Senate Committee to Investigate Organized Crime in Interstate Commerce
Passenger and Crew Lists of Vessels Arriving at New York, New York, 1897–1957, Year: 1939; Arrival: New York, New York; Microfilm Serial: T715, 1897–1957; Microfilm Roll: Roll 6273; Line: 21; Page Number: 15. National Archives Microfilm Publication, digital image, ancestry.com, accessed July 10, 2017
National Urban League Papers
University of Illinois at Chicago Special Collections
M. H. Bickman Papers
Schomburg Center for Research in Black Culture, New York Public Library, New York, New York
St. Clair Drake Papers
University of Chicago Special Collections
Ernest W. Burgess Papers
Special Collections, University of Illinois, Chicago
Kennelly Collection

Government Reports, Legal Documents, and Unpublished Sources

Barrett, Brenetta Howell. *The Policy Numbers Game Study Committee.* Springfield, IL, June 1975.
Bullock, Henry Allen. "The Urbanization of the Negro Church." Report to the Earhart Foundation for Community Leadership. Typewritten manuscript, 1935.
City of Chicago. Municipal Court. *Fifth Annual Report of the Municipal Court of Chicago: For the Year December 5, 1910, to December 3, 1911, Inclusive.* Chicago, n.d.
Chicago Municipal Code, 4-6-270. "Home Occupations." Chicago Decoded. https://chicagocode.org/4-6-270, accessed December 12, 2017.
Gary, Joseph E. *Laws and Ordinances Governing the City of Chicago, January 1, 1866, With an Appendix, Containing the Former Legislation Relating to the City and Notes of Decisions of the Supreme Court of Illinois Relating to Corporations.* Chicago: Bulletin Printing Company, 1866.
Laws of the State of Illinois Enacted by the Forty-Fourth General Assembly. Springfield: Illinois State Journal Company, State Printers, 1905.
McCabe, Jno. R., City Clerk. *All Amendments to The Revised Municipal Code of Chicago of 1905 (passed March 20, 1905): And All New General Ordinances and Ordinances Creating Prohibition and Local Option Districts Passed . . . from March 20, 1905, to January 1, 1909. Supplement number III.* Catalog Hathi Trust.
The Penal Code of the State of New York: In Force December 1, 1882. New York: Banks and Brothers, 1895.
People of the State of Illinois ex rel. John J. Stamos, State's Attorney of Cook County, Plaintiff-Appellee, v. 1965 Chevrolet Chevy II, 99 Ill. App.2d 201, 202 (Ill. App. Ct. 1968).

The People of the State of Illinois v. Rexford Clark, 9 Ill.2d 400, 137 N.E.2d 820 (Ill. App. Ct. 1956).

The People of the State of Illinois v. Barbara Heard et al. 47 Ill. 2d 501 (Ill. 1970).

The People of the State of Illinois v. Charles Wright et al. 41 Ill.2d 170, 171 (Ill. 1968).

People v. William H. Rhoden, case 105634, March 25, 1914.

People v. Willie Scott, case 105630, March 20, 1914.

Slaughter v. Johnson. 181 Illinois Appellate Court 693, 694 (1st District, 1913).

Treat, Samuel H., Walter B. Scates, and Robert S. Blackwell. *The Statutes of Illinois Embracing All of the General Laws of the State Complete to 1865, with Marginal Notes, Showing the Contents of Each Section, and a Reference to the Decisions of the Supreme Court upon the Construction of Each Statute.* Chicago: E. B. Myers and Chandler, 1866.

Books and Articles

Bachin, Robin. *Building the South Side: Urban Space and Civic Culture in Chicago, 1890–1919.* Chicago: University of Chicago Press, 2004.

Baldwin, Davarian. *Chicago's New Negroes: Modernity, the Great Migration, and Black Urban Life.* Chapel Hill: University of North Carolina Press, 2008.

———. "Comment." The Triangle African American History Colloquium. Durham, NC: Duke University, 2008.

Balto, Simon. *Occupied Territory: Policing Black Chicago from Red Summer to Black Power.* Chapel Hill: University of North Carolina Press, 2019.

Best, Wallace. *Passionately Human, No Less Divine: Religion and Black Culture in Chicago, 1915–1952.* Princeton, NJ: Princeton University Press, 2013.

Biles, Roger. *Big City Boss in Depression and War: Mayor Edward J. Kelly of Chicago.* DeKalb: Northern Illinois State University Press, 1984.

Black, Joel Elan. "Idlers, Outliers, and Dependents: The Free Labor Order in Industrial Chicago, 1870–1930." PhD diss., University of Florida, 2010.

Black, Timuel D., Jr. *Bridges of Memory: Chicago's First Generation of Black Migration—An Oral History.* Evanston, IL: Northwestern University Press, 2004.

———. *Bridges of Memory: Chicago's First Wave of Black Migration.* Evanston, IL: Northwestern University Press, 2003.

Blair, Cynthia M. *I've Got to Make My Livin': Black Women's Sex Work in Turn-of-the-Century Chicago.* Chicago: University of Chicago Press, 2010.

Blassingame, John W. *The Slave Community: Plantation Life in the Antebellum South.* New York: Oxford University, 1972.

Botkin, B. A. *Lay My Burden Down: A Folk History of Slavery.* Chicago: University of Chicago Press, 1945.

Brundage, Edward J. *The Chicago Code of 1911.* Chicago: Callaghan and Company, 1911.

Caldwell, Lewis A. H. "The Policy Game in Chicago." PhD diss., Northwestern University, 1940.

———. *The Policy-Numbers Game Study Committee* (Springfield, 1975). State of Illinois, transcript of floor debate, "House of Representatives, Seventy-Eighth General Assembly, Fiftieth Legislative Day, May 8, 1973.

Carby, Hazel V. "It Jus Be's Dat Way Sometime: The Sexual Politics of Women's Blues." *Radical America* 20, no. 4 (1986): 9–24.

———. "Policing the Black Woman's Body in an Urban Context." *Critical Inquiry* 18, no. 4 (1992): 738–55.

Carlson, Gustav G. "Number Gambling: A Study of a Culture Complex." MA thesis, University of Michigan, 1940.

Chatelain, Marcia. *South Side Girls: Growing Up in the Great Migration*. Durham, NC: Duke University Press, 2015.

Chicago Commission on Race Relations. *The Negro in Chicago: A Study of Race Relations and a Race Riot*. Chicago: University of Chicago Press, 1972.

Chicago Vice Commission. *The Social Evil in Chicago: A Study of the Existing Conditions with Recommendations*. Chicago: Vice Commission of Chicago, 1911.

Chicago Women's Liberation Movement. *Jane: Documents from Chicago's Clandestine Abortion Service, 1968–1973*. Baltimore: Firestarter Press, 2004.

Chireau, Yvonne P. *Black Magic: Religion and the African American Conjuring Tradition*. Berkeley: University of California Press, 2003.

Cooley, Will. "Jim Crow Organized Crime: Black Chicago's Underground Economy in the Twentieth Century." In Weems and Chambers, *Building the Black Metropolis*, 147–70.

Cooper, Brittney C. *Beyond Respectability: The Intellectual Thought of Race Women*. Urbana: University of Illinois Press, 2017.

Corocos, Christine. "Seeing It Coming since 1945." *Thomas Jefferson Law Review* 37, no. 1 (2014): 39–114.

Courage, Richard A., and Christopher Robert Reed, eds. *The Roots of the Chicago Black Renaissance: New Negro Writers, Artists, and Intellectuals, 1893–1930*. Urbana: University of Illinois Press, 2020.

Cressler, Matthew J. *Authentically Black and Truly Catholic: The Rise of Black Catholicism in the Great Migration*. New York: New York University Press, 2017.

Daly, Richard M., Mayor, and Commissioners of Police. *Chicago Police Department Annual Reports, 1960–1968*. Chicago: City of Chicago, 1960–1968.

Davis, Bridgett M. *The World According to Fannie Davis*. New York: Little, Brown, 2019.

Davis, James C. *Commerce in Color: Race, Consumer Culture, and American Literature, 1893–1933*. Ann Arbor: University of Michigan Press, 2007.

Deegan, Mary Jo. "Williams & Black Feminist Pragmatism." In Courage and Reed, *Roots of the Chicago Black Renaissance*, 57–77.

Dodge, L. Mara. *"Whores and Thieves of the Worst Kind": A Study of Women, Crime, and Prisons, 1835–2000*. Dekalb: Northern Illinois University Press, 2002.

Drake, St. Clair. *Churches and Voluntary Associations in the Chicago Negro Community*. Chicago: Works Progress Administration, District 3, 1940 (Report of Official Project 465-54-3-386, conducted under the auspices of the Works Progress Administration, Chicago, December 1940).

Drake, St. Clair, and Horace Cayton. *Black Metropolis: A Study of Negro Life in a Northern City*. New York: Harcourt, Brace and World, 1945. Reprint, Chicago: University of Chicago Press, 1993. Citations refer to the 1993 edition.

Du Bois, W.E.B. *The Philadelphia Negro*. Philadelphia: University of Pennsylvania Press, 1899.

———. *The Souls of Black Folk*. New York: Dover Publications, 1903.

Duncan, Otis, and Beverly Duncan. *The Negro Population of Chicago: A Study of Residential Succession*. Chicago: University of Chicago Press, 1965.

Eliot, Charles W., Louis D. Brandeis, Moorfield Storey, Adolph J. Rodenbeck, and Roscoe Pound. *Preliminary Report on Efficiency of the Administration of Justice*. Boston: Caustis-Claflin Co., Printers, 1914.

Fabian, Ann. *Card Sharps and Bucket Shops: Gambling in Nineteenth Century America*. London: Routledge Press, 2013.

Ferman, Louis, and P. Ferman. "The Structural Underpinnings of the Irregular Economy." *Poverty and Human Resources Abstracts* 8 (1978): 3–17.

Fischer, Anne Gray. "Centering Women in *Occupied Territory*," *Black Perspectives*, April 7, 2020. https://www.aaihs.org/centering-women-in-occupied-territory/.

Fishburne, Laurence, and Larenz Tate. "Episode 3." *Bronzeville* (podcast). February 21, 2017. http://bronzevilleseries.com.

Ford, Tanisha C. *Liberated Threads: Black Women, Style, and the Global Politics of Soul*. Urbana: University of Illinois Press, 2015.

Franklin, John Hope, and Evelyn Brooks Higginbotham. *From Slavery to Freedom: A History of African Americans*. 9th ed. New York: McGraw Hill, 2011.

Gans, Herbert. *The War against the Poor: The Underclass and Antipoverty Policy*. New York: Basic Books, 1995.

Garb, Margaret. *Freedom's Ballot: African American Political Struggles in Chicago from Abolition to the Great Migration*. Chicago: University of Chicago Press, 2014.

Gill, Tiffany. *Beauty Shop Politics: African American Women's Activism in the Beauty Industry*. Urbana: University of Illinois Press, 2010.

Goudie, Chuck. "The End of the Line." *ABC-7 Eyewitness News*. https://abc7chicago.com/.

Green, Adam. *Selling the Race: Culture, Community, and Black Chicago, 1940–1955*. Chicago: University of Chicago Press, 2007.

Gross, Kali N. *Colored Amazons: Crime, Violence, and Black Women in the City of Brotherly Love, 1880–1910*. Durham, NC: Duke University Press, 2006.

Grossman, James. *Land of Hope: Chicago, Black Southerners, and the Great Migration*. Chicago: University of Chicago Press; 1989.

Haley, Sarah. *No Mercy Here: Gender, Punishment, and the Making of Jim Crow Modernity*. Chapel Hill: University of North Carolina Press, 2016.

Haller, Mark H. "Historical Roots of Police Behavior: Chicago, 1890–1925." *Law and Society Review* 10, no. 2 (1976): 303–325.

Harding, Philip, and Richard Jenkins. *The Myth of the Hidden Economy: Towards a New Understanding of Informal Economic Activity*. Maidenhead, Berkshire, UK: Open University Press, 1989.

Harley, Sharon. "Working for Nothing but for a Living: Black Women in the Underground Economy." In *Sister Circle: Black Women and Work*, ed. Sharon Harley and the Black Women and Work Collective, 48–67. New Brunswick, NJ: Rutgers University Press, 2002.

Harris, Albert. *The Negro as Capitalist*. Philadelphia: American Academy of Political and Social Sciences, 1936.

Harris, LaShawn. "Dream Books, Crystal Balls, and 'Lucky Numbers': African American Female Mediums in Harlem, 1900–1930s," *Afro-Americans in New York Life and History* 35 (2011): 74–110.

———. "Playing the Numbers: Madame Stephanie St. Clair and African American Policy Culture in Harlem." *Black Women, Gender, and Families* 2, no. 2 (2008): 53–76.

———. *Sex Workers, Psychics, and Numbers Runners: Black Women in New York City's Underground Economy*. Urbana: University of Illinois Press, 2017.

Harris, Paisley Jane. "Gatekeeping and Remaking: The Politics of Respectability in African American Women's History and Black Feminism." *Journal of Women's History* 15, no. 1 (2003): 212–20.

Harvey, J. H. *Wehman's Complete Dancing Master and Call Book Containing a Full and Complete Description of All the Modern Dances, Together with the Figures of the German*. New York: H. J. Wehman, Publisher, monographic, 1889. https://www.loc.gov/item/musdi.091/.

Hayner, Don. *Binga: The Rise and Fall of Chicago's First Black Banker*. Evanston, IL: Northwestern University Press, 2020.

Helgeson, Jeffery. *Crucibles of Black Empowerment: Chicago's Neighborhood Politics from the New Deal to Harold Washington*. Chicago: University of Chicago Press, 2014.

Hendricks, Wanda A. *Gender, Race, and Politics in the Midwest: Black Club Women in Illinois*. Bloomington: Indiana University Press, 1998.

Hicks, Cheryl D. "Confined to Womanhood: Women, Prisons, and Race in New York State, 1890–1935." PhD diss., Princeton University, 1999.

———. *Talk with You Like a Woman*. Chapel Hill: University of North Carolina Press, 2010.

Higginbotham, Evelyn Brooks. *Righteous Discontent: The Women's Movement in the Black Baptist Church, 1880–1912*. Cambridge, MA: Harvard University Press, 1993.

Hine, Darlene Clark. *Hine Sight: Black Women and the Re-construction of American History*. Bloomington: Indiana University Press, 1997.

———. "Rape and the Inner Lives of Black Women in the Middle West." *Signs: Common Grounds and Crossroads: Race, Ethnicity, and Class in Women's Lives* 14, no. 4 (1989): 912–20.

Hinton, Milton, and David G. Berger. *Playing the Changes: Milt Hinton's Life in Stories and Photographs*. Nashville, TN: Vanderbilt University Press, 2008.

"History." Chicago Police Department. https://home.chicagopolice.org/about/history/.

Horne, Gerald. *The Rise and Fall of the Associated Negro Press*. Urbana: University of Illinois Press, 2017.

Howard, Robert. "The Rise and Fall of Jesse Binga: A Black Chicago Financial Wizard." In Weems and Chambers, *Building the Black Metropolis*, 61–79.

Illinois Association for Criminal Justice. *The Illinois Crime Survey*. Chicago: Blakely Printing, 1929.

Illinois General Assembly Oral History Program. "Corneal A. Davis Memoir, Volume I." Springfield, IL: Legislative Studies Center of Sangamon State University, 1984.

Johnson, Charles. *Middle Passage*. New York: Scribner, 1990.

Jones, Jacqueline. *Labor of Love, Labor of Sorrow: Black Women, Work, and the Family from Slavery to the Present*. New York: Basic Books, 2009.

Kallick, Maureen et al. "A Survey of American Gambling Attitudes and Behavior." Appendix 2, in Commission on the Review of the National Policy toward Gambling, *Gambling in America*. Washington, DC: Government Printing Office, 1976.

Katz, Michael B. *The Undeserving Poor: America's Enduring Confrontation with Poverty*. Oxford, UK: Oxford University Press, 2013.

Kefauver, Estes. *The Kefauver Committee Report on Organized Crime*. New York: Didier, 1951.

Kelly, Edward J., Mayor, and James P. Allman, Commissioner of Police. *Chicago Police Department Annual Reports, 1941–1946*. Chicago: City of Chicago, 1941–1946.

Kennelly, Martin H., Mayor, John C. Prendergast and Timothy J. O'Connor, Commissioners of Police. *Chicago Police Department Annual Reports, 1947–1955*. Chicago: City of Chicago, 1947–1955.

Kimble, Lionel. *A New Deal for Bronzeville: Housing, Employment, and Civil Rights in Black Chicago, 1935–1955*. Carbondale: Southern Illinois University Press, 2015.

King, Shannon. *Whose Harlem Is This Anyway? Community Politics and Grassroots Activism during the New Negro Era*. New York: New York University Press, 2015.

Kittrels, Alonzo. "'The Dream Book' Fed Dreams of Riches." *Philadelphia Tribune*, December 18, 2011. https://www.phillytrib.com/lifestyles/the-dream-book-fed-dreams-of-riches/article_359afoac-8dac-53aa-9b87-7231b638925b.html.

Knupher, Anne Meis. *Toward a Tenderer Humanity and a Nobler Womanhood: African-American Women's Clubs in Turn-of-the-Century Chicago*. New York: New York University Press, 1996.

Konje, Uriah [Herbert Gladstone Parris]. *H. P. Dream Book*. n.p., 1926.

Lab-Line Instruments Inc. *Analytical Chemistry* 26, no. 4 (1954): 7A.

Langland, James. *The Chicago Daily News Almanac and Year Book for 1910*. Chicago: Chicago Daily News, 1909.

Levine, Gordon V., and Ceil Misles-Reinglass. "Procedural Disarray in Illinois Ordinance Prosecution." *DePaul Law Review* 24, no. 2 (1975): 588–89.

Lindsey, Treva B. *Colored No More*. Urbana: University of Illinois Press, 2017.

Long, Carolyn Marrow. *Spiritual Merchants: Religion, Magic, and Commerce*. Nashville: University of Tennessee Press, 2001.

Mather, Frank Lincoln. Ed. *Who's Who of the Colored Race: A General Biographical Dictionary of Men and Women of African Descent*. Vol. 1. Chicago: State Historical Society of Wisconsin, 1915.

McCall, George M. "Symbiosis: The Case of Hoodoo and the Numbers Racket." In *Mother Wit from the Laughing Barrel: Readings in the Interpretation of Afro-American Folklore*, edited by Alan Dundes, 419–28. Jackson: University Press of Mississippi, 1990.

McCammack, Brian. *Landscapes of Hope: Nature and the Great Migration in Chicago*. Cambridge, MA: Harvard University Press, 2019.

Mollison, Willis E. *The Leading Afro-Americans of Vicksburg: Their Enterprises, Churches, Schools, Lodges, and Societies*. Vicksburg, MS: Biographia Publishing, 1908.

Osthaus, Carl R. "The Rise and Fall of Jesse Binga, Black Financier." *Journal of Negro History* 58, no. 1 (1973): 39–60.

Patrick, Jeremy. *Faith or Fraud: Fortune-Telling, Spirituality, and the Law*. Vancouver: University of British Columbia Press, 2020.

Peiss, Kathy. *Cheap Amusements: Working Women and Leisure in Turn-of-the-Century New York*. Philadelphia: Temple University Press, 2001.

Perez, Victoria. "Defending My People and My Culture." In *Chicanas of 18th Street: Narratives of a Movement from Latino Chicago*, edited by Leonard G. Ramirez, 118–36. Urbana: University of Illinois Press, 2011.

Pietruska, Jamie L. *Looking Forward: Prediction and Uncertainty in Modern America*. Chicago: University of Chicago Press, 2017.

Powell, Sallie L. "Elizabeth B. Slaughter." In *The Kentucky African American Encyclopedia*, edited by Gerald L. Smith, Karen Cotton McDaniel, and John A. Hardin. Lexington: University of Kentucky Press, 2015, 458.

Reckless, Walter. *Vice in Chicago*. Chicago: University of Chicago Press, 1933.

Redding, J. Saunders. "Playing the Numbers." *North American Review* 238, no. 6 (1934): 533–42.

Reed, Christopher Robert. *Black Chicago's First Century*. Vol. 1: 1833–1900. Columbia: University of Missouri Press, 2005.

———. *The Chicago NAACP and the Rise of Black Professional Leadership, 1910–1966*. Bloomington: Indiana University Press, 1997.

———. *The Depression Comes to the South Side: Protest and Politics in the Black Metropolis, 1930–1933*. Bloomington: Indiana University Press, 2005.

———. "Early Black Chicago Entrepreneurial and Business Activities from the Frontier Era to the Great Migration: The Nexus of Circumstance and Initiative." In Weems and Chambers, *Building the Black Metropolis*, 27–43.

———. "The Rise of Black Chicago's Culturati." In Courage and Reed, *Roots of the Chicago Black Renaissance*, 22–42.

———. *The Rise of Chicago's Black Metropolis, 1920–1929.* Urbana: University of Illinois Press, 2014.

Richings, G. F. *Evidences of Progress among Colored People*, 11th ed. Philadelphia: Ferguson, 1902.

Robb, Frederic H. H., ed. *1927 Intercollegian Wonder Book, or, The Negro in Chicago, 1779–1927.* Chicago: Washington Intercollegiate Club of Chicago, 1927.

Satter, Beryl. *Family Properties: How the Struggle over Race and Real Estate Transformed Chicago and Urban America.* New York: Picador Press, 2009.

Savannah Unit, Georgia Writers' Project, Works Projects Administration. *Drums and Shadows: Survival Studies among the Georgia Coastal Negroes.* Athens: University of Georgia Press, 1940.

Schlabach, Elizabeth Schroeder. *Along the Streets of Bronzeville: Black Chicago's Literary Landscapes.* Urbana: University of Illinois Press, 2013.

Shafton, Anthony. *Dream Singers: The African American Way with Dreams.* New York: Wiley and Sons, 2002.

Sherman, Richard B. *The Negro and the City.* New York: Prentice Hall, 1970.

Smith, Chris M. *Syndicate Women: Gender and Networks in Chicago Organized Crime.* Oakland: University of California Press, 2019.

Smoot, Harry Edward. *Manual of Juvenile Laws, Juvenile Protective Agency of Chicago.* Chicago: Hale-Crossley Printing, 1916.

Spear, Allan. *Black Chicago: The Making of a Negro Ghetto.* Chicago: University of Chicago Press, 1967.

Spiotto, James E. "Search and Seizure: An Empirical Study of the Exclusionary Rule and Its Alternatives." *Journal of Legal Studies* 2 (1973): 243–78.

Stone-Gordon, Tammy. "'Fifty-Cent Sybils': Occult Workers and the Symbolic Marketplace in the Urban U.S., 1850–1930." PhD diss., Michigan State University, 1998.

Strickland, Arvarh E. *History of the Chicago Urban League.* Columbia: University of Missouri Press, 1966.

Sundstrom, William. "Last Hired, First Fired? Unemployment and Urban Black Workers during the Great Depression." *Journal of Economic History* 52, no. 1 (1992): 415–29.

Taylor, Keeanga-Yamahtta. *From #BlackLivesMatter to Black Liberation.* New York: Basic Books, 2017.

Thompson, Nathan. *Kings: The True Story of Chicago's Policy Kings and Numbers Rackets, An Informal History.* Chicago: Bronzeville Press, 2006.

Thompson, Patrick H. *The History of Negro Baptists in Mississippi.* Jackson, MS: R. W. Baily Printing Co., 1898.

Tokman, Victor E. "The Informal Sector in Latin America: From Underground to Legality." In *Beyond Regulation: The Informal Economy in Latin America*, edited by Victor E. Tokman. Boulder, CO: Lynne Rienner Publishers, 1992, 3–4.

Travis, Dempsey. *An Autobiography of Black Chicago*. Chicago: Bolden, 1981.

Trotter, Joe William, Jr. *Workers on Arrival: Black Labor in the Making of America*. Berkeley: University of California Press, 2019.

Van Cleve, Nicole Gonzalez. *Crook County: Racism and Injustice in America's Largest Criminal Court*. Stanford, CA: Stanford University Press, 2017.

Vaz, Matthew. "The Jackpot Mentality: The Growth of Government Lotteries and the Suppression of Illegal Numbers Gambling in Rio de Janeiro and New York City," PhD diss., Columbia University, 2011.

——. *Running the Numbers*. Chicago: University of Chicago Press, 2020.

——. "'We Intend to Run It': Racial Politics, Illegal Gambling, and the Rise of Government Lotteries in the United States, 1960–1985." *Journal of American History* 101, no. 1 (2014): 71–96.

Venkatesh, Sudhir Alladi. *Off the Books: The Underground Economy of the Urban Poor*. Cambridge, MA: Harvard University Press, 2006.

Watkins-Owens, Irma. *Blood Relations: Caribbean Immigrants and the Black Working Class*. New York: Free Press, 1996.

Weems, Robert. *Black Business in the Black Metropolis: The Chicago Metropolitan Assurance Company, 1925–1985*. Bloomington: Indiana University Press, 1998.

——. *Desegregating the Dollar: African American Consumerism in the Twentieth Century*. New York: New York University Press, 1998.

Weems, Robert, and Jason P. Chambers, eds. *Building the Black Metropolis: African American Entrepreneurship in Chicago*. Urbana: University of Illinois Press, 2017.

White, Deborah Gray. *Ar'n't I a Woman? Female Slaves in the Plantation South*. New York: W. W. Norton, 1999.

White, Shane, Stephen Garton, Stephen Robertson, and Graham White. *Playing the Numbers: Gambling in Harlem between the Wars*. Cambridge, MA: Harvard University Press, 2010.

Wilkerson, Isabel. "Fresh Air Interview: Journalist Isabel Wilkerson." *National Public Radio*, September 13, 2010.

——. *The Warmth of Other Suns: The Epic Story of America's Great Migration*. New York: Vintage Books, 2011.

Williams, Rhonda Y. *The Politics of Public Housing: Black Women's Struggles against Urban Inequality*. New York: Oxford University Press, 2004.

Willrich, Michael. *City of Courts: Socializing Justice in Progressive Era Chicago*. New York: Cambridge University Press, 2003.

Wolcott, Victoria W. "The Culture of the Informal Economy: Numbers Runners in Inter-War Black Detroit." *Radical History Review* (Fall 1997): 46–75.

——. "Mediums, Messages, and Lucky Numbers: African-American Female Spiritualists and Numbers Runners in Inter-War Detroit." In *The Geography of Identity*, edited by Patricia Yeager. Ann Arbor: University of Michigan Press, 1996.

———. *Remaking Respectability: African American Women in Interwar Detroit.* Chapel Hill: University of North Carolina Press, 2001.

Wood, Sharon E. *The Freedom of the Streets: Work, Citizenship, and Sexuality in a Gilded Age City.* Chapel Hill: University of North Carolina Press, 2005.

Work, Nathan Monroe. "Negro Real Estate Holders of Chicago." PhD diss., University of Chicago, 1903.

Wright, Richard. *Black Boy (American Hunger).* New York: Harper Perennial Deluxe Edition, 2008.

Index